"A GIFT OF PEACE"

~~NOT TO BE OPENED UNTIL CHRISTMAS~~

TO BE OPENED IMMEDIATELY!

PRINCE OF PEACE

By
William Sears

BAHÁ'Í PUBLISHING TRUST
POST BOX 19
NEW DELHI – 110 001 INDIA

Copyright © 1986 by National Spiritual
Assembly of the Bahá'ís of India

First Published
December 1986

ISBN 81-85091-10-2

Printed in India

REJOICE

"Ho, everyone that thirsteth, come ye to the waters, and he that hath no money; come ye, buy, and eat; yea come, buy wine and milk without money and without price...

"Incline your ear, and come unto me: hear, and your soul shall live; and I will make an everlasting covenant with you...

"Seek ye the Lord while he may be found, call ye upon him while he is near...

"For ye shall go out with joy and be led forth with peace: the mountains and the hills, shall breakforth before you into singing, and all the trees of the field shall clap their hands."

(Isaiah 55:1-12)

THE STORY AS IT HAPPENS

CONTENTS
THE STORY AS IT HAPPENS

INTRODUCTION

Chapter		Page
	THE STORY BEGINS	
1.	Before Your Very Eyes	3
2.	On Course!	7
	WELCOME BACK!	
3.	Behold And Wonder Marvelously!	13
	WHO IS THE PRINCE OF PEACE?	
4.	The Prince of Peace	19
5.	The Theme of the Symphony	24
6.	Blessed Detour	28
	DIALOGUES OF DELIVERANCE	
7.	Gateway to the Prince of Peace	33
8.	Drama of the Kingdom	37
9.	The Inseparable Link	40
10.	Lo, He is Come With Conclusive Proof	44
11.	Fulfilled!	47
	YULETIDE MYSTERY UNFOLDS	
12.	Joy to the World	51
	"AND THE GOVERNMENT SHALL BE UPON HIS SHOULDERS"	
13.	Well-Wishers of the Governments of the World	57
14.	The All-Powerful Physician	61
	"WONDERFUL! COUNSELLOR!"	
15.	The Strong Fortress	67
16.	Hearken, O Ye That Dwell on Earth!	72
17.	The All-Knowing Physician	78
18.	Beautify Your Tongues	82

THE CHALLENGE

| 19. | Prelude | 87 |
| 20. | Yes? Or, No! | 92 |

"AS THE WATERS COVER THE SEA"

| 21. | Incoming Tide | 99 |

THE BÁB

22.	The Great Parallel	103
23.	The Downpour Begins.	111
24.	An Isolated Thunderstorm	115
25.	The Sacrifice	120

BAHÁ'U'LLÁH

26.	The Tidal Wave	127
27.	The Tidal Wave Continues	132
28.	The Tempest	135
29.	Life-Rafts For Humanity	141
30.	The Cloudburst	147

'ABDU'L-BAHÁ

31.	The Beloved Master	153
31.	Rising Tide in America	157
33.	The Kingdom of God on Earth, A Beginning	163
34.	Rising Tide in the Holy Land	170

THE GUARDIAN AND THE UNIVERSAL HOUSE OF JUSTICE

| 35. | Flood Tide | 177 |

THE BAHÁ'ÍS OF THE WORLD

| 36. | Flood Tide Continues | 187 |
| 37. | Hip! Hip! Hurray! | 191 |

"UNION OF NATIONS"

38.	The First Attempt	203
39.	Second Attempt	209
40.	Summon the Nations to God!	216
41.	"Look Chinaward!"	222

RETURN TO: "WONDERFUL! COUNSELLOR!"

42.	Wonderful! Counsellor!	229

"THE EVERLASTING FATHER"

43.	The Pure Mirrors	239
44.	The Lightning Flash	244
45.	The Sacred Fold of the Father	247
46.	Reborn!	251
47.	The Thrust of the Spear	256
48.	The Everlasting Father	260

"THE PRINCE OF PEACE"

49.	The Bahá'í Peace Program	267
50.	The Promised Day Is Come!	270
51.	Administer the Infallible Remedy	277
52.	Sing Out the Song of the Kingdom	283

EPILOGUE

TWO GARDENS

1.	Two Gardens	291

O LITTLE TOWN OF BETHLEHEM

2.	The Father and the Son	297

THE PRINCE OF PEACE

3.	The Prince of Peace	301

Errata

Page	Line	Now reads	Should read
47	16	and walk straight to the *close*	and walk straight to the *door*
61	9	from the *recovering* and grave illness	from the *recurring* and grave illness
81	Last line	his or her *choice*	his or her *chance*
124	12	five hundred years	five hundred *thousand* years
141	1	endless *floor* of Councels	endless *flood* of Councels

INTRODUCTION

When Bill (Sears) began this story five years ago, he asked me to write an introduction. Patiently I kept updating my introduction every year because I knew when it was finished, you would begin one of the most fascinating, beguiling Christmas stories ever told since the beauty of Bethlehem.

I found *Prince of Peace* to be simple, tender, and beautiful. It is a Yuletide tale for all mankind: men, women and children. It is a message of hope and encouragement filled with good cheer and good news. You are in for a pleasant, delightfully surprising, and an exciting few hours.

This Christmas story will warm and comfort your troubled heart. It will bring serenity and peace into your home exactly as promised in those words of *Isaiah:* "Ho! Everyone that thirsteth come to the waters" and drink your fill, "free and without a price."

The story about to unfold before your eyes comes at exactly the right time in history. It will reassure, comfort and console a puzzled and disillusioned world. It will set things on the right path once again.

Prince of Peace is brief, entertaining and astonishing — no, amazing — and has been specially "gift-wrapped" for you and your family.

No wonder the gift-package shown earlier was so plainly marked: "To be opened immediately!" You will soon see why.

What could be more exciting and hopeful than to receive such a Christmas present and to be told such a Christmas Story?

Once you have heard this melody, your life may never again be the same. It is a song of joy and rapture from the lips of the long-awaited, desperately needed *Prince of Peace*. It is sung here in these pages in all its majesty and splendor. Some of it for the very first time.

Open your "Gift" and begin the story.

Merry Christmas!

Robert Quigley (*)
Beverly Hills, California
December 25, Today

(*) Robert Quigley who wrote the introduction to this book has been described as one of Television's original thinkers. A truly gifted writer and producer of daytime-television programs on CBS, NBC, and ABC. Bob has a shelf full of Awards and Emmys to testify to his long and successful career. He is even better known throughout the world as one of the pioneers for the Bahá'í Faith. He has served in both Africa and the United States as a member of the Auxiliary Board for Southern Africa and the Islands of the Indian Ocean. The Guardian of the Bahá'í Faith said that he and Bill (Sears) should work together as "they made a good team." Hence this Introduction by Bob to Bill's book.

THE STORY BEGINS

"The world's most amazing unsolved mystery."

1.

Before Your Very Eyes

Each Christmas morning in many of the Christian churches of the West, the Bible is opened to the Book of *Isaiah, chapter nine, verse six:*

> "For unto us a child is born, unto us a son is given: and the government shall be upon his shoulder: and his name shall be called Wonderful, Counsellor, the mighty God, the everlasting Father, the Prince of Peace."*(Isaiah 9:6)*

These beautiful words are read to honor Jesus.
The red-letter edition of the King James Version of the Bible shows this entire paragraph as referring to Christ.
Hidden in this magical verse of *Isaiah,* will be found the most glorious "Christmas Present" that could possibly be given to a discouraged and disillusioned mankind: *Peace on earth.*
Permanent and planetary. Guaranteed.
Who would believe it?
Yet, we shall see that it is true. Word for word.

For almost a century and a half, the most amazing mystery of our time has been taking place all over the world. It is going on right now even as you read these pages.
For nearly one hundred and fifty years, a worldwide enduring Peace among all the nations of the earth has been entirely within the grasp and capability of the human race. This planetary Peace could literally have been established by now. We already could

have been living under its protection.

True. Every word. No matter how astonishing.

It is the sort of wild-sounding irresponsible statements that automatically makes one shut himself off. Subconsciously we reject such ideas as being too preposterous, improbable or ridiculous to waste our time on.

Don't feel too badly for dismissing such comments out of hand so casually. That has been the attitude of the peoples of the world for the best part of one hundred and fifty years. However, the fact, remains, that the statement is absolutely true. And can be proved.

Perhaps this time, before we discard both the mystery and solution in such a cavalier fashion, we should take another look at the world around us. Is it the sort of world we can all be proud of? A safe, secure and happy place for our children to grow up in? Can we look to the future with glowing hope, confident that it is daily improving and getting better each day?

Exactly!

That is why I wish to repeat the above astonishing statement one more time. Underlined. With an exclamation mark.

<u>It has been completely within the competence of the present nations of the world to have raised up and maintained a planetary Peace at any time during the past one hundred years. An enduring, self-perpetuating World Peace!</u>

In the pages ahead you will find both a crystal-clear explanation of the mystery of peace that has long baffled most of mankind, as well as an acceptable, comforting and soul-satisfying solution to that mystery. Once and for all.

Now brace yourself for another shock.

All the prophecies made in the Holy Books of the past concerning the coming of the *Kingdom of God on earth* have all been fulfilled.

In our day.

Today.

Furthermore, the prophecies of *Isaiah* in his famous so-called

THE STORY BEGINS

Yuletide-prophecy, already quoted, have also been fulfilled.
To the last word.
Every phrase.
Without exception.
With the exactness of the stars.
That is even harder to swallow, but it is true. Every word. And can also be proved. And will be in these pages.

The *Prince of Peace,* the *Wonderful,* the *Counsellor,* the Everlasting Father of *Isaiah's* prophecy has already transformed the lives of thousands upon thousands of individuals all across the face of the planet. They are all busily engaged in raising up that *Kingdom of God on earth* foretold by Christ.

A radical change for the better has already taken place in a myriad of individual and personal lives, with the same improvement gradually beginning to make itself felt in the collective life of Bahá'ís working together. A controlled "microcosm" is going on all around you. Wherever it has been tried, it has proved to be eminently successful.

Without doubt both the people and the places which have been associated with this test of the Prince of Peace have improved remarkably. The people have become better persons and finer human beings, which is the goal of every Bahá'í everywhere. The part of our society in which these Bahá'ís move has acquired to a far greater degree the qualities and virtues of integrity and responsibility. Even spirituality.

We are now about to unravel a centuries-old mystery. Agatha Christie, P.D. James, Michael Innes or Katherine Aird have never even come close to such disclosures, however excitingly they write. The beauty of our story is that it is all true. Every blessed word.
And can be proved.
Our mystery has taken thousands of years to come to its climax,

but that hour is here now.

In our time.

You have a special opportunity to be in at the end of a Yuletide story that affects the welfare of all mankind.

It can happen to you this very weekend. Right here in your own hometown. Before your very eyes.

> *"See with your own eyes, and not through the eyes of your neighbor."*

2.

On Course!

The mystery itself is quite simple.

It has been described in Scripture as a "marvelous work" and "wonder".

Now, in our time, it is racing toward its world-healing, world-redeeming fulfillment.

Yes, I know. Such language as "world-healing, world-redeeming" puts you off. Especially since our world is apparently neither healed nor redeemed. Perhaps even such a word as Scripture makes you skeptical. You become less eager and interested in following up what certainly seems to be a fantasy, or more likely a cruel hoax of some kind. It pays to be cautious. The world is filled with weird and unpleasant things these days.

That's all part of the mystery.

It's not surprising that you feel the way you do. Doubtful. Annoyed. Even antagonistic.

You're supposed to feel that way. That itself is Scripture.

Both the *Old Testament* and the *New Testament* says that you *would* feel that way whenever someone told you about the "marvelous work" and "wonder".

Isaiah, Habakkuk, and *St. Paul* agreed that these incredible events would take place at the *time of the end.*

That's now. Right now. In our time. Yours and mine. We're not talking about something that happened long ago. This is as fresh as today's headlines. Scripture also agreed that people such as ourselves would not "believe" the wondrous story even when it was taking place right before our very eyes.

That's very hard to believe, isn't it?

I'll share with you the three puzzling quotations that let loose this great mystery upon the world. When you're finished reading the quotations, perhaps you and I can find a way to work out the solution to the mystery and, as a result, perhaps improve the world a little. It's promised that we can. If we try.

Do you have anything better to do this weekend?

If not, let's hear the quotations about this "marvelous work" and "wonder":

Then figure out what we're going to do about it.

> ISAIAH: "Therefore, behold, I will proceed to do a marvelous work among these people, even a marvelous work and a wonder; for the wisdom of their wise men shall perish, and the understanding of their prudent men shall be hid."
> (*Isaiah 9:14*)
>
> HABAKKUK: "Behold... and regard, and wonder marvelously: for I will work a work in your days, which ye will not believe though it be told to you." (*Habakkuk 1:5*)
>
> ST. PAUL: "Behold, ye despisers, and wonder, and perish: for I work a work in your days, a work which ye shall in no wise believe, though a man declare it unto you."(*)
> (*Acts 13:41*)

As you meditate and think about these quotations, ask yourself this question:

(*) (*Isaiah 29:1-24*) (*Habakkuk 1:5, 2:2-3*) (*St. Paul, Acts 13:40-41*) St. Paul's words poignantly remind us that they failed to "believe" in Christ's day, too, even "though a man declared" the truth unto them.

This wonderful Event takes place, of course, with the coming of every new Messenger of God, such as Christ, Buddha, Krishna — all of them without exception. All the peoples of the world in that Day should "Behold!" and "wonder marvelously", yet they do not "believe" the *wondrous story* even when it is being

THE STORY BEGINS

Did you know that the "Kingdom of God on earth" foretold by Christ in His *Lord's Prayer* was already established in its earliest beginnings? Right now? In our time? In more than one hundred thousand places across the surface of the earth?

I thought not.

Among people of all five races of mankind? From the Harvard Psychiatrist to the humblest Bushman? From the doctor to the ditch-digger? From the school teacher to the housewife? Without preference, without prejudice, without exception? And that the people who, already working in this Kingdom of God, all believe the story is true. And are devoting their lives and all they hold dear to make it come true for you, too.

Did you know that?

I thought not.

If all of this is still news to you, you'd better start making your move.

Before our Yuletide Drama comes to an end, you will have ample opportunity to hear the full story, or, as Scripture says, to "Behold! and wonder marvelously!"

Can you think of a more intriguing way to spend a weekend? Or a more exciting Yuletide mystery to solve?

All the pieces of the puzzle will be in your hands.

You will meet the *Wonderful*, the *Counsellor*, the *Everlasting Father*, the *Prince of Peace* of *Isaiah's* prophecy. He will offer you convincing proofs that He is the One Who He says He is. And the One Who *Isaiah* says He is.

In His own Words, He encourages you to be independent and courageous in your search, challenging everything. He urges you to:

"...look into all things with a searching eye"[1]

"told" to them, and is happening before their very eyes. In this Day, *the time of the end*, with the coming of Bahá'u'lláh, it is of supreme importance to the world since this is the Day of all fulfillment, the Day of the one fold and one shepherd, of the culmination of the promises of all the Prophets and Messengers of the past. In the end, of course, the peoples of the world will "Behold!" and "Believe".

The purpose of this book is to save everyone much travail and suffering, by opening their eyes now.

He wants you to study and search so that you will:

> ". . .see with thine own eyes and not through the eyes of others, and shall know of thine own knowledge and not through the knowledge of thy neighbor."[2]

Call a few of your friends. Read the book together. Pick it apart. Not as a hostile and pre-prejudiced opposer, but as a sincere, open-minded seeker after truth. When you're through, then you decide its value and worth.

Give it your best shot.

We'll wait right here until you're ready.

Just in case.

WELCOME BACK!

"Fishers of men, and quickeners of society."

3.

Behold And Wonder Marvelously

Welcome!

I had faith in you. We appreciate the gallant open mind you've displayed by coming back to read on. Let's make one thing clear to all of us from the outset. This "wondrous story" does not, and will never, take anything away from the greatness and majesty of Christ.

It does not diminish in any way the high and glorious station of Jesus. Quite the opposite. In fact, it elevates Christ and His Mission on earth to an even more lofty plane. One that will rejoice His loved ones.

That should be good news for every lover of Christ. He was always a fundamental part of the "marvelous work" and "wonder" from the very beginning. He played, and is still playing, a major role in our Yuletide Drama.

Christ announced the *Kingdom of God on earth* in His *Lord's Prayer*. The *Prince of Peace* Whom we study in these pages, came to establish that Kingdom in all its beauty. Without Christ there would have been no mystery to solve, no possible solution, and no *Kingdom of God on earth*.

It should come as no surprise to anyone who has carefully examined the words of *Isaiah* in the *ninth chapter* of his book, and the Words of Christ, to learn that most of the titles in this prophecy of *Isaiah* do not refer to Jesus.

Most of them were never intended to refer to Christ. In fact, some of the titles Christ Himself clearly and categorically repudiated, as we shall see. In His, Christ's, own Words.

For example:

> "... and the government shall be upon his shoulders."
> *(Isaiah 9:6)*

This prophetic phrase from that so-called famous Yuletide Prophecy, makes it unmistakably clear that these words quite plainly were never intended to refer to Christ at all.

The Words which Christ Himself spoke to His followers show us unquestionably that these words of *Isaiah* were not meant to describe Him, Christ.

Christ made it plain that the "government" would *not* be upon His "shoulders" when he said:

> "My kingdom is not of this world." *(John 18:36)*

Christ's *Kingdom* was clearly not an earthly Kingdom. Nor was it to be a worldly government which would be established here on earth by Christ. His, Christ's, Kingdom would be "in the hearts of men." He said so clearly.

Nothing could be plainer than Christ's own Words. His Kingdom was *personal* and *spiritual*. It was not *social*. At least not in the worldwide sense of reforming human society. That reform would have to await the day of Christ's Return in the "glory of his Father." *(Matt. 16:27)*

This great work, the "marvelous work" and "wonder" would have to await the coming of that *Spirit of Truth* foretold by Christ, that wondrous One Who would lead men "into all truth".

That would be the work of the *Prince of Peace*. He would not only be the *Spirit of Truth* foretold by Christ, but also the *Wonderful*, the *Counsellor*, the *Everlasting Father* and the *Prince of Peace* envisioned by *Isaiah*.

Jesus said unmistakably:

> "My kingdom is not of this world" *(John 18:36)*

He also said:

> "The Kingdom of God is within you" *(Luke 17:21)*

And still again:

> "Render therefore unto Caesar the things which be Caesar's, and unto God the things which be God's." *(Luke 20:25)*

The Message of Christ was for the individual, not for society as a whole. Christ Himself said that he came to make His followers "fishers of men". Later, they would be "quickeners of society".

The spiritualization of the planet with a worldwide "government" would have to await the coming of that Great One envisioned by *Isaiah,* that Great Figure yet to come. It would include the responsibility of taking the "government" of the world "upon His shoulders" and establishing worldwide, enduring Peace.

Could the *Prince of Peace* do less?

If the prophecies of *Isaiah* in *chapter nine, verse six,* of his book, did not refer to Christ, to Whom did they refer?

Specifically?

By name?

We need to know that.

It is essential to our understanding and full appreciation of this unique mystery, this incredible Yuletide Drama we are about to unfold. We "need to know" some of the background concerning this *Spirit of Truth* foretold by Christ, this *Prince of Peace,* Who would change and transform both the world and its peoples. Did He give us any clear proof that He was such a Personage?

Furthermore, the information must be presented to us in a way that would win our confidence and remove our doubts. After centuries of thinking about these things in quite a different way, it would not be easy to change our minds. To reverse our way of thinking.

Before we are through with our Yuletide Drama, we shall examine in detail every single word of that prophecy of *Isaiah*. We shall take it apart phrase by phrase. We shall probe until we discover the incredible truth that lies behind this story of "Peace on earth". We fully expect to find that truth disclosed in unexpected richness and fullness. All the truth, every last mystery, every secret hidden within those sacred words of *Isaiah* will be brought to light.

This information will be compleletly germane to that "marvelous work" and "wonder" of Scripture which we are investigating. Therefore, before we begin with the opening strains of *Isaiah* from *chapter nine, verse six,* let us first turn the searchlight on that all important question: **Who is the Prince of Peace?**

WHO IS THE PRINCE OF PEACE?

"And about time."

4.

The Prince of Peace

This is one of the most fascinating and enchanting parts of *Isaiah's* entire prophecy. We shall also be discussing that Figure referred to by Christ as the "Spirit of Truth," the One Whom Christ promised would lead this world of ours into "all truth". He, too, this wondrous Figure, will dominate the dramatic story of "Peace on earth" from this point on.

Why?

Because, in the end, He will prove to be One and the same Person, embracing all of the virtues foretold by both *Isaiah* and Christ for the *Spirit of Truth* and the *Prince of Peace.*

It is only fitting that we should meet this *Prince of Peace* now, and follow the course of those dramatic events surrounding Him right through to the very conclusion of our glorious Christmas story.

After all, He is the *Prince of Peace.* And we intend to prove it.

This long-awaited Supreme Redeemer of men, will clearly demonstrate that He is also the *Wonderful,* the *Counsellor,* and the *Everlasting Father* of *Isaiah's* incredible prophecy.

The "government" of the peoples of the world will indeed be "upon His shoulders". This, too, will be only *one* of the "marvelous works" and "wonders" which God had destined for Him to achieve in His spiritual conquest of the planet and upliftment of the hearts of mankind.

He, acting in His capacity as the *Spirit of Truth,* in leading mankind "into all truth" as Christ foretold He would do, will bring hope and assurance to all the peoples of the world; all, without exception — every man, woman, youth and child of every race, nation, religion and class of society.

He will demonstrate that He has fulfilled each and every one of the promises of both Christ and of *Isaiah*. This truly is a Christmas gift for each one of us. A precious package of love and unity which we shall hold to our hearts forever.

Perhaps one of the best answers to our question, "Who is this Prince of Peace?" can be found in the words of a well-known Christian Clergyman and Scholar, Reverend Dr. T. K. Cheyne, who, in his book, *The Reconciliation of Races and Religions,* declared:

"If there has been any prophet in recent time, it is to Bahá'u'lláh [Founder of the Bahá'í Faith] that we must go. Character is the final judge. Bahá'u'lláh was a man of the highest class — that of prophets."[1]

Those Christians who might be startled by this sudden and unexpected revelation, this powerful declaration by a Christian clergyman, may be more astonished when they read in his same book that Dr. Cheyne made an even more profound statement:

"There was living quite lately a human being of such consummate excellence that many think it is both permissible and inevitable even to identify him mystically with the invisible Godhead."[2]

This is not one of the followers of Bahá'u'lláh speaking, not a Bahá'í, but a renowned Christian clergyman. Dr. Cheyne was again referring to Bahá'u'lláh, Founder of the Bahá'í Faith.

The more we learn about Bahá'u'lláh, the more fascinating *Isaiah's* prophecy in the *ninth chapter* of his book becomes. Especially when we see for ourselves that Bahá'u'lláh has indeed fulfilled every one of the words of *Isaiah* in his famous so-called Yuletide prophecy. In rich abundance, and in penetrating detail.

Bahá'u'lláh's Name means "the glory of God" or "the glory of the Lord". These are all titles which *Isaiah,* whose prophecy concerning the *Prince of Peace* we are now reviewing, used on many other occasions when referring to the Promised Messiah yet to come.(*)

Dowager Queen Marie of Rumania wrote of Bahá'u'lláh saying that His "wondrous Message" was "Christ's Message taken up anew". Bahá'u'lláh's Teachings, the Queen declared, bring "peace to the soul and hope to the heart". Bahá'u'lláh's Teachings were to Queen Marie, she said, a "star" that could lead a bewildered mankind to "peace and good will with all men".

And about time.

That same Dowager Queen Marie of Rumania, who in her later years became a follower of Bahá'u'lláh, wrote of the wonderful Message of Peace and Love which the Bahá'í Writings brought to her when she first encountered them:

"The Writings of Bahá'u'lláh's Faith...are a great cry toward peace, reaching beyond all limits or frontiers...It teaches that all hatreds, intrigues, suspicions, evil words, all aggressive patriotism even, are outside the one essential law of God, and that special beliefs are but surface things whereas the heart that beats with divine love knows no tribe or race."[3]

"Search out Bahá'u'lláh's Books" she wrote, "and let their glorious, peace-bringing, love-creating words and lessons sink into your hearts as they have into mine."(**)[4]

Professor E. G. Browne, renowned Orientalist and Christian scholar (not a Bahá'í), also wrote of Bahá'u'lláh in the Holy Land and recorded his impressions of that first meeting with Bahá'u'lláh as follows:

(*) See *Isaiah 35:2; 40:5*. *Isaiah* in the thirty-fifth chapter of his book declares that "Carmel" and "Sharon" shall see the "glory of the Lord". The plain of "Sharon" lies behind the Bahá'í properties on that holy mountain "Carmel" where the Shrine of the Herald of the Bahá'í Faith is established, a site Bahá'u'lláh Himself chose for the Báb's Resting Place. Bahá'u'lláh walked and taught there on the side of God's Holy Mountain. It was on the side of that holy Mountain that Bahá'u'lláh announced the fulfillment of the prophecies of the past, and gave the charter for all the world Institutions to be raised there for the future benefit of all mankind. It is there that the Supreme Administrative Body of the Bahá'í Faith has its Seat in the World Center of the Faith of Bahá'u'lláh. This is but one more of the mysteries and wonders of this fantastic Christmas Story which, sad to say, there is no time to tell here in full detail. Happily you can study it in all its richness, glory and delight at your leisure.

(**) From the Toronto, Canada, Star, May 4, 1926

"No need to ask in whose presence I stood, as I bowed myself before one who is the object of a devotion and love which kings might envy and emperors sigh for in vain."[5]

David R. Williams, also not a Bahá'í, in his book *World Religion and Hope for Peace* gives a description of Bahá'u'lláh, Founder of the Bahá'í Faith, which I share with you here. Perhaps, unwittingly, Mr. Williams has given us a picture of the *Prince of Peace* envisioned by *Isaiah* in his famous prophecy.

"In the year 1892, there passed away in a Turkish penal colony at the foot of Mount Carmel in Palestine, one of the bravest spirits, one of the broadest minds, one of the noblest characters who ever graced this planet.

"Today several millions of people throughout the world hail this person as the hope of World Peace and the Savior of all mankind. These people can be found among all creeds and races.

"Bahá'u'lláh, in the judgment of many, possessed the tenderness of St. Francis, the courage of Socrates, the meekness of Moses, the sanity of Confucius, the missionary vigor of Muḥammad, the moral majesty of Isaiah, the compassion of Buddha and the saintliness of Jesus.

"This sounds like extravagant praise and you may reasonably question whether there is any such evidence that such an individual lived. But there is overwhelming evidence that such an individual did live and lived for seventy-five years, and under such trying conditions that if there had been any weakness in his mind or character, they were bound to be disclosed. But thus far, not even the enemies and persecutors of this man have ventured to say a word."[6]

Joseph Klausner, in his book, *The Messianic Idea in Israel*, speaks of the coming Messiah of "Peace" and "Justice", saying of those *last days* yet to come:

"The Jewish Messiah is a redeemer strong in physical power, and spirit, who in the final days will bring complete redemption, economic and spiritual, to the Jewish peoples and along with this eternal peace, material prosperity and ethereal perfection to the whole human race. The Jewish Messiah is truly human in origin of flesh and blood like all mortals, a Messiah, full of spirit, wisdom and understanding. He has a special feeling for justice. He shall smite the land with the rod of his mouth and with the lips shall he slay the wicked."

Klausner goes on:
"When the King Messiah is revealed to Israel, he will not open his mouth, except for peace, as it is written *(Isaiah 52:7)*. How beautiful upon the mountains are the feet of the messengers of good tidings that announceth peace. Also, the Messiah shall be peaceful in his very name as it is written *(Isaiah 9:6):* 'Everlasting Father, Prince of Peace.' "[7]

Former President Eduard Benês of Czechoslovakia was simple and direct in his praise of the "spirit" and capacity of the Bahá'í Faith to heap benefits upon mankind in its search for world peace.

President Benês declared that the "Bahá'í Teaching is one of the spiritual forces now absolutely necessary to put the spirit first in this battle against material forces." Benês described the Teachings of Bahá'u'lláh's Faith as "one of the great instruments for the final victory of the spirit and of humanity."

Benês said that he had followed the Bahá'í Faith both during and after the great War, and considered it to be "One of the great moral and social forces in all the world today." High praise indeed. Benês concluded his tribute, saying, "Such a movement as the Bahá'í Cause which paves the way for universal organization of peace is necessary."[8]

Professor E.G. Browne of Cambridge University, mentioned earlier, visited Bahá'u'lláh in the Holy Land and interviewed Him on four separate occasions. Browne wrote that Bahá'u'lláh made a ringing Call for that greatly needed world peace on earth. He, Bahá'u'lláh, said to Professor Browne on that occasion:

> "We desire but the good of the world and the happiness of the nations ... that the bonds of affection and unity between the sons of men should be strengthened; that diversity of religion should cease, and differences of race be annulled ... Yet so it shall be; these fruitless strifes, these ruinous wars shall pass away, and the 'Most Great Peace' shall come ..."[9]

"Christ knew it, and said so."

5.

The Theme of the Symphony

There is an entire volume of such glowing tributes to Bahá'u'lláh, the Founder of the Bahá'í Faith.(*) Before we come to the end of this astonishing, long-neglected, soul-uplifting, heart-comforting Christmas Story *The Prince of Peace*, we shall share several more of these remarkable tributes to Bahá'u'lláh made by outstanding leaders in all fields: Religion, Government, Education, Science, Politics, Business, Literature, and many others, including Presidents of countries as well as Universities.

Through all these tributes, like the theme of a symphony, runs the melody of *Peace on earth* from the *Prince of Peace*, Bahá'u'lláh.

This Yuletide Drama of *Christ and Bahá'u'lláh* is told with consummate beauty in a book of that same name. It was written by a once highly placed leader of the Christian Church.

George Townshend, Sometime Canon of St. Patrick's Cathedral in Dublin, Ireland, and Arch Deacon of Clonfert, also in the Emerald Isle, produced a remarkable book of great power. It is called: *Christ and Bahá'u'lláh.*(**) George Townshend dwelt briefly on this astonishing story of Bahá'u'lláh as the *Prince of Peace*.

Townshend, after a deep and careful study of the life and teachings of Bahá'u'lláh, left his high position in the Church, and be-

---

(*) See *Appreciations of the Bahá'í Faith*. Bahá'í Publishing Trust, Wilmette, Illinois.

(**) *Christ and Bahá'u'lláh*, George Townshend, Publisher George Ronald, 46 High Street, Kidlington, Oxford, England, OX5 2DN. Every year it becomes more of a "run away" best seller.

came a follower of Bahá'u'lláh. He devoted his life to the Bahá'í Faith. He urged his fellow-Christian clergymen to follow his example in embracing the Faith of Bahá'u'lláh. In a special document which he addressed to all of them called "The old Churches and the New World Order", Townshend shared with them the reasons Bahá'u'lláh had captured his heart.

Townshend has been described as the greatest Bahá'í writer in the West. A perusal of his book *Christ and Bahá'u'lláh* will greatly enrich your appreciation of the message of love and unity which Bahá'u'lláh has brought to the world in fulfillment of the promises of Christ.

In fact, this book of George Townshend, *Christ and Bahá'u'lláh*, was the inspiration for this expanded version of his brief glimpse into the story of the *Prince of Peace*.

Townshend pointed out that the Christian world unwittingly honored Bahá'u'lláh on the day they had set aside to commemorate the birth of Christ, by erroneously using these titles which more truly belong to Him, Bahá'u'lláh, than to His Holiness Christ, as we shall continue to see.

Throughout this entire Yuletide Drama, we shall become more and more aware that Bahá'u'lláh and Christ are one in Spirit, so that anything which honors Bahá'u'lláh, also honors Christ. And vice versa.

Bahá'u'lláh is plainly shown to be the Return of Christ. This is yet another "Gift" to mankind, supported by an almost endless fulfillment of prophecies from the sacred Scriptures of the past. A veritable downpour.(*)

So in one sense, these titles *do* belong to Christ as well, when understood in this symbolic manner.

(*)See *Thief in the Night*, some 300 pages of arresting and revealing prophecies fulfilled by the appearance of Bahá'u'lláh taken from the pages of the Holy Books of the past. All testify to this glorious and magnificent truth. Publisher, George Ronald, 46 High Street, Kidlington, Oxford, England, OX5 2DN

Christ's words, however, "My kingdom is not of this world" clearly show that the "government" of the future was never intended to be upon His "shoulders". Christ knew it, and said so.

Bahá'u'lláh, on the other hand, from the very beginning of His Mission, was deeply involved, on a continuing basis, in the establishment of a "just government" of peace and stability throughout the world.

Bahá'u'lláh took positive progressive steps to bring about this peace and justice. Upon such a Justice, Bahá'u'lláh said world peace must ultimately be based.

Already, in more than one hundred thousand Centers all over the world, the beginning of that foundation of Justice has been laid down. Thousands upon thousands of Local Spiritual Assemblies will become Local Bahá'í Houses of Justice in the future, they are functioning vigorously and successfully with ever-increasing expansion and strength in so many places in the world.

Bahá'u'lláh, as already indicated, gave to the world the laws, principles, agencies and institutions necessary to establish this "reign of justice" foreseen by *Isaiah*, promised by Christ, and now being established everywhere in the world by Bahá'u'lláh.

In almost every part of the world, through the teaching work and sacrifice of the Bahá'ís, those energetic followers of Bahá'u'lláh, the early beginnings of the "Christ-promised Kingdom of God on earth" are sinking deep roots into the soil of human hearts.

Most important of all, Bahá'u'lláh has brought the guidance and spiritual power to inspire the human race to *want* to accomplish this vital task. Not by His, Bahá'u'lláh's desire, but through that power and spirit born of God, the knowledge, wisdom and truth which Christ had promised would be brought to the world by the *Spirit of Truth*.

Bahá'u'lláh has offered all the "truth" needed to assure the fulfillment of God's plan for a *Kingdom* here on earth "as it is in

Heaven".

No man-made peace could hope to take the place of the *Peace Plan* sent down by God through His Messenger for that exact purpose, and have any hope of succeeding.

We have already witnessed the many continued failures of man in trying to go it alone, without the help of God, His Messengers, and His peoples.

Look at the condition of the world around you. Then examine this story from the pages of sacred Scripture — *Old* and *New Testament*, and all the Holy Books of the past — the story of Christ, *the Son* and Bahá'u'lláh, *the Father*.

Then you decide where your own future lies.

"I will send Him."

6.

Blessed Detour

Out of respect and consideration for those Christian friends who before reading this book, may not yet have heard all the details of this wondrous story of Bahá'u'lláh, the *Prince of Peace*, I have deliberately delayed our Yuletide Drama even a little longer before penetrating directly into the heart of our story of *Isaiah* and the *ninth chapter* of his book.

This further delay will greatly add to the ultimate appreciation of our Christian friends as they see the uniqueness of the unity, oneness and love which motivates both Christ and Bahá'u'lláh, and Christianity and the Bahá'í Faith. They will see, to their surprise, how the two Religions are linked together inseparably on behalf of all the peoples of the world.

This truth can be demonstrated clearly in this premonitory glimpse at Their own Words as spoken by Christ and Bahá'u'lláh.

> *CHRIST:* "Nevertheless I tell you the truth; It is expedient for you that I go away: for if I go not away, the Comforter will not come unto you; but if I depart, I will send him unto you. (*John 16:7*)

> *BAHÁ'U'LLÁH:* "O Kings of Christendom! Heard ye not the sayings of Jesus, the Spirit of God, 'I go away, and come again unto you?' Wherefore, then did ye fail, when He did come again unto you in the clouds of heaven, to draw nigh unto Him, that ye might behold His face, and be of them that attained His presence?"[1]

WHO IS THE PRINCE OF PEACE

CHRIST: "I have yet many things to say unto you, but ye cannot bear them now. Howbeit when he, the Spirit of truth, is come, he will guide you into all truth ..." (*John 16:12-13*)

BAHÁ'U'LLÁH: "O Kings of Christendom! ... in another passage, He (Jesus) saith: 'When He, the Spirit of truth is come, He will guide you unto all truth.' And yet, behold how when He did bring the truth, ye refused to turn your faces toward Him and persisted in disporting yourselves with your pastimes and fancies. Ye welcomed Him not, neither did ye seek His presence, that ye might hear the verses of God from His own mouth, and partake of the manifold wisdom of the Almighty, the All-Glorious, the All-Wise."[2]

Perhaps you are among those who are still inclined to say: "If this Faith of Bahá'u'lláh is so wonderful, why haven't I heard of it before? Surely, if there were a *Prince of Peace* on the planet, I would have known. I would have been informed about it long ago by my own religious leaders whose business it is to know about these things. The Scriptures are what they live by. Right?"
Wrong.
One would certainly think it should be as you describe, yet the Scriptures disagree with you. Entirely. This is one of the most fascinating parts of our Christmas Story. It is also one of the easiest doubts and worries to remove from your mind.
Scripture says clearly, definitely and unmistakably that mankind will *not* know the truth in this day. Even when it is staring them straight in the face.
It is all part of that "marvelous work" and "wonder" which God promised to accomplish in the *last days*. Mankind in general, except for that already promised "alert" and "awake" and "ready" miniscule minority, would not "believe" the story even when it was being "told" to them.
Face to face.
That's Scripture.
Remember?(*)

They wouldn't believe because their "eyes" and "ears" would be covered over. The "wisdom" of their "Wisemen" would be withdrawn. The "meaning of the books" would be "sealed" and "closed up" until the *time of the end*.

That's what would happen. And it would take place today.

In our time.

And, it's Scripture.

Although in far better and more elegant language than mine.

These facts of Scripture can't be repeated too often if we hope to rescue the potential *Elect* and *Chosen* who may still be among us with the potential to be able to see and hear. Hopefully, that group may even include ourselves.

Don't be discouraged if you yourself are skeptical and doubtful. You're supposed to feel that way. And probably will continue to do so right up to the very end. Most of mankind remains totally unaware of their great deprivation and loss. They have lived so long by the gratification of their physical senses and material pleasures, that they have lost the capacity to recognize and respond to the spiritual impulses surrounding them every day of their lives.

Or, as Scripture says, they are caught in the grasp of that deep "sleep like unto death."

I don't want that to happen to you.

Therefore, this temporary delay in our Yuletide Drama is very worthwhile. You might call it a blessed detour. I am now about to share with you quite an original device. It was tremendously helpful to me. Perhaps it will be to you, too. Let me tell you about it.

It is a unique Dialogue between Christ, *the Son*, and Bahá'u'lláh, *the Father*. It may set your heart on fire. As it did mine.

(*)Chapter 2, page 7. No doubt by this time, you have already read those words from the pages of Scripture yourself.

DIALOGUES OF DELIVERANCE

"You have the key to the only way the world can be made over."

7.

Gateway to the Prince of Peace

I am going to place the Words of Christ and the Words of Bahá'u'lláh side by side, one following the other, as in the dialogue of a play, until they reach their dramatic climax.

This comparison of the Words of Christ and the Words of Bahá'u'lláh will not be found in other Bahá'í books. This is a first time for us both. But it was such a thrilling thing for me, in my search for the *Prince of Peace*, I wanted to share the experience with you.(*)

It is important to understand from the outset that these dialogues are entirely of my own fashioning. Don't misunderstand. The quotations from both Christ and Bahá'u'lláh are completely authentic and accurate. The Words are Their Words and no one else's. It is the dramatic positioning of these quotations that is mine.

These dialogues inspired me (electrified me, really) to such a degree, that I wanted to share them with you.

I felt sincerely that if I did, you would never again have any doubts about the oneness and unity of the Missions of Christ and Bahá'u'lláh. You would see at once Their common shared purpose in raising up the *Christ-promised Kingdom of God on earth*. Trans-

---

(*)The dialogues in *All Flags Flying*! were taken from this book *Prince of Peace* which has been in the process of writing for over six years. These pages were first written in 1979.

forming both the inner and outer life of mankind, until it would be here "on earth" as it is "in heaven".

It would be a life dedicated to the service of God and our fellowman; developing and utilizing all of our God-given talents, enabling us to become better persons and finer human beings; balanced, mature, fulfilled human beings as was intended for all of us by God from the beginning.

Establishing this *Kingdom of God on earth*, was the "great work" of the Mission of both Christ, *the Son*, and Bahá'u'lláh, *the Father*.

So astonishing and delightful were these arranged dialogues between Christ and Bahá'u'lláh, and so many, so expansive, and so abundant were Their shared Words and Concepts, that I eventually made up an entire book of them called: "Dialogues of Deliverance".

I have since used these remarkable quotations from the lips of Christ and Bahá'u'lláh in other books.

Once the dialogues shared here between Christ, *the Son*, and Bahá'u'lláh, *the Father*, have ended, we shall return to our Yuletide Story of the *Prince of Peace* and follow it to its surprising and satisfying conclusion.

The Station of Bahá'u'lláh, as revealed in these dialogues, is confirmed, not by the love and admiration of Bahá'ís, but by the tributes which Christian scholars, educators, scientists and religious leaders have paid to Him. The knowledge of these tributes will not only bring comfort to the Christian seeker after truth, but will enrich the dialogues themselves which are yet to come.

It was a Christian clergyman, not a Bahá'í, who first introduced the Faith of Bahá'u'lláh to America. Dr. Henry H. Jessup, D.D. addressed the Columbian Exposition of 1893 at Chicago, and pointed out that Bahá'u'lláh had recently been visited by a Cambridge University scholar and educator in the Holy Land. At that time, Jessup told his audience, Bahá'u'lláh had given "utterance to sentiments" that were both "noble" and "Christlike". So much so, that Jessup used those words of Bahá'u'lláh in his closing remarks to that famous Exposition in the Parliament of Religions.[1]

It was not a Bahá'í, but a Christian scholar and scientist, Dr. George Washington Carver, not a White man but a Black man, who spoke movingly about the gifts of peace, love and unity which the Bahá'í Faith had brought to the world:

"I am so happy to know that the Christlike Gospel of good will is growing throughout the world.

"You hold in your organization [the Bahá'í Faith] the key that will settle all of our difficulties, real and imaginary.

"May God bless, keep and prosper you."[2]

The following are a few more of those countless glowing "tributes" to the greatness and value of the Teachings of Bahá'u'lláh which, to this very day, continue to flow in from all parts of the world.

Dr. Raymond Frank Piper, another Christian educator and scholar, while serving in the Philosophy Department of the Syracuse University, declared: "The Bahá'í Faith is laden with the goods we so direly need in this catastrophic era."[3]

The renowned American historian, also a Christian, Dr. Herbert Adams Gibbons, after carefully examining the Bahá'í Teachings on the reformation of human society, stated:

"I have had on my desk, and have read several times, the three extracts from the Bahá'í Writings on Social Regeneration. Taken together, they form an unanswerable argument and plea for the only way the world can be made over. If we could put into effect this program, we should indeed have a new world order."[4]

And lastly, because there is no end to the words of praise honoring Bahá'u'lláh, it was not a Bahá'í, but yet another Christian clergyman, not a Westerner, but an Oriental, the Reverend K.T. Chung, who in the preface to the Chinese version of *Bahá'u'lláh and the New Era*, said plainly:

"Should the Truth of the Bahá'í Faith be widely disseminated among the Chinese people, it will naturally lead to the coming of the Kingdom of Heaven. Should everybody again exert his efforts toward the extension of this beneficent influence throughout the world, it will then bring about world peace and the general welfare of humanity."⁵

Every sincere seeking Christian heart should now feel much more confident in our Yuletide Drama. They can be comforted by the fact that Bahá'u'lláh not only found favor in the eyes of the Bahá'ís of the world, but also among prominent sincere Christian clergymen, scholars and students. Many of them have become followers of Bahá'u'lláh because of the impact His Message had upon their hearts.

So enthusiastic did they become, that they are now busily engaged in every corner of the world in helping to raise up the "Kingdom of God on earth" foretold by Christ.

Enough of the suspense.

It is now time to share our *Dialogues* between Christ and Bahá'u'lláh and between Christianity and the Bahá'í Faith.

Perhaps the final barriers will be removed from every potential *Elect* and *Chosen*, such as ourselves. May we no longer be numbered among the many who were "called", but among the few who were "chosen".

Our destiny: To carry out the "great work" of both Christ, *the Son*, and Bahá'u'lláh, *the Father*.

Bahá'u'lláh Himself calls out to every such willing and receptive Christian heart:

> "O people of the Gospel! They who were not in the Kingdom have now entered it, whilst we behold you, in this day, tarrying at the gate. Rend the veils asunder by the power of your Lord, the Almighty, the All-Bounteous, and enter, then, in My name, My Kingdom."⁶

Let our Dialogues, the gateway that leads to the *Prince of Peace*, begin.

"Into all truth!"

8.

Drama of the Kingdom

This revealing Dialogue concerning the *Comforter* and the *Spirit of Truth*, taken from the Words of both Christ, *the Son*, and Bahá'u'lláh, *the Father*, is intended to furrow the soil of every Christian and Bahá'í heart, and prepare them to accept the seeds of the world unity planted by the *Prince of Peace*.

The Dialogues are designed to inspire us to arise and serve this Scriptural-promised Kingdom of the *Announcer*, Christ and the *Fulfiller*, Bahá'u'lláh.

The Son speaks and *the Father* replies:

> CHRIST: "Nevertheless I tell you the truth; It is expedient for you that I go away: for if I go not away, the Comforter will not come unto you; but if I depart, I will send Him unto you. (*John 16:7*)

> BAHÁ'U'LLÁH: "The Comforter Whose advent all the Scriptures have promised is now come that He may reveal unto you all knowledge and wisdom. Seek Him over the entire surface of the earth, haply ye may find Him."[1]

> CHRIST: "I have yet many things to say unto you, but ye cannot bear them now." (*John 16:12*)

> BAHÁ'U'LLÁH: "This is the Word which the Son (Jesus) veiled when He said to those around Him that at that time they could not bear it ..."[2]

CHRIST: "Howbeit when he the Spirit of truth is come, he will guide you unto all truth ..." (*John 16:13*)

BAHÁ'U'LLÁH: "Verily the Spirit of Truth is come to guide you into all truth."[3]

CHRIST: "And when he is come, he will reprove the world of sin, and of righteousness, and of judgment: Of sin, because they believe not on me ..." (*John 16:8*)

BAHÁ'U'LLÁH: "Beware that thou disputeth not with Him [Bahá'u'lláh] even as the Pharisees disputed with Him [Jesus] without a clear token of proof ... Consider those who opposed the Son [Christ] when He came unto them with a sovereignty and power ... yet when the fragrance of His beauty was unveiled, they turned aside from Him and disputed with Him."[4]

CHRIST: "He will reprove the world ... because they believe not on me." (*John 16:8-9*)

BAHÁ'U'LLÁH: "Ponder ye, and be not of them that are veiled and fast asleep. He that wedded not (Jesus) found no place wherein to dwell or lay His head, by reason of that which the hands of the treacherous had wrought."[5]

CHRIST: "He shall glorify me ..." (*John 16:14*)

BAHÁ'U'LLÁH: "Know thou that when the Son of Man [Christ] yielded up His breath unto God, the whole creation wept with a great weeping. By sacrificing Himself, however, fresh capacity was infused into all created things."[6]

CHRIST: "He shall glorify me ..." (*John 16:14*)

BAHÁ'U'LLÁH: "The deepest wisdom which the sages have uttered, the profoundest learning which any mind hath unfolded, the arts which the ablest hands have produced, the influence exerted by the most potent rulers, are but manifestations of the quickening power released by His [Christ's] transcendent, His all-pervasive, and resplendent Spirit."[7]

CHRIST: "He shall glorify me ..." (*John 16:14*)

So that there should never, for all time, remain any doubt of the holy link of love between them, Bahá'u'lláh replied with His own Name:

BAHÁ'U'LLÁH: "He [Bahá'u'lláh] is the One Who glorified the Son [Jesus] and exalted His Cause."[8]

Our dialogue between Christ and Bahá'u'lláh, races on towards its appointed end.

*"He hath testified of Me, and
I do testify of Him."*

9.

The Inseparable Link

Our dialogue continues:

CHRIST: "... he shall testify of me." (*John 15:26*)

BAHÁ'U'LLÁH: We testify that when He [Christ] came into the world, He shed the splendor of His glory upon all created things. Through Him the leper recovered from the leprosy of perversity and ignorance. Through Him the unchaste and the wayward were healed. Through His power, born of Almighty God, the eyes of the blind were opened, and the soul of the sinner sanctified ... He it is Who purified the world. Blessed is the man who, with a face beaming with light, hath turned towards Him."[1]

CHRIST: "... he shall testify of me." (*John 15:26*)

BAHÁ'U'LLÁH: "Say, verily, He hath testified of Me, and I do testify of Him."[2]

CHRIST: "... he shall testify of me." (*John 15:26*)

BAHÁ'U'LLÁH: "Consider those who rejected the Spirit [Christ] when He came unto them with manifest dominion. How numerous were the Pharisees who had secluded themselves in synagogues in His name, lamenting over their separation from Him, and yet when the portals of reunion were flung open and the divine Luminary [Christ] shone resplendent from the Dayspring of Beauty, they disbelieved in God, the Exalted, the Mighty. They failed to attain His [Christ's] presence, notwithstanding that His Advent had been promised in the Book of *Isaiah* as well as in the Books of the prophets and Messengers. No one from among them turned his face towards the Dayspring of divine bounty except such as were destitute of any power amongst men. And yet, today, every man endowed with power and invested with sovereignty prideth himself on His Name Christian."[3]

And still another time:

> *BAHÁ'U'LLÁH:* "Moreover, call thou to mind the one who sentenced Jesus to death, He was the most learned of His Christ's age in His own country, whilst he who was only a fisherman believed in Him. Take good heed and be of them that observe the warning."[4]

> *CHRIST:* "... he shall testify of me." (*John 15:26*)

> *BAHÁ'U'LLÁH:* "Verily He Who is the Spirit of Truth is come to guide you unto all truth. He speaketh not as prompted by His own Self, but as bidden by Him [God] Who is the All-Knowing, the All-Wise."[5]

> *CHRIST:* "... he shall testify of me." (*John 15:26*)

> *BAHÁ'U'LLÁH:* "Open the doors of your hearts, He Who is the Spirit [Christ] verily standeth before them. Wherefore keep ye afar from Him Who hath purposed to draw you nigh unto a Resplendent Spot? Say: We, in truth, have opened unto you the gates of the Kingdom. Will ye bar the doors of your houses in My face? This is naught but grievous error. He, verily, hath again come down from heaven, even as He [Christ] came down from it the first time."[6]

And on yet another occasion, Bahá'u'lláh addressed the entire "concourse of Christians" and admonished them to accept what

Christ Himself had foretold.

> *BAHÁ'U'LLÁH:* "O concourse of priests! Leave the bells, and come forth, then, from your churches. It behooveth you, in this day, to proclaim aloud the Most Great Name among the nations. Prefer ye to be silent, whilst every stone and every tree shouteth aloud: 'The Lord is come in His great glory!' Well is it with the man who hasteneth unto Him. Verily, he is numbered among them whose names will be eternally recorded and who will be mentioned by the Concourse on High."[7]

Wouldn't you like to be numbered among them? Among the people described by Bahá'u'lláh as those who "summoneth men in My Name" and who will "show forth that which is beyond the power of all that are on earth."

And finally still upon our theme "he shall testify of me" as foretold by Jesus.

> *CHRIST:* "... he shall testify of me." (*John 15:26*)

> *BAHÁ'U'LLÁH:* "Say, Lo! The Father is come, and that which ye were promised in the Kingdom is fulfilled! This is the Word which the Son [Christ] concealed, when the appointed time was fulfilled and the Hour had struck, the Word shown forth above the horizon of the Will of God. Beware, O followers of the Son that ye cast it not behind your backs. Take ye fast hold of it. Better is this for you than all that ye possess. Verily, He is nigh unto them that do good. The Hour which We had concealed from the knowledge of the peoples of the earth and of the favored angels hath come to pass. Say, verily, He hath testified of Me, and I do testify of

Him. Indeed, He [Christ] hath purposed no one other than Me. Unto this beareth witness every fair-minded and understanding soul."[8]

Having established the close and inseparable ties that bind together Christ, *the Son*, and Bahá'u'lláh, *the Father*, we now come to our final unique and revealing Dialogoue.

"Things to come"

10.

Lo, He Is Come With Conclusive Proof

One of the most fascinating and challenging things said by Christ in all these "fashioned" dialogues which I have prepared for you between Christ, *the Son,* and Bahá'u'lláh, *the Father,* concerns the subject of "things to come."

"*The Son* speaks and *the Father* replies" comes to a close with this chapter. It should empty our cup of all pre-conceived ideas about the relationship between Christ and Bahá'u'lláh, and between Christianity and the Bahá'í Faith.

Both Christ and Bahá'u'lláh made it unmistakably clear that these amazing "things to come" foretold by Christ, and to be fulfilled by Bahá'u'lláh, the *Spirit of Truth,* would come only by inspiration from on High.

Christ said of the Spirit of Truth:

> *CHRIST:* "... he shall not speak of himself, but whatsoever he shall hear, that shall he speak ..." (*John 16:13*)

> *BAHÁ'U'LLÁH:* "Verily, He Who is the Spirit of Truth is come to guide you unto all truth. He speaketh not as prompted by His own Self, but as bidden by Him [God] Who is the All-Knowing, the All-Wise."[1]

Christ announced the *Kingdom of God* in His *Lord's Prayer.* Bahá'u'lláh proclaimed that Kingdom of Christ, and called for its establishment everywhere on the planet.

Bahá'u'lláh addressing the leaders and people of Christianity called out:

BAHÁ'U'LLÁH: "Lo! He is come in the sheltering shadow of Testimony, invested with conclusive proof and evidence, and those who truly believe in Him regard His presence as the embodiment of the Kingdom of God. Blessed is the man who turneth towards Him..."[2]

Our Dialogue continues and concludes.

CHRIST: "... and he [the Spirit of Truth] will shew you things to come." (*John 16:13*)

BAHÁ'U'LLÁH: That Dawning Place of Revelation [Christ] saith that on that Day He Who is the Promised One will reveal the things which are to come. Accordingly... most of the things which have come to pass on this earth have been announced and prophesied by the Most Sublime Pen [Bahá'u'lláh]."[3]

CHRIST: "... he will shew you things to come."
(*John 16:13*)

BAHÁ'U'LLÁH: "Though the clearest proofs attest the truth of His Cause; though the prophecies He [Bahá'u'lláh], in unmistakable language hath made have been fulfilled ... yet, behold how this generation hath rejected His authority, and rebelled against Him! ... God grant that, with a penetrating vision and radiant heart, thou mayest observe the things that have come to pass and are now happening, and, pondering them in thine heart, mayest recognize that which most men have, in this Day, failed to perceive."[4]

How could the peoples of the world have missed such a *Headline Story?* How many Anchor-men were asleep when the story broke? How could it have gone unnoticed?
Easily.

They were numbered among those that would not "believe" the story even when it was being "told" to them. They would "behold" and "wonder marvelously", sigh, then go on with their drab daily lives of "business as usual". They would vaguely be aware they were missing something quite unique, but never knowing what it was.(*)

Aren't we lucky?
We're getting another chance.

(*)A perfect description of our days, today, is found in *II Timothy, 3:7:* "Ever learning, and never able to come to the knowledge of the truth". In those days described in the *Acts of the Apostles* of Christ as: "Perilous times ... for men shall be lovers of their own selves, covetous, boasters, proud, blasphemers, disobedient to parents, unthankful, unholy, without natural affection, truce-breakers, false accusers, incontinent, fierce, despisers of those who are good. Traitors, heady, high-minded, lovers of pleasures more than lovers of God, having a form of godliness, but denying the power thereof: from such turn away." (*II Timothy, 3:1-5*)

I should think so. It sounds like any modern-day city, doesn't it? Chicago, Rio, Los Angeles, Hong Kong, New York, London, Moscow or Tokyo.

What hope would they have for "truth" without the *Spirit of Truth* foretold by Christ to "lead mankind into all truth."

Bahá'u'lláh is His Name. It means: *The Glory of God.*

Better learn how to spell it and pronouce it.

It will come in "oh so handy!" when the sky of chicken-little is finally falling!

"Things to come"

11.

Fulfilled

This is the dramatic story of those "things to come" which Bahá'u'lláh foretold in fulfillment of the prophetic words of Christ. Some of these events have already taken place. Many are now happening around you. Others will take place in the future. But all will inevitably come to pass.

Ask yourself, as you read about these dramatic events, who among your Christian friends except yourself is even vaguely aware that Christ, when he foretold the inevitable coming of the *Spirit of Truth*, also promised the world that this *Spirit of Truth* would "show" to the peoples of the world those "things" that were yet "to come"? So they might confidently "believe" in Him. And become numbered among the *Elect* and the *Chosen*, those "prepared souls" who would recognize the "marvelous work" and "wonder" for exactly what it was: *the Kingdom of God on earth*.

They would "Behold!" and "wonder marvelously!" and "believe" and walk straight to the close with the big sign:

KINGDOM OF GOD ON EARTH
("ENTER HERE")

If you didn't have "eyes to see", that blurred-sign would read: *EXPRESS DOWN!*

How many Christians know that Bahá'u'lláh actually acknowledged Christ's Words, and answered them? Or that Bahá'u'lláh actually spoke of these "things to come" to which Christ had referred.

We shall therefore review a few of those "things to come" promised by Christ, and shown to the world by Bahá'u'lláh, as a further preparation to *Isaiah's* famous prophecy about the *Wonderful*, the *Counsellor*, the *Everlasting Father*, the *Prince of Peace*.

You will ask yourself "Who else could He be? If not Bahá'u'lláh? Who else has shown us any of those wonderful things? Who else has offered such proofs? And left it entirely up to us, saying: "Believe it or not, as you choose." When He should have said: "Read 'em and weep!"

Let us now examine these:

THINGS TO COME
(Described by Bahá'u'lláh's Pen and recorded in the Writings of His Faith)

(1) The calling for a vast assemblage of Nations both great and small to protect the rights of all countries and peoples. The United Nations Charter and Declaration of Human Rights are filled with echoes of the Principles and Teachings which Bahá'u'lláh gave to the world over a hundred years ago.

(2) The coming of that terrible and destructive nuclear-force which could "poison the atmosphere" and "destroy the cities".

(3) The downfall of Kings and the passing of their dynasties.

(4) The inevitability of both the First and Second World Wars.

(5) The unprecedented persecution of the Jews on the European continent following the first World War.(*)

(*)Following World War I which was yet another among the "things to come" foretold by the Writings of Bahá'u'lláh's Faith, Europe and the world were warned about the terrible persecution of the Jews that would take place on European soil because Bahá'u'lláh's Teachings were still not put into effect. Following that same War, a Message was sent from the Bahá'í World Center in the Holy Land to the Great Peace Conference held at the Hague. Once again Bahá'u'lláh's Teachings on Peace were shared with that Conference. Even the title "Union of Nations" was given in that Message, and the type of Body needed to assume the leadership

(6) The graft, corruption, crime and lawlessness at a never before equalled pitch of intensity which would seize and paralyze the cities of the world were also among those "things to come" foreseen and warned against by Bahá'u'lláh long before the event.

(7) The disastrous consequences that would follow the use of habit forming drugs, and the terrible affect of alcohol upon the human body and spirit.

(8) The alarming number of broken marriages. The increasing divorce rate. How nearly half of all marriages would be dissolved upon the flimsiest of pretexts, endangering the stability of human society. The family and the home were the basic unit of society, and would lose their prestige and honor. All warnings of Bahá'u'lláh.

(9) The rapid rise of the Movement of the Left which would spread its influence into all parts of the world.

(10) A radical transformation in human society.

(11) The rolling up of the present day Order in the world.

(12) The weakening of the pillars of religion.

(13) The development of terrible weapons of war.

(14) The burning of cities.

(15) The contamination of the atmosphere of the earth.

(16) The fundamental changes affecting the structure of the governments of the world.

(17) The spread of tyranny.

(18) Political conflict, racial animosity, class antagonism, immorality, irreligion — all the attendant events that proclaim the ineffectiveness and obsolescence of the institutions of a morally bankrupt society.

These warnings are all found in the Writings of the Faith of the

among the nations of the world if Peace were to be established and maintained was carefully described. The reply from the nations of the world was silence. What a loss! What a tragedy for mankind! What a fulfillment of Scriptures! It foreshadowed the suffering and struggle that still lay ahead for an unrepentant society. Pity is, it was all so unnecessary. It was among the "things to come" foretold by Christ and fulfilled by Bahá'u'lláh.

Prince of Peace, Bahá'u'lláh. He constantly directed the eyes of the world to the one remedy that could shelter and protect mankind in this day against the onslaught of such ungodly assaults on their lives — both material and spiritual.

> *BAHÁ'U'LLÁH:* "The whole of mankind is groaning, is dying to be led to unity, and to terminate its age-long martyrdom. And yet it stubbornly refuses to embrace the light and acknowledge the sovereign authority of the one Power that can extricate it from its entanglements and avert the woeful calamity that threatens to engulf it.[1]

With those clear warnings behind us, and that essential background describing the majesty and greatness of Bahá'u'lláh, *the Glory of God*, and the sole hope of present-day society, let us return directly to our astonishing *Yuletide Prophecy*.

OUR YULETIDE MYSTERY UNFOLDS

"Some great Figure yet to come."

12.

Joy to the World

We shall now resume where we left off in our review of *Isaiah's* prophecy in the *ninth chapter* of his book. We shall examine that *ninth chapter* phrase by phrase in a much more hopeful manner.

The story begins with Christ and Bahá'u'lláh. Yet, throughout, these glorious references symbolically and figuratively refer to both Christ and Bahá'u'lláh.

They are One and inseparable in Spirit.

Christ announced the *Kingdom of God on earth* and Bahá'u'lláh is now establishing it everywhere in the world. Through His followers. These Bahá'ís have already laid the foundation for that *Kingdom* in more than one hundred thousand places in all parts of the planet.

Did you know that?

Honestly?

We shall see before our Yuletide Drama comes to an end, how each one of these promised titles of *Isaiah*, while still honoring Christ, have been fulfilled in lavish abundance by Bahá'u'lláh.

With the exactness of the stars.

Let us begin at the very beginning.

The first words of that *sixth verse* in *Isaiah's chapter nine*, say:

> "For unto us a child is born, unto us a son is given..."
> *(Isaiah 9:6)*

The first part of this prophecy would quite clearly appear to apply to His Holiness Christ alone. He came in the Station of the Son. In fact, *Isaiah*, two chapters earlier, speaking of the *first* coming of Christ, declares plainly:

> "Therefore the Lord himself shall give you a sign; Behold, a virgin shall conceive, and bear a son, and shall call his name Immanuel."(*) (*Isaiah, 7:14*)

What a beautiful and powerful picture that provides of His Holiness Christ. His Name? Immanuel, God is with us!

Nothing could be plainer or more comforting than that.

After this opening phrase, the prophecy of *Isaiah* switches back to the future and the *time of the end*. The very next phrase speaks of "the government" being "on his shoulders", something which Christ categorically denied as referring to Him.

Thus, the opening strains of this peerless and unique Christmas symphony of *Isaiah*, quite clearly refer to both Christ and Bahá'u'lláh. To *the Son*, Christ, in time of His first coming, and to *the Father*, Bahá'u'lláh in the time of His, Christ's Return in the glory of *the Father*. The day when "the government" shall indeed be upon His "shoulders" as we shall clearly see.

The truth is, the two stories (Christ and Bahá'u'lláh) are interwoven throughout this book as the melodies of one single theme: *The Kingdom of God on earth.*

After the opening line of *Isaiah's* so-called Christmas prophecy, the remainder speaks almost exclusively of the future and those promised days of fulfillment for the world through this Great Figure yet to come: The "Wonderful", the "Counsellor", the "Everlasting Father", the "Prince of Peace".

Before you have finished reading *"The Prince of Peace"*, we feel sure you will believe in your heart that these words could refer to none other than Bahá'u'lláh.

Christ Himself will help make this truth unmistakably clear to each one of us.

It is this Yuletide Story of total fulfillment which we shall now

---

(*)Literal meaning: "God is with us."

unfold before your eyes. As promised at the outset, it will bring to the world that longed-for hour when the heart of every man shall once again "rejoice", because of this "Gift of Peace" which He, Bahá'u'lláh brings each one of us; exactly as it was foretold and promised in sacred Scriptures.

It is ours, this *GIFT OF PEACE*. Why shouldn't we have it? With no further delay.

Joy to the world!

"AND THE GOVERNMENT SHALL BE UPON HIS SHOULDERS"

"These things are not optional, they are obligatory."

13.

Well-wishers of the Governments of the World

We are now back in the flow of *Isaiah's* famous Yuletide prophecy.

"... and the government shall be upon his shoulders."
(Isaiah 9:6)

We have already seen in chapter three of this book that Christ made it unmistakably clear that the "government" was never intended to be upon His, Christ's, "shoulders."

That accomplishment would await the "great work" to be achieved by the *Spirit of Truth*, Bahá'u'lláh foretold by Christ.

We shall now see how the "government" quite unmistakably was always intended to be Upon His, Bahá'u'lláh's, "shoulders."

Already, in more than one hundred thousand places all over the planet, that "Kingdom of God" foretold by Christ, that "spiritual government" from on High, has already put down deep roots. In the fullness of time that Kingdom will "be on earth as it is in heaven."

Just Government and the Peace of the World were always among the principal concerns of Bahá'u'lláh. How could it be otherwise? Bahá'u'lláh made it plain to the world from the very beginning of His Mission that it was the wish of God that the world's religious and civil leaders would "unitedly arise for that reformation of this age and rehabilitation of its fortunes."

Bahá'u'lláh, writing to one of the world's religious leaders, re-emphasized this social aspect of His Message. Bahá'u'lláh declared that His purpose at all times was to assist both the governments of the world, and their citizens, to obtain and preserve a full and rich life of peace, security and happiness.

Bahá'u'lláh wrote:

> "This Wronged One hath, at all times, aimed and striven to exalt and advance the interests of both the government and the people..."[1]

The Writings of Bahá'u'lláh's Faith express this principle clearly as one of the basic instructions to be followed by every Bahá'í:

> "... the Bahá'ís must obey and be well-wishers of the governments of the land..."[2]

So vital and important was the principle of "just government" that Bahá'u'lláh gave clear instructions to all mankind, as well as His own followers, as they labored to raise up that long-awaited, eagerly-anticipated and desperately needed Christ-promised Kingdom of God on earth.

Bahá'u'lláh said:

> "It is incumbent upon every man, in this Day to hold fast unto whatever will promote the interests, and exalt the station, of all nations and just governments. Through each and every one of the verses which the Pen of the Most High hath revealed, the doors of love and unity have been unlocked and flung open to the face of men."[3]

Bahá'u'lláh has given us a glimpse into the future showing what it might be like in a country which was inspired by His Teachings, and where the hearts of the people were motivated by the spirit of His Faith. It was a day which He, Bahá'u'lláh, foretold was close at hand and rapidly drawing nearer and nearer.

Bahá'u'lláh proclaims:

"The day is approaching when God will have exalted His Cause and magnified His testimony in the eyes of all who are in the heavens and all who are on the earth."[4]

And again:

"The day is approaching when all the peoples of the world will have adopted one(*) universal language and one common script. When this is achieved to whatsoever city a man may journey, it shall be as if he were entering his own home ... It is incumbent upon every man of insight and understanding to strive to translate that which hath been written into reality and action."[5]

Bahá'u'lláh adds to these Words, saying:

"That one indeed is a man who, today, dedicateth himself to the service of the entire human race. The Great Being saith: Blessed and happy is he that ariseth to promote the best interests of the peoples and kindreds of the earth. In another passage He hath proclaimed: It is not for him to pride himself who loveth his own country, but rather for him who loveth the whole world. The earth is but one country and mankind its citizens."[6]

(*)This international language would be taught in each land in addition to the mother-tongue, so the beauty and glory of each nation's own language would never be lost. Yet, at the same time every man would be able to converse with ease, comfort and accuracy with every other person on the planet.

This is all the work of the *Prince of Peace*, is it not? Bahá'u'lláh undertook it willingly on behalf of all the nations, peoples, and governments of the world. To the leaders of men Bahá'u'lláh said that these things were not optional, they were mandatory. They were not a suggestion, but a command.

Bahá'u'lláh declared:

"These things are obligatory and absolutely essential."[7]

> *"Peace-loving, law-abiding, non-violent citizens."*

14.

The All-Powerful Physician

We thus see how boldly Bahá'u'lláh took this "government" envisioned by *Isaiah* upon His "shoulders". Bahá'u'lláh addressed a special Message to the "elected representatives of the people of every land", those who were in a position to play such a vital and dominating role in the governments of their own countries.

Bahá'u'lláh understood only too well the weaknesses and needs of present-day civilization. He offered the leaders of mankind the remedy which these key-figures in the affairs of the world could use to help save the world from the recovering and grave illness of disunity from which it constantly suffered.

Bahá'u'lláh declared:

> "O ye the elected representatives of the people in every land! Take ye counsel together, and let your concern be only for that which profiteth mankind, and bettereth the condition thereof."[1]

Bahá'u'lláh pointed out the frailties and weaknesses of a human leadership which had withdrawn from the work of God and the Word of God. He warned about the danger of being ruled by such leaders who sought to benefit personally at the expense of their country and its peoples. Sweet hopes of a better land and a better time of life for their subjects were dashed to pieces by such cruel leaders. Such greedy rulers left behind a disillusioned people with broken hopes and dreams. Such leaders had created a distrustful skeptical people who no longer believed any of their leaders. A people hard to move and inspire.

Bahá'u'lláh told these leaders, upon whom their innocent and trusting subjects had once depended so innocently and naively, exactly how they must act from now on toward their people.

Bahá'u'lláh warned them of the grave dangers for their "government", their peoples, as well as for themselves, if they did not behave with integrity and in a just manner at all times, as expected and required by God.

Bahá'u'lláh wrote:

> "O ye the elected representatives of the people in every land! ... Regard the world as the human body which, though at its creation whole and perfect, hath been afflicted, through various causes, with grave disorders and maladies. Not for one day did it gain ease, nay its sickness waxed more severe, as it fell under the treatment of ignorant physicians, who gave full rein to their personal desires, and have erred grievously."[2]

And yet again:

> "And if, at one time, through the care of an able physician, a member of that body was healed, the rest remained afflicted as before. Thus informeth you the All-Knowing, the All-Wise."[3]

Bahá'u'lláh denounced the selfishness which motivated a great number of today's leaders. He laid the burden of responsibility for many of the world's most serious ills upon such unenlightened leadership. They were all too often more interested in what would be pleasing to men and to themselves, rather than what would be pleasing to God. They ignored and neglected the needs of their nation which called for a leadership of concern, imagination, creativity and an incorruptible integrity.

In the slang phrase of a once outraged legislator, "They are more interested in the fleece than in the flock."

Bahá'u'lláh spoke of the sad state of the world, saying:

> "We behold it, in this day, at the mercy of rulers so drunk

with pride that they cannot discern clearly their own best advantage, much less recognize a Revelation so bewildering and challenging as this. And whenever any one of them hath striven to improve its condition, his motive hath been his own gain, whether confessedly so or not; and the unworthiness of this motive hath limited his power to heal or cure."[4]

Bahá'u'lláh never failed to praise those leaders and legislators who were sincere and labored for the welfare of their people. Such leaders were, He said, like a "breath of life" to the body of the world.[5]

Bahá'u'lláh then prescribed the only remedy that could solve these grave difficulties from which the world suffered. These afflictions which were threatening its very life needed an immediate, an all-powerful healing.

Bahá'u'lláh proclaimed:

> "O ye the elected representatives of the people in every land! ... That which the Lord hath ordained as the sovereign remedy and the mightiest instrument for the healing of all the world is the union of all its peoples in one universal cause, one common Faith. This can in no wise be achieved except through the power of a skilled, an all-powerful and inspired Physician."[6]

The followers of Bahá'u'lláh, the members of the Bahá'í Faith, are the "well-wishers" of every nation and government. They are loyal to the governments of their native lands. They are peace-loving, law-abiding, non-violent people. These are instructions of Bahá'u'lláh, the Founder of their Faith, the *Prince of Peace*. He has directed them to behave in this responsible manner at all times. Every Bahá'í must be both loyal and trustworthy. It is part of their religion. It can never be compromised, or put aside, even temporarily, for any reason whatsoever.

This spiritual "government", this *Kingdom of God* "on earth as it is in heaven", will eventually prevail no matter how hostile or opposed the actions of present-day leaders of man may be.

This is a promise, a vow really, upheld and frequently renewed in the Writings of Bahá'u'lláh's Faith. Such integrity was foretold as a certainty in the great Scriptures of the past for this very day.

Clearly, this first part of *Isaiah's* famous prophecy, "the government shall be upon his shoulders", refers to Bahá'u'lláh and not to Christ.

We have taken but one cup from the ocean of this Truth from the *Spirit of Truth*.

All the seas and pearls remain for your own later search and discovery as you probe deeper and deeper into the wonder of our Christmas Story.

I envy you as I remember only too well the excitement, joy and rapture that gradually enveloped me as the story unfolded before my own eyes.

To cite the words of a famous Bahá'í historian, on another far greater occasion, as the majesty and greatness of Bahá'u'lláh's story was unveiled to him and his companions on the Eve of Bahá'u'lláh's *Declaration* of His Mission to the world:

"O for the joy of those days, and the gladness and wonder of those hours!"[7]

May they soon be yours, too.

"WONDERFUL! COUNSELLOR!"

"O people of the earth!"

15.

The Strong Fortress

The prophecy of *Isaiah* continues:

"... and his name shall be called Wonderful, Counsellor ..." (*Isaiah 9:6*)

Christ made it plain to His disciples who the *True Counsellor* would be.

Jesus said:

"I have yet many things to say unto you, but ye cannot bear them now.
"Howbeit when he, the Spirit of truth, is come, he will guide you into all truth..." (*John 16:12-13*)

The coming Great One, the *Spirit of Truth*, would *Counsel* the whole world with His wonderful Words of wisdom and guidance. The *Spirit of Truth* would guide mankind toward the true path of world peace, and would show them how to achieve it.

All this was implicit in Christ's promise. Among the most important "truths" into which man desperately needed to be led was the achieving of World Peace. No one would contest that Truth.

Bahá'u'lláh left no doubt about the One to Whom Christ was referring when He spoke of the *Spirit of Truth*. Bahá'u'lláh addressed the ruling monarchs of the Christian world, saying:

"O kings of Christendom! Heard ye not the sayings of Jesus, the Spirit of God ... 'When He, the Spirit of Truth, is come, He will guide you into all truth.' And yet behold how, when He did bring you the truth, ye refused to turn your faces towards Him ... Ye welcomed Him not, neither did ye seek His Presence, that ye might hear the verses of God from His own mouth, and partake of the manifold wisdom of the Almighty ... Ye have by reason of your failure, hindered the breath of God from being wafted over you ..."[1]

Most of the entire world has been deprived of this "Breath of God" and "hindered" from receiving this outpouring of "Truth". Exactly as foretold in Scripture, they still did not "believe", and were thus deprived and rendered "obsolete" and useless in helping mankind.

The world cries out for peace, but there is no peace. How can there be peace when the *Prince of Peace* has been withheld, even obstructed, in administering His healing God-given remedy?

His *"Counsels"* are the guidance promised to the world in sacred Scripture, *Counsels* which have been sent to protect and shelter all the peoples of the world. What a tragedy for the world if mankind continues to be "hindered" from hearing, accepting, and acting upon what God had destined for man in this day simply because of the spiritual "blindness" and "deafness" of those who Christ Himself condemned because they refused to "enter" into the Truth in His day. Instead, they had "hindered" those prepared souls who were trying to "enter". (*Luke 11:52*)

Bahá'u'lláh declared:

> "Every man of insight will, in this day, readily admit that *the counsels* which the Pen of this Wronged One hath revealed constitute the supreme animating power for the advancement of the world and exaltation of its peoples."[2]

Bahá'u'lláh offered ample evidence that He was that *true Counsellor* promised by Christ, the "Spirit of Truth". He came to guide a bewildered and unshepherded world into "the truth" that would revive and rescue it. Bahá'u'lláh called upon the world to study

His Teachings and His *Counsels* to mankind before dismissing them so carelessly.

The power, logic and relevance of these Teachings to deal with the current needs of this afflicted world, would help the peoples of the world to become aware of the value and significance of the guidance which Bahá'u'lláh was offering as the *Counsellor* of the human race, as *the Spirit of Truth*.

They had it all in the palm of their hand, at their fingertips. Every single solution to their most horrendous problems was theirs.

Yet, the world for over a century has continued to neglect and reject Bahá'u'lláh's *Counsels*. Thus, each day the world has added to the measure of its own suffering. This planetary grief cannot improve, but can only deepen and worsen, unless and until the Plan given to mankind for this day by God's appointed Messenger is adopted. In its entirety.

Nothing should have been plainer than that to anyone familiar with sacred Scripture and interested in the story of the *Prince of Peace*. And who had taken the time to find out.

Bahá'u'lláh's Pen had a plaintiff sound as He wrote:

> "Though the world is encompassed with misery and distress, yet no man hath paused to reflect what the cause or source of that may be. Whenever the True Counsellor uttered a word in admonishment, lo, they all denounced Him as a mover of mischief and rejected His claim."[3]

Bahá'u'lláh counselled all men and women to change their lives, to improve their characters, so that they might become trusted citizens of their country, people whose integrity was unquestioned by their fellowman.

Especially did He thus address His own followers. Only such a transformed people would be sufficiently worthy, and capable, of raising up the *Christ-promised Kingdom of God on earth*, the sovereign remedy for the desperate state of the world.

Every Bahá'í on the planet, without exception, is striving each day to achieve this goal of becoming a better person, a finer human being. There are no exceptions. Only in this way Bahá'u'lláh tells us can we hope to change the world.

First we must change ourselves.

These are all *Counsels* from the *Prince of Peace*.(*)

Becoming a better person and a finer human being, Bahá'u'lláh declared, was the true purpose in life for every human being. This is what Scripture meant when it said that man was created in the "image and likeness of God". We must acquire God-like virtues: Trustworthiness, integrity, kindliness, compassion, love and justice, among others.

These are all *Counsels* from the Pen of Bahá'u'lláh, given to the world for its understanding and betterment.

Bahá'u'lláh declared:

> "Beautify your tongues, O people, with truthfulness, and adorn your souls with the ornament of honesty. Beware, O people, that ye deal not treacherously with anyone. Be ye the trustees of God amongst His creatures, and the emblems of His generosity amidst His people ... Such are the counsels which I bequeath unto you. Would that ye might follow My counsels!"[4]

How could the Christ-promised Kingdom of God on earth be established by lesser people? Only the *Elect* and the *Chosen* could do that.

And again, in the Words of the *Counsellor*, Bahá'u'lláh:

> "From the heaven of God's Will, and for the purpose of ennobling the world of being, and of elevating the mind and souls of men, hath been sent down that which is the most effective instrument for the education of the whole human race ... Incline your hearts, O people of God, unto the counsels of your true, your incomparable Friend."[5]

In one of His more than one hundred volumes, each one of

(*)The underlining in all instances throughout this book are those of the author. They are used merely for emphasis.

which has been described as a treatise on morality, integrity and trustworthiness, Bahá'u'lláh calls out:

> "O people of the earth! ... Hearken to the advice of this oppressed One. Abandon that which ye hold, and adhere unto what the trustworthy counsellor commands. Deprive not yourselves of that which is created for you."[6]

Bahá'u'lláh's Words make it clear that the time has come for man not only to "do unto others as you would have them do unto you", but to be among those "blessed" ones who "prefer" his brother *before* himself.

Bahá'u'lláh says of His *Counsels* to the world:

> "Each one of the revealed commands is a strong fortress for the protection of the world. Verily, this oppressed One only wishes your security and elevation."[7]

The story of *Isaiah's* prophecy concerning the *Prince of Peace* continues, and will demonstrate ever more clearly that Bahá'u'lláh is indeed the one to Whom *Isaiah* was referring when he spoke of the "Wonderful!", the "Counsellor!".

> *"Counsels that can satisfy the needs of all mankind."*

16.

Hearken, O Ye That Dwell on Earth!

Bahá'u'lláh made it clear that only the Word of God could bring about the changes needed to improve the world today. If mankind continued to ignore the *Counsels* of the *Spirit of Truth* sent by God to help them, obviously the world's problems would only intensify and worsen until they did listen.

Bahá'u'lláh wrote:

> "The One true God beareth Me witness ... Before the face of all men I have arisen ... My object is none other than the betterment of the world and the tranquillity of its peoples. The well-being of mankind, its peace and security, are unattainable unless and until its unity is firmly established. This unity can never be achieved so long as the counsels which the Pen of the Most High hath revealed are suffered to pass unheeded."[1]

Such inspiring Words as these help us see that Bahá'u'lláh was indeed not only the *Counsellor* referred to by *Isaiah*, but the *Wonderful*, as well.

The "well-being" and welfare of all humanity, every soul upon the surface of the planet, was Bahá'u'lláh's primary concern, one to which Bahá'u'lláh devoted His entire life and Mission.

Bahá'u'lláh is the Gift-giver from God Who came for the protection and happiness of the peoples of the world. The sacred Writings of the Bahá'í Faith say of Bahá'u'lláh, the Supreme Redeemer of men:

"He is the One to Whom none can compare, Whose utterance mortal man can never rival. He it is Who from everlasting hath been established upon the seat of ascendancy and might, He from Whose lips have gone out counsels that can satisfy the needs of the whole of mankind ..."[2]

How marvelous these Words ring out when they are taken together with the words of *Isaiah* in his *fortieth chapter*, words which *Isaiah* uses to speak of the "Counsellor" Whom God will raise up and direct for the rescue and redemption of mankind.
Isaiah declares:

"To whom then will ye liken me, or shall I be equal? saith the Holy One." (*Isaiah 40:25*)

Bahá'u'lláh, the Holy One foretold, echoed yet another time those words of *Isaiah* when He wrote:

"Who is the man amongst you that can rival Me in vision or insight? Where is he to be found that dareth to claim to be My equal in utterance or wisdom? No, by My Lord, the All-Merciful! All on the earth shall pass away; and this is the face of your Lord, the Almighty, the Well-Beloved."[3]

Shouldn't somebody have listened? Wasn't there anyone worthy to hear either the Words of Christ, *the Son* or Bahá'u'lláh, *the Father*? Shouldn't you, yourself, struggle to be among the rescued before you, spiritually speaking "go down for the third time"?

Isaiah, in that same chapter, mentions the very title of Bahá'u'lláh, the *Glory of the Lord*, which shall be "revealed" to the world; the One Who will bring solace and hope to mankind;

the "Comforter" promised by Christ.
Isaiah says:

> "Comfort ye, comfort ye my people, saith your God ... the *glory of the Lord* shall be revealed, and all flesh shall see it together: for the mouth of the Lord hath spoken it."
> (*Isaiah 40:1,5*)

It was the same promise given by *Habakkuk* who said that "the knowledge of the *Glory of the Lord* shall cover the earth as the waters cover the sea."

In a little less than one hundred and fifty years, the "knowledge" of Bahá'u'lláh, Whose Name means the *Glory of the Lord* or the *Glory of God,* has been spread to all parts of the planet, on land and in the islands of the seven seas. Not just the *knowledge* of His Teachings, but the foundation of His Kingdom of Peace which is already being built upon a Local, National and International basis.

In well over three hundred countries, territories and islands, and in more than one hundred thousand Centers around the world, the roots of this *Christ-promised Kingdom of God on earth* which Bahá'u'lláh has come to establish, have already been planted.

The fact that the leaders of mankind still do not know of this "great work" of the Lord, shows only too clearly how blind, deaf, and sleeping humanity has been to the call of God's "Counsellor", the *Prince of Peace.*

That this very neglect was destined to happen is also Scripture. So don't feel too badly. Yet.

Just because such a state of spiritual catalepsy was prophesied for the generality of mankind in this day, does not mean that you yourself have to remain in such unaware state of spiritual deprivation. You can still hearken to the words of *Isaiah* which he spoke about this very time in which we, you and I, are now living.

Isaiah states plainly:

> "Who hath directed the Spirit of the Lord, or being his counsellor hath taught him?
> "With whom took he counsel, and who instructed him, and taught him in the path of judgment, and taught him

knowledge, and showed to him the way of understanding?"
(*Isaiah 40:13-14*)

Bahá'u'lláh echoed these words of *Isaiah*:

> "Can any one of you race with the Divine Youth in the arena of wisdom and utterance, or soar with Him into the heaven of inner meaning and explanation? Nay, by My Lord, the God of mercy! ... Can the one possessed of wooden legs resist him whose feet God hath made of steel?"[4]

Bahá'u'lláh tried to awaken those souls who had the potential to help build the *Christ-promised Kingdom on earth*. He couldn't bear to lose even one single soul. God created them all. God wanted them all.

Bahá'u'lláh cried out:

> "O people of the earth! ... give ear unto the counsels of this Wronged One. Abandon the things current amongst you and adopt that which the faithful Counsellor biddeth you.
>
> "Deprive not yourselves of the bounties which have been created for your sake."[5]

Bahá'u'lláh urged the peoples of the world to arise and seize their chance so they might bettter both their social and individual lives through the *Counsels* which He, in answer to the Summons of God, had brought to the earth for their welfare and benefit.

> "Arise, O people, and by the power of God's might, resolve to gain the victory over your own selves, ... Do not busy yourselves in your own concerns; let your thoughts be fixed upon that which will rehabilitate the fortunes of mankind and sanctify the hearts and souls of men. This can best be achieved through pure and holy deeds, through a virtuous life and a goodly behavior."[6]

Bahá'u'lláh goes on:

> "Incline your hearts, O people of God, unto the counsels

of your true, your incomparable Friend. The Word of God may be likened unto a sapling, whose roots have been implanted in the hearts of men. It is incumbent upon you to foster its growth through the living waters of wisdom, of sanctified and holy words, so that its root may become firmly fixed and its branches may spread out as high as the heavens and beyond."[7]

Bahá'u'lláh made certain that the people of the world understood that His *Counsels* were for the entire world, and not merely for His own followers. Bahá'u'lláh didn't come to the Bahá'ís, He came to the world. Bahá'u'lláh was addressing all humanity, the masses of mankind, when He wrote:

"The summons and the message which We gave were never intended to reach or to benefit one land or one people only. Mankind in its entirety must firmly adhere to whatsoever hath been revealed and vouchsafed unto it. Then and only then will it attain unto true liberty ... Incline your hearts, O people of God, unto the counsels of your true, your incomparable friend."[8]

And again:

"O ye that dwell on earth! ... We have, on the one hand, blotted out from the pages of God's holy Book whatsoever hath been the causes of strife, or malice and mischief amongst the children of men, and have, on the other, laid down the essential prerequisites of concord, of understanding, of complete and enduring unity. Well is it with them that keep My Statues."[9]

Bahá'u'lláh not only brought *Counsels* to benefit and enrich the lives of individuals; but, to re-emphasize, He brought the Teachings, the Laws, the Agencies and the Institutions which if properly established and maintained, would assure the peace and tranquillity of mankind.

He was not only the *Counsellor* of *Isaiah*, but the *Prince of Peace* as well.

Above all Bahá'u'lláh brought that special power of the *Holy Spirit* to the peoples of the world, which would enable each one of them to raise up this better world in an eager, willing manner, "on fire!" with its truth in a way, and with an enthusiasm, that would make it work better and function properly and continuously. Not in theory alone, but with practical answers and solutions to the world's grave problems. They would be surrounded by the *Spirit* all the days of their lives, if they arose to serve.

These Bahá'í Institutions have already been established around the world in their primary stages, both National and Local. The roots are down. They are already working, growing and developing for the future welfare of all humanity.

Thanks to their "True" and incomparable friend, their "Counsellor", Bahá'u'lláh, the *Kingdom of God on earth* is already underway!

> *"Incline your hearts to the Counsels of your incomparable Friend."*

17.

The All-Knowing Physician

We read these powerful, moving Words from the Pen of Bahá'u'lláh concerning the *Counsels* which He poured out uninterruptedly for half a century for the betterment of the world. In more than one hundred volumes, Bahá'u'lláh showered His Words of love, unity and guidance upon mankind. Every phrase proclaimed His Station as the *Wonderful,* the *Counsellor* of *Isaiah.*

Bahá'u'lláh Himself declared:

> "Each one of the ordinances We have revealed is a mighty stronghold for the protection of the world of being."[1]

And again, repeat:

> "He it is ... from Whose lips have gone out counsels that can satisfy the needs of the whole of mankind ..."[2]

Yet, Bahá'u'lláh points out, we should carefully observe how the world remains blind and indifferent to the one truth that can rescue and redeem it.

Bahá'u'lláh writes:

> "Behold the disturbances which, for many a long year, have afflicted the earth, and the perturbation that hath

seized its people. It hath either been ravaged by war, or tormented by sudden and unforeseen calamities. Though the world is encompassed with misery and distress, yet no man hath paused to reflect what the cause or source of that may be. Whenever the True Counsellor uttered a word in admonishment, lo, they all denounced Him as a mover of mischief and rejected His claim."[3]

How can the world, with both its leaders and peoples asleep and entrapped in a paralyzing materialism, hope to recover by its own unaided efforts? They have neglected and fought against the one Power which God has sent to rescue, redeem, and restore them to a peaceful, progressive fruitful life? It would, naturally, be difficult, if not impossible to overcome such neglect and indifference.

Bahá'u'lláh denounced such faithless, false leaders exactly as Christ Himself had denounced them. They "do not enter" the Faith "themselves", Christ warned, but instead, they "hinder" others whose hearts are touched and attracted, and prevent *them* from "entering". Such leaders of men are unworthy of their high stations.

Bahá'u'lláh appealed to those sincere and prepared souls, those potential *Elect* and *Chosen*. He told them to trust only their own heart, and not to be misled by such "bats of darkness" as those who abhor the Light of God's Truth.

Bahá'u'lláh, *the Father,* echoed the Words of Christ, *the Son.* In every Day in which a Messenger of God appears, He, too, Whoever He may be, and to whatever people, or segment of society He may appear, is also the *Wonderful,* the *Counsellor* for that age. Bahá'u'lláh is speaking as the Counsellor promised for these *last days,* the *time of the end,* the Day of the *One Fold and One Shepherd,* the day of fulfillment. Bahá'u'lláh speaks for each and every one of these Prophets and Messengers of the past Who had gone before Him.

Christ said:

> "I am the resurrection, and the life: he that believeth in me, though he were dead, yet shall he live: And whoso liveth and believeth in me shall never die." *(John 11:25-26)*

Every Word Christ spoke was true.

Bahá'u'lláh, speaking to the sincere souls who might still help others to become "awakened" in this Day, the promised Day foretold in all the Scriptures of the past, refers to that same spiritual theme. Bahá'u'lláh declared:

> "Arise, and lift up your voices, that haply they that are fast asleep may be awakened. Say: O ye who are as dead! The Hands of divine bounty proffereth unto you the Water of Life. Hasten and drink your fill. Whoso hath been re-born in this Day, shall never die; whoso remaineth dead, shall never live."[4]

Such a spiritual re-birth comes to the follower of every past religion in this Day, the Day of the *Wonderful,* the *Counsellor* of *Isaiah's* prophecy. Every human being who hears and obeys His *Counsels,* is a "re-born Christian", a "re-born Buddhist", a re-born soul of every Religion.

Some have caught a glimpse of this spirit, but never solved the Mystery of what a wonderful thing it was that they were "Re-born" into!

A spiritual human being who has become "reborn" in every way today, is now qualified to be numbered with the *Elect* and the *Chosen* in this critical, crucial, all-important day. Hopefully, you are numbered among them, the builder of the *Kingdom of God on earth*.

That is the most glorious destiny which any human being can achieve — the goal and purpose of life.

Hurray for you!

We can't let anyone take it from you.

Bahá'u'lláh urges all mankind, each one of these transformed and recreated souls, to join in the "great work", and to apply

God's healing-remedy to this sick, afflicted world.

Such is the value and power of His *Counsels*.

This is not only the salvation for all society, it is also the only salvation and hope for every individual human being.

For *you*.

How can we make sure we all succeed? That everyone, every human being on the planet has his or her choice.

"And so you shall."

18.

Beautify Your Tongues

Bahá'u'lláh urges each one of these transformed, reborn and recreated souls to join in the "great work" and to apply God's healing remedy to this sick, afflicted world.

> "The All-Knowing Physician hath His finger on the pulse of mankind. He perceiveth the disease, and prescribeth, in His unerring wisdom, the remedy."[1]

Bahá'u'lláh reveals the planetary remedy which He, the *Spirit of Truth,* has come to administer to the crying needs of our present-day society. He directs the eyes of man to His world-unifying, world-healing Teachings on all aspects of modern society. Bahá'u'lláh declares:

> "Through the movement of Our Pen of glory We have, at the bidding of the omnipotent Ordainer God, breathed a new life into every human frame, and instilled into every word a fresh potency. All created things proclaim the evidences of this worldwide regeneration. This is the most great, the most joyful tidings imparted by the pen of the wronged One to mankind."[2]

And again:

> "Incline your hearts, O people of God, unto the counsels of your true, your incomparable Friend. The Word of God may be likened unto a sapling, whose roots have been im-

planted in the hearts of men. It is incumbent upon you to foster its growth through the living waters of wisdom, of sanctified and holy words, so that its roots may become firmly fixed and its branches may spread out as high as the heavens and beyond."[3]

Bahá'u'lláh calls out to every individual:

"Beautify your tongues, O people, with truthfulness, and adorn your souls with the ornament of honesty. Beware, O people, that ye deal not treacherously with any one. Be ye the trustees of God amongst His creatures, and the emblems of His generosity amidst His people ..."[4]

It becomes almost incomprehensible that this sophisticated and materially brilliant world of ours, which can conquer space, walk on the moon, watch television, work computers, transplant human organs, arrest cancer, cure tuberculosis, could miss the greatest story of all: The transformation of human character that would result in the raising up of the *Christ-promised Kingdom of God on earth.*

What "marvelous work" and "wonder" could be greater than that?

Or compare to it in any way?

Bahá'u'lláh, the *Wonderful!* the *Counsellor!* declares:

"Such are the counsels which I bequeath unto you. Would that you might follow My counsels!"[5]

We *shall* follow them. Now! We have no other hope. Our very survival and that of our family and our friends depends upon it.
That is what the next crucial chapters are all about:
Our survival!
Can we meet the challenge of a skeptical world, or not?

THE CHALLENGE

"The Conquest of the Elect and the Lost"

19.

Prelude

A full comprehension of the words of *Isaiah, Habakkuk* and *St. Paul* is not only germane, but essential to our understanding of "As the waters cover the sea". Let us examine their words once again, one after the other.

We have heard their warnings, now let us hear about the blessings that will be showered upon those who develop *spiritual eyes* and *spiritual ears* in these last days.

Isaiah described the complete change that would take place in the hearts and souls of those who turned a "believing" ear to the Lord.

In *Isaiah's* own words:

> "And in that day shall the deaf hear the words of the book, and the eyes of the blind shall see out of obscurity and out of darkness." (*Isaiah 29:24*)

Isaiah goes on with his glad-tidings:

> "The meek also shall increase their joy in the Lord, and the poor among men shall rejoice in the Holy One of Israel...
> "They also that erred in spirit shall come to understanding, and they that murmured shall learn doctrine." (*Isaiah 29:24*)

Hurray for our side!

And How about *Habakkuk*?

Habakkuk encouraged everyone to forget the past, and to wait for that coming day of victory.

Habakkuk says:

> "And the Lord answered me, and said: Write the vision, and make it plain upon tables, that he may run that readeth it.
>
> "For the vision is yet for an appointed time, *but at the end it shall speak*, and not lie though it tarry, wait for it; because it will surely come, it will not tarry." (*Habakkuk 2:2-3*)

In the very same chapter *Habakkuk* gives us the good news:

> *HABAKKUK:* "For the earth shall be filled with the knowledge of the glory of the Lord, as the waters cover the sea."(*)
> (*Habakkuk 2:14*)

You see? You do have a chance.
Even now.
Especially now. If you "believe" at last.

St. Paul also warned the "despisers" to "Behold" this "work" being accomplished by God in their day because if they didn't, *St. Paul* warned them of their perilous state.

> *ST. PAUL:* "Beware therefore, lest that come upon you, which is spoken of in the prophets." (*Acts, 13:40-41*)

You see?

(*)We learned earlier that "the glory of the Lord" was one of the titles bestowed upon Bahá'u'lláh. It was the actual meaning of His Name in English. Bahá'u'lláh: *Glory of God* or *Glory of the Lord*.

Straighten up, fly right, or else.
No one has a better chance than you. Forewarned is forearmed.
In the words of *St. Paul*, which were not only for his day, but for our day, too, for all time.

> *ST. PAUL:* "How shall we escape, if we neglect so great salvation..." (*Hebrews 2:3*)

Christ foretold that the day would come when He would no longer speak in parables, but would show the people openly of *the Father*. Christ promised that those things which had been "whispered in closets" would in that day be proclaimed "from the housetops".

That day has come at last.

"Never since the beginning of the world," Bahá'u'lláh Himself affirms, "hath the Message been so openly proclaimed."¹

Sincere "prepared" souls like yourself are out there, everywhere, waiting with willing eager hearts to serve the Lord for whom they have been waiting.

This is their day. Your day.

Bahá'u'lláh spoke tenderly about such heroic souls who were trying their best to shake off this material world, and become better in their lives:

> "Let thy soul glow with the flame of this undying Fire that burneth in the midmost heart of the world, in such wise that the waters of the universe shall be powerless to cool down its ardor." ²

Bahá'u'lláh made it clear that no matter what the world might think, these pure-hearted souls were not fanatical in any way. They were mature, balanced human beings who represented the very best, and most competent, in their chosen fields whatever their profession or trade might be. The world might think them fanatical, but the shoe was really on the other foot.

These Bahá'ís were successful in their chosen fields, dependable and trustworthy because of their spiritual nature. Because to them: "Work is worship to God."

They endeavor to fulfill their job-responsibilities to the best of their abilities as a service to their fellowman, and as a tribute to God. Their daily work accomplished in this spirit is the finest kind of prayer possible. It is also the most competent and professional manner in which to handle the job, and whatever task may be assigned to them.

Over and above their integrity and dependability, what makes these Bahá'ís everyone's choice to accomplish whatever work needs to be done, is that they are lovers of God more than lovers of man. They are exactly the opposite of the kind of people Scripture warned the world to "turn away" from in this day if we wanted to stand out as a useful and upright citizens of our home town.

Remember?

Timothy? 3:1-5?

Such sincere, well-balanced souls would sooner or later be numbered among the *Elect* and the *Chosen*. People popular with everyone because they were helpful, kind and helpful. Bahá'u'lláh was always hoping that the *Elect* might help Him capture the hearts of the *Lost*.(*) He called upon His followers to help Him awaken spiritually sleeping souls wherever they were found. And tell them what day they were living in, and to "wake up!"

Bahá'u'lláh declared:

> "Make, then, mention of thy Lord, that haply the heedless among Our servants may be admonished through thy words, and the hearts of the righteous be gladdened." 3

(*)Bahá'u'lláh never forgot to mention and praise every soul that tried. Each soul who might hear and recognize the truth of His Mission and arise to help Him better the spiritual condition of every other human being, and the world as a whole. God wants them all, not just *some*. Because He created them all. Each soul was a special beautiful prize worthy of entering the Kingdom of God, Bahá'u'lláh was determined not to lose any of them. Including you.

Happily, for the "children of the Prince of Peace", the number of new believers in the Bahá'í Faith is growing like a rising tidal river.

"The Challenge: And the Verdict."

20.

Yes? Or No!

A favorite expression one frequently hears from an unbelieving world when discussing this theme, is this:

"But if Scripture says that the peoples of the world won't believe the story even when it's being told to them, can those people really be held responsible? Or be blamed for not hearing it?"

"Scripture is to blame, not the people."

"God *said* they wouldn't believe, and they *don't*. They can't. It's not their fault. You can't go against God."

"Right?"

Wrong.

This is a new time in history now. *Scripture* is on your side at last. Why? Because it's the *last days*, the *time of the end*, when the *blind* and *deaf* can see at last. When the truth is so plain that even the person who runs can "read" it and understand, this is the time of that "great salvation" at last. Just as it was promised to us in the Scriptures. The "glory of the Lord" will fill us with all the knowledge we need to become part of the *Kingdom of God on earth*.

Halellujah!

Up until now, the overwhelming number of people didn't even know there *was* a Scripture which said they wouldn't "believe" Even when the "wondrous story" was happening before their very eyes. In fact, they didn't even know there *was* a "wondrous story".

The first time many such Christians learned there was something wonderful in the world which they should "Behold" and wonder at "marvelously" was when they read about it here in this book for the first time.

Of course, it comes as a shock. But a little shock-therapy may be just what the world needs. Spiritually speaking. If they hope to make a little spiritual life-saving progress.

Isn't it a blessing to learn about the Scripture in which Christ Himself tells us to be "awake" and "alert" and not "sleeping" at the *time of the end* and during the *last days*? Without Christ's warning we might have been "cast asunder" and our "portion would be appointed with the hypocrites."

Nobody wants that!

Right?

If we had been "awake" today, right now, in our time, we'd have had every right to expect that we might be among those who would "see" and "hear" and "believe" the wondrous story and become numbered with the *Elect* and the *Chosen*.

From total loser to total winner. Like snapping our fingers.

Perhaps we should hear Christ's own Words one more time. Just to make sure we're on the right path this time. And know what we are expected to do, in this day, if we want to be part of the Christ's promised *Kingdom of God on earth*. We've waited long enough for it. Let's not lose it. Each one of us can appraise our own position when we're through. Or lack of it. And see where we really stand.

Christ made this point plainly and unmistakably to the Christian world. Not only for that day, but for this day as well, for all time. He was speaking to us. And said so.

These are His Words of warning:

> "Take ye heed, watch and pray: for ye know not when the time is ... Lest coming suddenly he find you sleeping.
> "And what I say unto you I say unto all, Watch."
> *(Mark 13:33-37)*

Everybody can figure out their own present position easily enough. Did you "heed"? Did you "watch"? Did you "pray" about it? Or is this all bad news to you?

Well then.

Fortunately for the Cause of God, and for humanity, thousands and thousands *did* heed, watch and pray. And were ready to go. And do something constructive about it.

Where do you think all those thousands, and hundreds of thousands, and millions of the followers of Bahá'u'lláh came from? The ones who even as you read these words are sacrificing their lives right now, for you. All over the planet. Doing your work. Raising up the *Christ-promised Kingdom of God on earth?*

Your job, really.

But theirs, too, because they love it. And they could use a little *help*.

If anyone among you were to say now, that in spite of all our good-natured nudges:

"If this 'story' is so *marvelous* and so filled with that magic Scriptural *wonder*, why haven't I heard about it before? Finding out about it now, for the first time, is not enough."

"If the Bahá'í Faith is that big and that prominent in the world, I want it proved to me. In black and white. As I'm not going to change anything in my life. Either today or tomorrow."

At least now, after reading this far, you know who to blame.

And who not to blame.

Right?

Wrong?

You say you're still not sure?

Good.

I like that.

Hold firm.

You shouldn't be sure yet.

We've hardly started on the "wondrous story." In fact, we are just now about to begin our proof. You'll soon have the answer to your question: "Has the Bahá'í Faith told the *wondrous story* to the peoples and nations of the world."

Or not?

Yes? or No?
It all comes down to that one thing.
Who's right and who's wrong.

Our job now is to prove to you beyond a shadow of a doubt that the "wondrous story" of Bahá'u'lláh and Bahá'í Faith has been clearly and frequently "told" to the peoples and nations of the world. So clearly, so unmistakably, that no person "alive" and not "spiritually dead" could possibly have missed it.

Until we have proved that, we shall have to postpone that joyous and triumphant moment of victory we had our heart set on.

The "wonderful" and the "Counsellor" are now on *hold*.

"The Everlasting Father" and the "Prince of Peace," are waiting in the wings.

For your final verdict.

"AS THE WATERS COVER THE SEA"

"As the waters cover the sea"

21.
Incoming Tide

We are now about to undertake the task of demonstrating how completely and frequently the "wondrous story" has been told everywhere, and how indifferent the masses of humanity remained in spite of it.

Exactly as foretold in Scripture.

Up until this very day in which you and I are living in now, when it became a whole new ball game. Pardon the slang.

You can decide for yourself whether the "marvelous work" and "wonder" is already a reality on the face of the earth or not. Does mankind in general plod along on its way still unbelieving, even when they see their own neighbors arising by the thousands to serve as part of that "wondrous story" and leaving their homes to pioneer for Bahá'u'lláh and the Bahá'í Faith in every part of the world.

Surely there should be a "clue" there somewhere for the peoples of the world.(*)

The following words from the Writings of the Bahá'í Faith give us our first insight into the answer to our challenge. They announce

---

(*)See *All Flags Flying!* for a dramatic and fascinating account of this worldwide wave of Bahá'í pioneers, moving out into every corner of the globe to tell the "wondrous story"; and to remain and become a productive, deep-rooted new citizen of that part of the world, their new homeland. Ask any Bahá'í.

the onrushing hoofbeats of Bahá'u'lláh victorious battalions as the "waters" begin to cover the earth, and our "wondrous story" begins to unfold on every side.

Incoming Tide

"Under whatever conditions, the dearly loved, the divinely sustained, the onward marching legions of the army of Bahá'u'lláh may be laboring, in whatever theatre they may operate, in whatever climes they may struggle, whether in the cold and inhospitable territories beyond the Arctic circle, or in the torrid zones of both the Eastern and Western Hemispheres; on the borders of the jungles of Burma, Malaya and India; on the fringes of the deserts of Africa and of the Arabian Peninsula; in the lonely, far-away, backward and sparsely populated islands dotting the Atlantic, the Pacific and the Indian Oceans and the North Sea; amidst the diversified tribes of the Negroes of Africa, the Eskimos and the Lapps of the Arctic regions, the Mongolians of East and South East Asia, the Polynesians of the South Pacific Islands, the reservations of the Red Indians in both American continents, the Maoris of New Zealand, and the aborigines of Australia; within the time-honored strongholds of both Christianity and Islam, whether it be in Mecca, Rome, Cairo, Najaf or Karbila; or in towns and cities whose inhabitants are either immersed in crass materialism, or breathe the fetid air of an aggressive racialism, or find themselves bound by the chains and fetters of a haughty intellectualism, or have fallen prey to the forces of a blind and militant nationalism, or steeped in the atmosphere of a narrow and intolerant eclesiasticism — to them all, as well as to those who, as the fortunes of this fate-laden Crusade prosper, will be called upon to unfurl the standard of an all-conquering Faith ... in the jungles of the Amazon, scale the mountain-fastnesses of Tibet, establish direct contact with the teeming and hapless multitudes in the interior of China, Mongolia and Japan, sit with the leprous, consort with the outcasts in their penal colonies, traverse the steppes of Russia or scatter throughout the wastes of Siberia, I direct my impassioned appeal to obey, as befits His [Bahá'u'lláh's] warriors, the summons of the Lord of Hosts, and prepare for that Day of Days when His victorious batallions will ... celebrate the hour of final victory."¹

The above Message was first written by a descendent of the Báb, the Herald of the Bahá'í Faith. He is also a great-grandson of Bahá'u'lláh Himself, the Founder. His name is Shoghi Effendi Rabbani, the Guardian of the Bahá'í Faith. He is the author of the above powerful paragraph. He saw almost every word of that Message come true before his passing in 1957, after thirty-six years as the World Head of the Bahá'í Faith. Whenever I hear his name or think of his books, his some 23,000 personal letters to the Bahá'í Assemblies (multiplied a thousand fold to the individual Bahá'ís, I consider every year of his Ministry of thirty-six years as a "Light-Year."

Much more has happened in the Bahá'í world since that time, and the "story" of Bahá'u'lláh and the Bahá'í Faith has been carried into the most remote parts of the world as well as into the teeming cities everywhere.

Peoples from all nations, races, religions and classes — especially among the Youth of the world — are answering that Call and Summons of Bahá'u'lláh to arise and help build a better world for mankind under the banners of *Justice* and *Peace*; all keenly aware that they are raising up "The Christ-promised Kingdom of God on earth."

In the words of Bahá'u'lláh Himself:

> "The Word of God has set the heart of the world afire, how regrettable if ye fail to be enkindled with its flame." ²

THE BÁB

"As the waters cover the sea"

22.

The Great Parallel

No need to write the story of the Báb's life here. It is told in a dozen different books in more detail and with greater eloquence and power.(*)

Here we shall recall but a few of those moving episodes that led up to His arrest and martyrdom, but not until He had shaken to its foundations His native land, Persia.

His fame, both before and following His remarkable life, and His astonishing death, awakened half of the world to that "wondrous story" which He, the Báb, had brought to mankind.

There has never been a story like it. Before or since. As you shall see for yourself.

Ernst Renan who wrote a famous *Life of Christ*, in his *The Apostles*, refers to the persecutions of the followers of the Báb in Tihrán in 1852, saying it was "A day without parallel perhaps in the history of the world".[1]

"Tales of Magnificent Heroism"[2] is the written testimony of Lord Curzon of Kedleston.

The events surrounding the life and death of the Báb were unique among all these events.

The Prime Minister insisted that drastic action be taken against

---

(*)Read *The Dawn Breakers*, Nabíl's dramatic history of those unforgettable days; or, *The Báb* by the fine scholar, Ḥasan Balyuzi; *Release the Sun;* or perhaps, preferable to them all, *God Passes By*, by Shoghi Effendi. Ask any Bahá'í.

the Báb. He cursed the laxity with which his predecessor had allowed so great a peril to grow. The Prime Minister was determined that this weak policy must cease at once. To allow the Báb to continue to gain in glory and prestige everywhere was unthinkable.

Comte de Gobineau himself in his history, says, of the Báb, "Those who came near him felt in spite of themselves the fascinating influence of his personality, of his manner and of his speech. His guards were not free from that weakness."

"Nothing," the Prime Minister told his people, "short of his public execution can, to my mind, enable this distracted country to recover its tranquillity and peace." [3]

The Prime Minister ordered the immediate transfer of the Báb to a death cell in the city barracks. He had the Báb's turban and sash, the twin emblems of His noble lineage, ripped off. He ordered Sam Khán the head of the execution regiment, to post ten special guards outside the door of the Báb's cell.

As the Báb was being led through the courtyard to His cell in the barracks, a young boy from Tabríz rushed forward from the crowd. He was but eighteen years old. His face was haggard, his feet were bare, his hair dishevelled. He forced his way through the mob, ignoring the peril to his own life which such an action involved. He flung himself at the feet of the Báb.

"Send me not from Thee, O Master," he implored. "Wherever Thou goest, suffer me to follow Thee."

The Báb smiled down upon him and spoke gently. "Muḥammad-'Alí, arise," He told the young man, "and rest assured that you will be with Me. Tomorrow you will witness what God hath decreed."

Dr. T.K. Cheyne writes: "It is no doubt a singular coincidence that both [the Báb] and Jesus Christ are reported to have addressed these words to a disciple: 'Today thou shalt be with me in Paradise.' " [4]

Early the next morning, the chief-attendant came to the barracks to conduct the Báb into the presence of the leading doctors of law in Tabríz. They were to authorize His execution by signing a death-warrant, thus relieving the Prime Minister of the entire responsibility.

The Báb was engaged in a confidential conversation with Siyyid Husayn, one of His closest followers, who had been serving as His secretary. Husayn had been with the Báb throughout His imprisonment. The Báb was giving him last minute instructions.

"Confess not your Faith," the Báb advised Husayn. "Thereby you will be enabled, when the hour comes, to convey to those who are destined to hear you, the things of which you alone are aware."

The Báb was thus engaged when the chief-attendant arrived. He insisted upon the Báb's immediate departure. The Báb turned and rebuked the chief-attendant severely.

"Not until I have said to him all those things I wish to say," the Báb warned, "can any earthly power silence me. Though all the world be armed against Me, yet shall they be powerless to deter Me from fulfilling, to the last word, My intention." [5]

Nothing in all the world, no person, no authority, and no power on earth could prevent the telling of the "wondrous story."

The chief-attendant was amazed at such a bold speech on the part of a prisoner. However, he still insisted that the Báb accompany him with no further delay. The conversation with Husayn was left unfinished.

The chief-attendant, having secured the necessary death-warrants, delivered the Báb into the hands of Sam <u>Kh</u>án, the leader of the Armenian Christian regiment that was to execute Him.

Sam <u>Kh</u>án found himself increasingly affected by the behavior of his Captive. He had placed a guard of ten soldiers about the Báb's cell door and had carefully supervised it himself. Throughout every step he felt an increasing attraction to this unusual Prisoner. He was in constant fear that his action in taking such a holy life might bring upon him the wrath of God. Finally, unable to bear this worry any longer, he approached the Báb and spoke to Him privately.

"I profess the Christian Faith," he said, "and entertain no ill-will against you. If your Cause be the Cause of Truth, then enable me to free myself from the obligation to shed your blood."

The Báb comforted him with these words: "Follow your instructions and if your intention be sincere, the Almighty is surely able to relieve you from your perplexity." 6

About ten thousand people had crowded into the public square. They were thronged on the roofs of the adjoining houses as well. All were eager to witness the spectacle. Yet each person was willing to change from an enemy into a friend at the least sign of power from the Báb. They were still hungry for drama, and He was disappointing them. Just as the crowd had stood on Golgotha, reviling Jesus, wagging their heads and saying, "Save thyself. If thou be the Son of God, come down from the cross". So, too, did the people of Tabríz mock the Báb and jeer at His seeming impotence.

As soon as the Báb and His companion were fastened to the pillar, the regiment of soldiers arranged itself in three files, each file having two hundred and fifty men.

The leader of the regiment, Sam Khán, could delay the command no longer. The Báb had told him to do his duty; therefore, it was apparently the will of God that his regiment should take the life of the Báb. This was a source of great sorrow to him.

Reluctantly he gave the command, "Fire!"

In turn, each of three files opened fire upon the Báb and His companion. One file prone, one kneeling, one standing discharged their seven hundred and fifty muskets until the entire regiment had fired its volley.

There were over ten thousand eye-witnesses to the electrifying spectacle that followed. One of the historical accounts of that staggering moment states:

"The smoke of the firing of the seven hundred and fifty old style muskets was such as to turn the light of noonday sun into darkness.

"As soon as the cloud of smoke had cleared away, an astounded multitude looked upon a scene which their eyes could scarcely believe.

"There, standing before them, alive and unhurt, was the companion of the Báb, whilst He, Himself, had vanished from their sight. Though the cords with which they had been suspended had been rent in pieces by the bullets, yet their bodies had miraculously escaped the volleys."

Cries of astonishment, confusion and fear rang out among the bewildered multitude.

"The Báb has vanished!"

"He is freed!" They shrieked.

"It is a miracle! He was a man of God!"

"They are slaying a man of God!"

An intense clamor arose on all sides. The crowd was already growing dangerous. The public square became a bedlam as a frantic search for the Báb was launched on all sides.

M.C. Huart, a French author who wrote of this episode, says: "The soldiers in order to quiet the excitement of the crowd which, being extremely agitated, was quite ready to believe the claims of a religion which thus demonstrated its truth, showed the crowds the cords broken by the bullets, implying that no miracle had really taken place."

"Look!" Their actions implied. "The seven hundred and fifty musket-balls have shattered the ropes into fragments. This is what freed them. It is nothing more than this. It is no miracle."

Uproars and shouts continued on all sides. The people still were not certain themselves what really had happened.

M.C. Huart, giving his view of that astonishing event, states: "Amazing to believe, the seven hundred and fifty bullets had not struck the condemned but, on the contrary, had broken the bonds and he was delivered. It was a real miracle."[7]

A.L.M. Nicolas also wrote of this episode, saying: "An extraordinary thing happened, unique in the annals of the history of humanity: the bullets cut the cords that held the Báb and he fell on his feet without a scratch." [8]

The frenzied search by the authorities for the Báb came to an end within but a few feet of the execution post. They found Him back in His cell in the barracks, in the same room He had occupied the night before. He was completing His conversation with his secretary, Siyyid Ḥusayn. He was giving to him those final instructions which had been interrupted that morning. An expression of unruffed calm was upon His face. The Báb's body, obviously, had emerged unscathed from the shower of bullets.

The Báb looked at the chief-attendant and smiled.

"I have finished My conversation," He said. "You may now proceed to fulfill your duty."

The chief-attendant was much too disturbed to resume his duties. He recalled vividly the words with which the Báb had rebuked him when he had earlier interrupted that conversation: "Though all the world be armed against Me, yet shall they be powerless to deter Me from fulfilling, to the last word, My intention."

The chief-attendant refused to continue with any part of the execution. He left the scene of that barracks cell, shaken to the core of his being. He resigned his post and cut himself off from the enemies of the Báb forever.

The head of the Christian regiment, Sam Khán, was likewise stunned by what had taken place. He, too, remembered clearly the words which the Báb had spoken to him: "If your intention be sincere, the Almighty is surely able to relieve you from your perplexity." Sam Khán had given the command to fire, yet the Báb had been freed. Surely the Lord had delivered him from the need to shed the blood of this Holy Man. He would not go on with the execution. Sam Khán ordered his regiment to leave the barracks square immediately. He told the authorities plainly that he was finished with this unjust act.

"I refuse," he said, "ever again to associate myself and my regiment with any act which involves the least injury to the Báb." As he marched his regiment out of the public square he swore before all of them: "I will never again resume this task even if it costs me my life." [9]

After the departure of Sam Khán and his regiment, a colonel of the bodyguard volunteered to carry out the execution.

On the same wall and to that same nail, the Báb and his youthful companion were lashed a second time. The new firing squad formed in line. As the regiment prepared to fire the final volley, the Báb spoke His last words to the gazing multitude.

"Had you believed in Me, O wayward generation," He said, "everyone of you would have followed the example of this youth who stood in rank above most of you, and willingly would have sacrificed himself in My path. The day will come when you will have recognized Me, but that day I shall have ceased to be with you."

A dead silence fell over the square. In omnious hush, the only sound was the metallic click of rifles being readied to fire. The crowd stirred restlessly. The rifles were raised, the command given and the rifles thundered. The bodies of the Báb and His youthful companion were shattered by the blast.

As Jesus had expired on the cross so that men might be called back to God, so did the Báb breathe His last against a barracks wall in the sun-drenched city of Tabríz, Persia, at high noon, July 9, 1850.

The historian A.L.M. Nicolas, in his account of those hours, writes, "Christians believe that if Jesus had wished to come down from the cross he could have done so easily; he died of his own free will because it was written that he should and in order that the prophecies might be fulfilled. The same is true of the Báb so [his followers] say ... He likewise died voluntarily because his death was to be the salvation of humanity. Who will ever tell us the words that the Báb uttered in the midst of the unprecedented turmoil which broke out ... who will ever know the memories which stirred his noble soul?"[10]

The Báb called out to mankind that it was God's will and not His own that impelled Him to "throw Himself headlong into that ocean of superstition and hatred which was fatally to engulf Him." Both Christ and the Báb uttered the same words of warning, "O wayward generation!"

The martyrdom of the Báb took place at noon on Sunday, July 9, 1850, thirty years from the time of His birth in Shíráz.

There is but one parallel in all recorded history to the turbulent ministry of the Báb. It is the passion of Jesus Christ. There is a remarkable similarity in the distinguishing features of Their careers. Their youthfulness and meekness; the dramatic swiftness with which their ministries moved toward their climax; the role which the religious leaders played as chief instigators of the outrages They were made to suffer; the indignities heaped upon Them; the suddenness of Their arrest; the interrogations to which They were subjected; the scourgings inflicted upon Them; Their passing first in triumph, then in suffering through the streets of the city where They were to be slain; Their public parade through the streets on the way to the place of martyrdom; Their words of hope and promise to a companion who was also to die with Them; the darkness that enveloped the land in the hour of Their martyrdom; and finally Their ignominous suspension before the gaze of a hostile multitude." [11]

"As the waters cover the sea"

23.

The Downpour Begins

"So momentus an event as the Martyrdom of the Báb could hardly fail to arouse widespread and keen interest even beyond the confines of the land in which it occurred."

So confident was the Báb of the worldwide spread of his Faith, that when things were seemingly the darkest He told Dr. McCormick, a European physician who attended Him when the lashes of the bastinado wounded His face as well as His feet, that He, the Báb, had no doubt whatsoever that in time all the people of the European continent would eventually embrace His Faith.

Isn't it about time?

One particularly moving document on the Báb points out:

"This illustrious soul arose with such power that he shook the supports of the religion, of the morals, the conditions, the habits, and the customs of Persia, and instituted new rules, new laws, and a new religion. Though the great personages of State, nearly all of the clergy and the public men arose to destroy and annihilate him, he alone withstood them and moved the whole of Persia." [1]

"Many persons from all parts of the world," one writer states, "set out for Persia and began to investigate wholeheartedly the matter."

A noted French publicist testifies: "All Europe was stirred to pity and indignation." "Among the litterateurs of my generation in the Paris of 1890", he said, "the martyrdom of the Báb was still as fresh a topic as had been the first news of his death. We wrote poems about him. Sarah Bernhardt entreated Catulle Mendes for a play on the theme of this historic tragedy." [2]

A drama was published in 1903 entitled "The Báb" and was played in one of the leading theatres of St. Petersburg. The drama was publicized in London and was translated into French in Paris and into German by the renowned poet Fiedler." [3]

M.J. Balteau in a lecture on the Faith of the Báb quotes M. Vambery's words spoken in the French Academy, words which testify to the depth and power of the Báb's teachings. The Báb, he states, "has expressed doctrines worthy of the greatest thinkers." [4]

The famous Cambridge scholar, Edward Granville Browne, wrote: "Who can fail to be attracted by the gentle spirit of [the Báb]? His sorrowful and persecuted life, his purity of conduct and youth; his courage and uncomplaining patience under misfortune ... but most of all his tragic death, all serve to enlist our sympathies on behalf of the young Prophet of Shíráz." [5]

"That Jesus of the age ... a prophet and more than a prophet" is the judgment passed by the distinguished English clergyman, Dr. T.K. Cheyne. "His combination of mildness and power is so rare," he states, "that we have to place him in a line with supernormal men." [6]

"A true Godman," is the verdict of a famous British traveler and writer.

"The finest product of his country", is the tribute paid to the Báb by a noted French publicist.

"The most important religious movement since the foundation of Christianity," is the profound possibility envisaged by a well-known Oxford scholar.

Sir Francis Younghusband in his book *The Gleam* has written: "The story of the Báb ... was the story of spiritual heroism unsurpassed ... The Bab's passionate sincerity could not be doubted, for he had given his life for his faith. And that there must be something in his message that appealed to men and satisfied their souls was witnessed to by the fact that thousands gave their lives in his cause and millions now follow him ... his life must be one of those events in the last hundred years which is really worth study." [7]

The French historian, A.L.M. Nicolas, wrote: "His life is one of the most magnificent examples of courage which it has been the privilege of mankind to behold ... He sacrificed himself for humanity, for it he gave his body and his soul, for it he endured privations, insults, torture and martyrdom. He sealed, with his very lifeblood, the covenant of universal brotherhood. Like Jesus, he paid with his life for the proclamation of a reign of concord, equity and brotherly love. More than anyone, he knew what dreadful dangers he was heaping upon himself ... but all these considerations could not weaken his resolve. Fear had no hold upon his soul and, perfectly calm, never looking back, in full possession of all his powers, he walked into the furnace."[8]

At last the clergy and the state prided themselves on having crushed the life from the cause which they had battled so long. The Báb was no more. His chief disciples were destroyed. The mass of His followers throughout the land had been beaten, exhausted, and silenced.

Yet, at that very moment in a suburb of the capital, Bahá'u'lláh was receiving a visitor, a friend who was soon to be the new Prime Minister.

He told Bahá'u'lláh: "The Báb has been slain. He has been put to death in Tabríz. It is all over. At last the fire which I feared might engulf and destroy you has been extinguished."

Bahá'u'lláh replied: "If this be true, you can be certain that the flame that has been kindled will by this very act, blaze forth more fiercely than ever and will set up a conflagration such as the combined forces of the statesmen of this realm will be powerless to quench." [9]

Of all those great figures who loved Him, the Báb, so dearly not one soul was left alive save Bahá'u'lláh, Who with His family and a handful of devoted followers was driven destitute into exile to a foreign land.

Bahá'u'lláh was banished from place to place until He reached the "Mountain of God" in the Holy Land. Bahá'u'lláh was exiled, still a prisoner, to the Fortress situated on the plain of 'Akká, and those startling words of the prophecy given several hundred years before about the "last days" of the Twin Messengers were literally fulfilled:

"All of them [the companions of the Herald] shall be slain except One Who shall reach the plain of 'Akká, the banquet Hall of God."[10]

This was Bahá'u'lláh, the One foretold with such staggering accuracy by His Herald the Báb; the One Whose coming *Isaiah* portrayed so beautifully and powerfully; the One Whose every step along that God-directed journey from Persia to Mount Carmel in the Holy Land was predicted by the *Old Testament* prophet *Micah.(*)*

Although the Faith of God had been crushed into the ground at such an early age and rudely trampled upon, this very process would bring about its germination. Buried in the earth, warmed by the blood of Its martyrs, the Bahá'í Faith of the Báb and Bahá'u'lláh would blossom out in glory at a later date with the brightness of the sun. It would fulfill prophecy after prophecy with the exactness of the stars.

The Dawn would give way to the Sun. The era promised to the earth since the beginning of time, the Day of the "One fold and the One shepherd" would be ushered in by the sacrifice of that gentle Youth from Shíráz: the Báb, the Gate of God.

No One ever told the "wondrous story" with such beauty, courage and sacrifice. Of course, He awakened the world. All except those who were still in that strange spiritual sleep of death.

(*)See *The Half-Inch Prophecy* by William Sears which tells one of the most incredible stories ever before told, from the amazing and thrilling verses of the sacred scriptures of the past. Ask any Bahá'í.

"As the waters cover the sea"

24.

An Isolated Thunder Storm

One of the most courageous and greatest of all the Báb's disciples was a woman. She carried the "wondrous story" into the remote capitals of Europe. Her name will live forever, not only among the followers of the Báb and Bahá'u'lláh, but among the women of the world who still honor her memory.

She was known as Ṭáhirih, which means "The Pure One". The members of her family ranked high among the religious leaders of Persia. Her father was one of the most famous of all. From her earliest childhood, Ṭáhirih was regarded by her fellow-townsmen as a prodigy. Her knowledge and gifts were so outstanding that her father was often heard to lament: "Would that she had been a boy, for he would shed illumination upon my household, and would have succeeded me."

Ṭáhirih has shed such an illumination upon that household which rejected and persecuted her, that her memory will live forever in every part of the planet, her illustrious reputation growing more famous and cherished with each passing year. Far beyond anything her famous father might ever have imagined for her had she been a son.

How little they knew about her! They didn't "believe" the story even when she was "telling" it to them. She paid with her life for her loving efforts.(*)

Ṭáhirih spoke with such power and eloquence that those who had seen and heard her before she became a follower of the Báb were amazed.

They said: "This is not the same woman we knew before."

One of the most outstanding of Ṭáhirih's characteristics was her ability to arouse a keen desire in her listeners to investigate the truth of the Báb's mission for themselves. Within an astonishingly short time her extraordinary attraction had won many supporters. A large number had followed her to Baghdád in order to attend her classes.

The priests of Baghdád became aroused as her magic words began to woo away their own followers. Ṭáhirih was emptying their classrooms. So many of the priests rose up against her that she challenged them publicly. Through the Governor she invited them all to meet her in a great public discussion upon the truth or falsehood of the Báb's Faith.

They refused. They made excuses. Finally, they complained to the government about the spiritual revolution she was stirring up in Baghdád.

A delegation of the ablest religious leaders in the city came to see her. Ṭáhirih's popularity had grown so remarkably and with such rapidity, that all the religious leaders of every denomination were against her. They were alarmed at the effect this one woman might have upon their people. Therefore, they united in their attacks upon her.

This particular delegation had representatives from the two leading sects of Islam and from the Jewish and Christian communities as well. Their mission was clear:

Silence Ṭáhirih!

"We have come," they informed her, "to convince you of the folly of your actions, and to turn you from your purpose."

(*)No need to tell here the story of Ṭáhirih, called "A wonder among women". Entire books have been written about her unique and dramatic life. You can read them at your leisure and be most fascinated and moved to the depths. Perhaps even to tears for this "first woman suffragette".

The bluntness and insolence of their approach made it clear how little respect they had for Ṭáhirih. She was, after all, merely a misguided woman. At least so they thought at first.

Prior to this meeting, these religious leaders had thought of Ṭáhirih as a beautiful, gifted woman whose enthusiasm for something new had overleaped the bounds of moderation. Her popularity, they felt sure, was based on novelty. They were confident that once she came face to face with a group of such eminent religious leaders as themselves, she would be subdued and humiliated to a sufficient degree for her to resume her humble place as a woman once again. Where she belonged.

Knowing Ṭáhirih's life before she came to Baghdád, one has to exert considerable discipline to keep from laughing out loud at their stupidity.

These eminent and august religious leaders were totally unprepared for Ṭáhirih's reckless indifference to their combined wisdom. They were startled by her cool and accurate appraisal of their motives.

Ṭáhirih knew exactly why they were there.

Following that meeting, these religious leaders looked upon Ṭáhirih with quite different eyes. They now looked upon her as a dangerous and powerful adversary.

Ṭáhirih was able to silence every protest they made. She astounded them with the force of her argument and the depth of her knowledge. She was not lowly and submissive before them as they had expected her to be. Instead, she was aflame with the love of God and the Báb. She burned away their flimsy reasoning with the fire of her words.

They were deeply embarrassed by their inability to subdue her. Disillusioned at their complete failure, they withdrew.

"She is no mere woman." They said, once they had left.

Such victories increased Ṭáhirih's fame on every side, and aroused a deeper hatred among her enemies. Eventually, after an illustrious proclamation of the Message of the Báb, she was condemned to death. She knew there could be no other path.

Dr. Jakob Polak, Austrian physician to the king, in a book written in 1856, states that he was an eye-witness to Ṭáhirih's last hours. She endured her death with "super-human fortitude," he said.(*)

Thus ended the life of Ṭáhirih. She was one of the greatest of the disciples of the Báb. No one told the "wondrous story" more often, more courageously, more eloquently than she. She was recognized by the world as the first woman-suffrage martyr as well.

As the hour of her death approached, she turned to the one into whose custody she had been placed, and declared boldly:

"You can kill me as soon as you like, but you cannot stop the emanciption of woman".[1]

Marianna Hainisch, the mother of one of Austria's president's declared: "The greatest idea of womanhood has been Ṭáhirih."

The famous French playwright, Catulle Mendes called Ṭáhirih the "Persian Joan of Arc."

Ṭáhirih's career was dazzling, brief, tragic and eventful. The fame of her deeds spread everywhere with the same astonishing swiftness as that of the Báb Himself, Who was the direct Source of all her inspiration.

The following tributes to her which close this matchless drama, will show us how widespread and popular the young poetess of Qazvin had become in the world. Her poetry is still read in Írán.

Lord Curzon in his book on Persia speaks of Ṭáhirih, and states bluntly: "Of no small account, then, must be the tenets of a creed that can awaken in its followers so rare and beautiful a spirit of

---

(*)Ṭáhirih was martyred under the most moving of circumstances. See *God Passes By*, pp. 73-77, by Shoghi Effendi, for a detailed account of this remarkable event. Ṭáhirih was strangled and cast into a well. Marguerite (Mrs. Sears) and myself have visited that site, once a garden, now so close to the Bank that houses the Crown Jewels of Iran. Their greatest Jewel, the immortal Ṭáhirih, rests there. She "told" them the "wondrous story" in the most eloquent of ways, but they did not "hear", nor did they *believe*. They still go on in their blindness unaware of the precious treasure beneath the dust of the heart of their city, Ṭihrán. They will, of course, one day know. To their sorrow and their distress, and their terrible deprivation.

self-sacrifice."2

One of the most penetrating comments of those historians who followed the life of Ṭáhirih, by Dr. T.K. Cheyne: "Looking back on the short career one is chiefly struck by her fiery enthusiasm and by her absolute unwordliness. This world was, in fact, to her ... a mere handful of dust."

Ṭáhirih justified all of these words of tribute to her by her heroic death in a quiet garden in the shadow of Persia's greatest city.

Lord Curzon summed up Ṭáhirih's life for all of us: "The heroism of the lovely but ill-fated poetess is one of the most affecting episodes in modern history."

Ṭáhirih was at the height of her beauty and power when she was slain in the Ílkhání garden in August, 1852. She was thirty six years old.

She has been called Qurratu'l-'Ayn — Consolation of the Eyes. Others had called her Zarrín-Táj — One "crowned in gold." But the name by which she lives forever in the hearts of the followers of the Báb and Bahá'u'lláh, is Ṭáhirih — The Pure.

"As the waters cover the sea"

25.

The Sacrifice

From the very first moment, the Báb, on the eve of May 23, 1844, linked His own Mission with that of Bahá'u'lláh.

Nabíl states in his history: "Did not the Báb, in the earliest days of His Mission allude, in the opening passages of His commentary of the Súrih of Joseph, to the glory and significance of the Revelation of Bahá'u'lláh? Was it not His purpose, by dwelling upon the ingratitude and malice which characterized the treatment of Joseph by his brethren, to predict what Bahá'u'lláh was destined to suffer at the hands of His brother and kindred?"[1]

In His farewell address to His chosen disciples, the Báb stated clearly that He was but the forerunner of a greater One yet to come.

"I am preparing you for the advent of a mighty Day," He told them in that parting message. "Scatter throughout the length and breadth of this land, and, with steadfast feet and sanctified hearts, prepare the way for *His* coming." [2]

The Báb also instructed His disciples to record the names of all the believers who accepted the Faith.

"Of all these believers I shall make mention in the Tablet of God," He told them, "so that upon each one of them the Beloved of our hearts may, in the Day when He shall have ascended the throne of glory, confer His inestimable blessing."[3]

It was from the names of these believers that the first followers of Bahá'u'lláh came, and upon whom He conferred His special blessing and love.

The Báb did everything in His power to assist His followers so that they would know where to turn after His own martyrdom. He clearly announced that He was the Promised One, but that He "stood in relation to a succeeding and greater [Messenger] as did John the Baptist to the Christ. He was the Forerunner of One more mighty than Himself. He [the Báb] was to decrease; that Mighty One was to increase. And as John the Baptist had been the Herald or Gate of the Christ, so was [He] the Báb the Herald or Gate of Bahá'u'lláh." [4]

"Ere nine [years] will have elapsed from the inception of this Cause," the Báb wrote in another place, pointing out even the exact hour of Bahá'u'lláh's coming, "the realities of all created things will not be made manifest ... Be patient until thou beholdest a new creation."

"In the year nine ye will attain unto the presence of God." [5]

Before nine years had elapsed, in fact during the ninth year [1853], Bahá'u'lláh's Mission began, thus fulfilling not only the promise of the Báb (and that of Shaykh Ahmad and Siyyid Kázim), but also the prophecy from the sacred writings of that land which said: "In the year [1844] the earth shall be illumined by His light... If thou livest until the year [1853] thou shalt witness how the nations, the rulers, the poeples, and the Faith of God shall have been renewed." [6]

The Báb's challenging words written at Mah-Ku seal forever the bond that unites Him with Bahá'u'lláh.

"Well is it with him who fixeth his gaze upon the Order of Bahá'u'lláh and rendereth thanks unto his Lord." "For He will assuredly be manifest." [7]

"I verily am a believer in Him," the Báb declares to the world, "and in His Faith, and in His Book ..." [8]

Bahá'u'lláh on His part had such a love for the Báb that He would not let the Báb suffer any pain, indignity, or humiliation in which He, Bahá'u'lláh, did not share.

The Báb was first confined in the house of the Chief Constable of Shíráz. Shortly after this Bahá'u'lláh was confined in the house of one of the religious leaders in Ṭihrán. The Báb's second imprisonment was in the castle of Mah-Ku; that of Bahá'u'lláh followed when He was imprioned in the residence of the governor of 'Amul. The Báb was scourged in the prayer-house in Tabríz. The very same punishment was inflicted shortly after this upon Bahá'u'lláh in the prayer-house at 'Amul. The Báb's third imprisonment was in the castle of Chihríq; that of Bahá'u'lláh followed in the "Black Pit" prison of Ṭihrán. The Báb was struck in the face with missiles in the streets of Tabríz. Bahá'u'lláh was pelted with stones on the streets of 'Amul, and struck in the face with a rock on His way to prison in Ṭihrán. The Báb was slain in the public square of Tabríz. Bahá'u'lláh underwent nearly half a century of living martyrdom. He was exiled and imprisoned for forty years. He was poisoned in the "Black Pit". He was set upon by assassins in Baghdád. He was poisoned again in Adrianople. He was approached by yet another assassin in the prison of 'Akká. To His grave Bahá'u'lláh carried the scars of great prison-chains which had torn the flesh from His shoulders.

Nabíl recounts in his history: "The Báb, Whose trials and sufferings had preceded, in almost every case, those of Bahá'u'lláh, had offered Himself to ransom His Beloved from the perils that beset that precious life; whilst Bahá'u'lláh, on His part, unwilling that He Who so greatly loved Him should be the sole sufferer, shared at every turn the cup that had touched His [the Báb's] lips.

"Such love no eye has ever beheld, nor has mortal heart ever conceived such mutual devotion. If the branches of every tree were turned into pens, and all the seas into ink, and earth and heaven rolled into one parchment, the immensity of that love would still remain unexplored, and the depths of that devotion unfathomed." [9]

Their Missions were bound together for eternity.

Thus it was that the Báb was able to leave the prison of Chihríq in peace and with eagerness, and begin what He knew would be His last journey on this earth. He had fulfilled His task. He was the Dawn, and He had faithfully prepared His followers for the coming of the Sun itself.

"I, verily, have not fallen short of My duty to admonish that people, and devise means whereby they may turn towards God ..., " He said. "If, on the day of His Revelation, all that are on earth bear Him allegiance, Mine inmost being will rejoice, inasmuch as all will have attained the summit of their existence, and will have been brought face to face with their Beloved ... I truly have nurtured all things for this purpose. How then can anyone be veiled from Him?"

"I have educated all men, that they may recognize this Relevation." [10]

The Báb's heart was turned toward Ṭihrán and Bahá'u'lláh when He wrote those moving words which foreshadowed the hours that were fast sweeping down upon Him:

"I have sacrificed Myself wholly for Thee; I have accepted curses for Thy sake, and have yearned for naught but martyrdom in the path of Thy love." [11]

The soldiers bearing the fatal edict from the Prime Minister which called for His execution were already at the gates of the prison-castle of Chihríq. The Báb, confident that He had expended every effort in the path of God, had already sent His Writings, His pen-case, His seals, and His ring to Bahá'u'lláh, along with a beautiful scroll filled with the praises and glory of His Name.

Now He calmly awaited His escort of death.

The wonder of it all, is not whether the Bahá'í Faith has "told" the *wondrous story*, but that we, you and I, should be alive in this Day even to hear such a story. It is all part of that "marvelous work" and "wonder" which God would bring about in the *last days*.

"The Faith of Bahá'u'lláh should indeed be regarded, if we wish to be faithful to the tremendous implications of its message, as the culmination of a cycle, the final stage in a series of successive, of preliminary and progressive revelations. These, beginning with Adam and ending with the Báb, have paved the way and anticipated with ever-increasing emphasis the advent of that Day of Days in which He Who is the Promise of All Ages should be made manifest." [12]

The Báb had closed the Cycle of Prophecy, the *Prophetic Cycle* which began with Adam and ended with the Báb. The *Cycle* prophesied of that *Great Day* of the coming of the *Promised One* foretold in prophecy by all the Messengers of God that went before Him. They prophesied of the *last days*, the *time of the end*, the Day of the *One Fold and One Shepherd*, the glorious Day of God when *Two* Messengers of God would come in swift succession.

The Báb and Bahá'u'lláh had come.

The *Prophetic Cycle* was ended!

The Báb also "opened" the *Cycle of Fulfillment* that would last for five thousand centuries, five hundred years! Until the world lives in the promised "golden age" of human kind.

Is that a "wondrous story"?

Is that as "marvelous work" and "wonder"?

Can you imagine the blessings and bounties showered upon the soul who *hears* and *believes*?

We now turn our gaze upon Him, Bahá'u'lláh, the Founder of the Bahá'í Faith, Whose Name means "*The Glory of the Lord*" who has made all of these marvelous promises come true.

BAHÁ'U'LLÁH

"As the waters cover the sea"

26.

The Tidal Wave

Let us first reflect upon the mysterious power "so august, so momentous" an outpouring as that released to the world by Bahá'u'lláh. "How vast, how entrancing the panorama" which the years 1844-1986 "unrolls before our eyes!"

"To merely contemplate this unique spectacle, to visualize, however dimly, the circumstances attending the birth and gradual unfoldment" of the Bahá'í Faith, can "overwhelm" the seeker.

"Dominating the entire range of this fascinating spectacle towers the incomparable figure of Bahá'u'lláh, transcendental in His majesty, serene, awe-inspiring, unapproachably glorious."

It is not surprising that the Cambridge University Professor and scholar, Edward Granville Browne, would say upon his first sight of Bahá'u'lláh when he visited Him in the Holy Land:

"The face of Him on Whom I gazed, I can never forget." Browne admitted frankly, "No need to ask in whose presence I stood, as I bowed myself before one who is the object of adoration and love which kings might envy and emperors sigh for in vain."[1]

It is the story of Bahá'u'lláh we tell next.

Bahá'u'lláh, the Founder of the Bahá'í Faith, Whose appearance among men had been foretold in all the holy Books of the past, but never with such beauty and accuracy as by the Báb.

Bahá'u'lláh immediately took up the task where the Báb had

left off. He, Bahá'u'lláh, informed and awakened the world to the significance of the day in which they were living. He continued to tell the "wondrous story" in Words and by examples such as the eyes of man have never before witnessed.

Bahá'u'lláh wrote with his own Pen to the kings, rulers, and the leaders of men in both the East and the West. They were the most renowned rulers in His Day. They held the destiny of their subjects in the palm of their hands.

To them all Bahá'u'lláh directed both personal and general Messages.

To some, not once, but twice.

You can read His Words and study these guidance-filled Messages to the leaders of men for yourself at another time. Here, we shall be specific as to names, if not as to details concerning the content of those powerful Letters of Bahá'u'lláh.

Their like had never before been received by such Heads of State in the history of the world, religious or civil.(*)

Bahá'u'lláh wrote to:
    Napoleon III of France
    Czar Alexander II of Russia
    Queen Victoria of England
    Kaiser Wilhelm I of Germany
    Emperor Francis-Joseph of Austria
    Sulṭán 'Abdu'l-'Azíz of Turkey
    Náṣiri'd-Dín Sháh of Persia
    The Rulers of America
    The Presidents of the Republics therein

Bahá'u'lláh also directed special Messages to:
    The Kings of Earth (Collectively)
    The Rulers of Earth (Collectively)
    The Leaders of Religion (Collectively)
    The Clergy and People of Various Faiths

(*)See *The Proclamation of Bahá'u'lláh,* an entire volume of Bahá'u'lláh's Messages to Kings, Emperors, Shahs, Sultans, the Legislators of the world, the Presidents of Republics in the West.

The Elected Representatives of the People of Every Land
The Concourse of Divines (Religious Leaders in the East)
The Concourse of Christians (Repeatedly)
The Great Announcement to Mankind
The Peoples and Kindreds of the Earth
The Children of Men
Contending Peoples of the Earth
Peoples of the World

The Books containing these Messages and Bahá'u' lláh's Proclamation to the world can now be found in both public and private libraries.

Bahá'u'lláh's call to the Nations, summoning them to world peace, has been presented again and again to the rulers and leaders of men on an International, National and Local level. Repeatedly, with each change of leadership. Not once, not twice, but countless times.

The process is continuous and unending. It is going on now, even as you read these words, in almost every part of the world. It will continue to do so as the followers of Bahá'u'lláh "tell" the "wondrous story" and acquaint all mankind with that "marvelous work" and "wonder" the coming of Bahá'u'lláh and the Bahá'í Faith, until every single person on the planet will have had his or her own chance to "Behold! and wonder marvelously!"

This challenge to the kings, rulers and leaders of the earth, was also foretold in Scripture.

Bahá'u'lláh called upon the Kings, Rulers, Heads of State, and Leaders of the people everywhere, to unite in an energetic worldwide effort so that all mankind might attain social justice and peace on earth.

Bahá'u'lláh demanded action, not merely good intentions.

To one such powerful ruler, Bahá'u'lláh gave a "counsel" which

He intended for all the leaders of men:

> "Arise thou amongst men in the name of this all-compelling Cause, and summon then, the nations unto God ... "[2]

The response of such selfish, self-centered rulers could be easily predicted. Their attitude was almost unanimous.

Why should any king pay attention to such "ravings"? Who would believe a madman, a condemned Prisoner at that, who had the audacity to announce publicly the collapse of the world's greatest kingdoms and dynasties if they failed to heed His "Counsels" for what He called the betterment of society?

How dare He pronounce on the steps which must be taken for the protection of the under-privileged and the establishing of "Peace on earth" without first consulting them?

They were the ones who knew how to bring such things about.

Not a condemned prisoner in exile.

If He couldn't even save Himself from prison, what hope could he have of freeing the peoples of the world from bondage and tyranny?

How could He possibly reform the world as He promised to do from the cell of a condemned prisoner?

How could such a helpless person confined in a mighty fortress called 'Akká, hope to control and guide the destinies of powerful kings?

Nonsense!

Even to think such a thing was madness.

Yet, that is precisely what Bahá'u'lláh did.

Kings were shut up in prison, and He, the Prisoner, was released. Monarchies were overthrown and vanished from the pages of living history, while the Prisoner's ideals and teachings have penetrated even into the remotest corners of the world and captured the hearts of peoples. The rulers were disgraced and He, Bahá'u'lláh, was honored. His Teachings and guidance on Peace have permeated the thinking of modern man.

This phenomenon has happened, and is still happening, with ever-increasing speed, in more than one hundred thousand places all over the world.

This process of the downfall of kings has taken place with frightening precision, step by step, until each hostile despot was dethroned. Each unjust king was shorn of his power. The dynasties of each of the deaf and blind Monarchs who opposed Bahá'u'lláh, the *Prince of Peace,* were forever extinguished.(*)

This was not only Scripture, it is history.

Bahá'u'lláh had indeed been "terrible to the kings of the earth" as the Bible centuries ago had warned He would be. *(Psalms 76:12)*

Job who said he knew his Redeemer would stand upon the earth in the "latter day", also said he would "break in pieces mighty men" in that day, and would "looseth the bond of kings" and "leadeth princes away spoiled, and overthroweth the mighty."

Bahá'u'lláh did all that, and far more.

(*)This story of unparalled drama is told in far greater detail in the *Promised Day is Come* with surpassing skill.

"As the waters cover the sea."

27.

The Tidal Wave Continues

It is impossible to speak of the planetary spread of the Bahá'í Faith, as this "marvelous work" and "wonder" unfolds before the eyes of mankind, without referring to Bahá'u'lláh's final Book, *The Epistle to the Son of the Wolf,* written about one year before His passing in 1892.

This book was written to a notorious enemy of the Bahá'í Faith. Bahá'u'lláh called upon him to repent of his cruel ways. Bahá'u'lláh offered clear and unmistakable proofs of the validity of His Mission. He quoted some of the most characteristic and celebrated passages from His own Writings. This Book was a veritable Compilation of Bahá'u'lláh's *Counsels* to the world.

This final Book of Bahá'u'lláh is but one of a hundred volumes from the Pen of the *Prince of Peace,* the Supreme Redeemer of men. This "precious achievement", as Bahá'u'lláh's final volume has been described, contains many of the "priceless pearls" of Bahá'u'lláh's utterance, His supreme gift to the world: *The Word of God for our time.*

No gift could ever compare to it.

With this Book, Bahá'u'lláh's appeal to the kings and rulers of men, and to all the peoples of the world, may be said to have practically terminated.

Bahá'u'lláh's Personal Call to Mankind had come to an end.

His Successor 'Abdu'l-Bahá, and Bahá'u'lláh's followers would of course, carry Bahá'u'lláh's *Counsels* and His Teachings into every corner of the planet until the entire world would be "illuminated" with His knowledge and Wisdom.

BAHÁ'U'LLÁH

This final volume of Bahá'u'lláh has been described in the Bahá'í Writings as being:

> "... replete with unnumbered exhortations, revolutionizing principles, world-shaping laws and ordinances, dire warnings and portentous prophecies, with soul-uplifting prayers and meditations, illuminating commentaries and interpretations, impassioned discourses and homilies, all interspersed with either addresses or references to kings, emperors and ministers of both the East and the West."[1]

No part of the world, no segment or sphere of human society and thought, was overlooked by Bahá'u'lláh in those incredible one hundred and more volumes of His writings.

Bahá'u'lláh directed his Messages to:
    Kings
    Emperors
    Ministers of State
    Legislators in every land
    Ecclesiastical and Religious leaders of all denominations

To Leaders in special spheres of:
    Intellectual Thought
    Political
    Mystical
    Commercial
    Humanitarian

To Scholars

Students

And to the masses of mankind in all parts of the planet[2]

Bahá'u'lláh Himself has testified:

> "We verily have not fallen short of Our duty to exhort men, and to deliver that whereunto I was bidden by God, the Almighty, the All-Praised. Had they hearkened unto Me, they would have beheld the earth another earth."[3]

And again:

> "Is there any excuse left for any one in this Revelation? No, by God, the Lord of the Mighty Throne! My signs have encompassed the earth, and My power enveloped all mankind, and yet the people are wrapped in a strange sleep."[4]

These same Words were used by Christ, *the Son:* "Lest coming suddenly, he find you sleeping." Bahá'u'lláh, *the father,* also found the peoples of the world, who should have been wide awake and "on fire!" with an eagerness to build the *Christ-promised Kingdom of God on earth,* asleep to the glorious opportunities which surrounded them.

Mankind was still wrapped in that "strange sleep" of spiritual death in spite of all the warnings of Scripture. It is not surprising that they did not hear the "wondrous story" even when it was being told to them.

No matter how many chances they had.

How many more chances would they yet have?

In the Words of Bahá'u'lláh:

"How long will ye sleep?"

"As the waters cover the sea."

28.

The Tempest

Bahá'u'lláh's Words, and His Faith, the Bahá'í Faith, are now, in this very hour (1986), infusing "into the entire body of mankind boundless potentialities." Under our very eyes it is "shaping the course of human society." That, of course, is the work of the *Prince of Peace.* And those are Words taken from the Writings of His Faith.

This is not surprising now that we realize who the Báb and Bahá'u'lláh were, those "Twin Fires of Heaven" that Scripture promised would appear in the *last days* at the *time of the end.*

The *last days* and the *time of the end* are tiresome words really when repeated over and over. But necessary.

Not *one* Messenger of God would appear at that time but two in swift succession. Exactly as Bahá'u'lláh appeared, just nine years after the *Declaration* of the Báb.

You can study all that we're saying here whenever you choose, at your leisure in *God Passes By, The World Order of Bahá'u'lláh, Thief in the Night.* Pages and pages of the "wondrous story" in book after book, each upon a new, delightful theme of the same one story.

Here we mention only a few prophesies in passing as one of the inevitable reasons that hundreds, then thousands, hundreds of thousands and millions are now attracted to the Faith of Bahá'u'lláh. Otherwise, how could it have spread itself with such lightning-like rapidity to the four corners of the earth? In less than one hundred and fifty years?

It has been a victory for the spirit and destiny of man. Yet, thus far a pyrrhic victory. For far too few have yet heard the "wondrous story" and arisen to help build the *Christ-promised Kingdom of God on earth*.

It becomes clearer and clearer every day that indeed the "story has been told", but that mankind in general still remains in that "deep sleep like unto death" surrounded by stultifying, paralyzing materialism.

It is clear from the Scriptures, that the final victory *will* be won by the *Prince of Peace*, but it is coming far too slowly. For all of us. The power is there but is still being used by too few of us.

This book has been written to try and increase that number tremendously, including yourself. It is a search for *awakened* and *prepared souls. Hence* this sharing of those unique prophecies from Scripture that have an impulse such as nothing else can.

We have tried man's way, now let us try God's.

Let me share with you a few more of those exceptional words from sacred Scripture that make us delighted to be exactly who we are, and exactly *where* we are in these exciting times.

We shall understand even more clearly why so many peoples of all previous religious conviction, have arisen to accept and to serve Bahá'u'lláh in so many parts of the world.

They have discovered the promises in the Scriptures of many lands foretelling the coming of *Two Messengers of God* in quick succession in the *time of the end*, the so-called "last days".

So many promises from so many different Sources, has strengthened the belief and confidence of seekers everywhere that this indeed is the time the entire world has been waiting for over such a long and unbroken period of *Expectation*.

Their hearts are cheered and comforted at last. There has been no sign on the horizon of present history that any help of any kind is coming from the leadership of man alone.

They take additional sustenance from the promises of the past Holy Books that the day will come when God will redeem His promises to them, and that a long reign of "righteousness and Peace" will come. And the Messiah of those days, the *Prince of Peace*, will win the victory over all His adversaries.

These promised *Two Messengers of God*, those "Twin Fires of Heaven", as They have been described, have already appeared, and their one, unifying Spirit is at work in the world to bring together the children of men.

Among them are:

Zoroastrian: Úshídar-Máh and the Sháh Bahrám.
Shí'ih Islam: The Qá'im and the Imám Husayn.
Sunni Islam: The Qá'im and Jesus the Christ.
Christianity: John the Baptist and Christ. Elijah and Christ.
Judaism: Messiah ben Joseph and Messiah ben David.
(Elias) and the Messiah.[1]

In Persia, the land where both the Báb and Bahá'u'lláh appeared, there are additional prophecies concerning the coming of "two holy Figures" in the *last days*.

One in particular:

> "Verily I say, after the *Qá'im* (He Who shall arise) the Qayyúm will be made manifest".[2](*)

(*)The Qá'im was the Promised One Who would bring about the spiritual Resurrection of men's hearts. The Qayyúm was the *second* Messenger of God Who would appear to continue this healing process. The "second" and "third woes" of the book of *Revelation*.

It is not surprising or strange that Persia is mentioned so prominently in these prophesies concerning the Promised One of the *last days*. It would be strange and surprising if Persia were *not* mentioned. The Mission of the *Twin Fires* of Heaven, the Báb and Bahá'u'lláh, could not otherwise have been true.

Jeremiah said God would set "His throne" in *Elam* and "destroy from thence the king and the princes, saith the Lord." (*Jeremiah, 49:38*)

Elam was the capital of ancient Persia.

Persia, according to *Daniel*, would be a "place of vision" at the *time of the end*. (*Daniel, 8:12, 17*)

The Christian clergyman, Reverend John Cumming, in his book about the last days, *The Great Tribulation*, quotes a prophecy of Zoroaster concerning the Messiah which states that this Messenger of God will come from the land of Núr in Persia.

Núr is the province of Mázindarán. It is the homeland of Bahá'u'lláh. His father, Mírzá Buzurg of Núr, was an honored Minister to the King of Persia (known as the Sháh).[3]

In the book *Religious Debates* by Nategh, are found the following prophecies of Zoroaster concerning the One who will come from the *East:*

1. 'God will give you (Persia) a good ending.'
2. 'If there is but one minute remaining in the whole world, I will send someone from this nation (Persia) who will renew religion.'
3. 'When Persia and the other countries are overtaken by the Arabs, I will choose one from the generation of the Kings of Persia, so that He will call the people of the world from East to West to worship one God.[4]

There is a prophecy of the Great Messiah to come which is known to the Buddhists. The prophecy is attributed to Buddha Gautama Himself, and states that in the fullness of time, there would arise:

'A Buddha named Maitreye, the Buddha of universal fellowship.'[5]

This great Messiah, the Buddhists believe, will come: *not from the East*, but *from the West*.

Mr. Edward Irving, a Christian clergyman of Britain, who was keenly anticipating the return of Christ during the millennial zeal of the 1800's said: "... What is very remarkable, a friend of mine, who ... stood on the Himalaya mountains in India, by the holy pool, where never Christian had dwelt before, found there also an expectation of a religion *from the west* which in the space of forty years was to possess the earth..."[6]

Bahá'u'lláh came from Persia which is to the *East* of Israel, but to the *West* of India. His ministry from the time of its beginning until His last days on earth was *forty years*.

The prophets of Syria and Palestine foretold the coming of the promised Messiah from the *East*. The prophets and seers from India and the Far East, said that He would appear in the *West*. Persia, the birthplace of Bahá'u'lláh lies in between these two, and fulfills the requirements of each.

In the book of *Enoch,* it is prophesied that the Messiah of the *last days* shall come from the East of Israel, and that He shall come from the land now known as Persia. Enoch foretells:

"And *in those days* the angels will assemble, and turn their heads *towards the East,* toward the people of *Parthia and Medea,* in order to excite the kings, and that a spirit of disturbance came over them and disturbed them from off their thrones."[7]

Parthia and Medea make up a part of what is now the land of Persia, the birthplace of Bahá'u'lláh.

The Jewish oracles, the Sibylline books, also mention the coming of the Messiah from the *East* saying:

"And then *from the sunrise* God shall send a king who shall give every land relief from the bane of war ... nor shall he do these things by his own counsel, but in obedience to the good ordinances of the Mighty God ."[8]

Joseph Klausner, in *The Messianic Idea in Israel,* writes:

"The 'king from the sunrise' is, without any doubt, the King-Messiah".

The prophet *Ezekiel* also foretold that the Messiah would come to the Holy Land, Israel, from the *East*. He even gave the title by which he would be known in that day: *The Glory of God*. Ezekiel recorded his vision of the *last days,* saying:

"And, behold, the *Glory of the God* of Israel came from the way of the *east* ..."⁹

In another place, Ezekiel says:

"And the *Glory of the Lord* came into the house *by way of the gate* whose prospect is toward *the east* ."¹⁰

We have already learned that the name of Bahá'u'lláh when translated into English means, the *Glory of God* or the *Glory of the Lord.*

His Herald was called the Báb. This when it is translated into English means, *the Gate.*

Such a Day had been promised in religious history since the beginning of time. The sacred Writings of the Bahá'í Faith say:

> "All the signs have been revealed; every prophetic allusion hath been manifested. Whatever hath been enshrined in all the Scriptures of the past hath been made evident. To doubt or hesitate is no more possible."¹¹

In yet another place:

> "Every proof and prophecy, every manner of evidence, whether based on reason or on the text of the scriptures and traditions, are to be regarded as centered in the persons of Bahá'u'lláh and the Báb. In them is to be found their complete fulfillment."¹²

With such an ocean of fulfillment, it is not surprising that the followers of Bahá'u'lláh would have flooded the earth with the glorious news of the "wondrous story".

"As the waters cover the sea."

29.

Life-Rafts for Humanity

Before we leave Bahá'u'lláh's endless floor of *Counsels* and guidance for the world, and such an unprecedented fulfillment of prophecy which has showered upon mankind by the appearance of both the Báb and Bahá'u'lláh. It is important for us to know, and to see for ourselves, the ocean of tribulations and sufferings which He, Bahá'u'lláh, willingly accepted for our sake, and for the sake of humanity.

A more tender and more intimate human story could not be found. In spite of its grief and sorrow.

Bahá'u'lláh was exiled like Abraham, stoned like Moses, scourged like Christ and persecuted for nearly half a century, from city to city, from country to country, from continent to continent.

Bahá'u'lláh was once scourged, twice stoned, three times poisoned, four times exiled. He was twice threatened by assassins.

Bahá'u'lláh, was the fulfillment of all that was brought by the Messengers of God from past ages. Bahá'u'lláh brought about the fulfillment of the hopes of all the Religions of days gone by. Therefore, He, Bahá'u'lláh, was forced to withstand the sufferings and persecutions with which all past Prophets before Him had been afflicted. As the Promised One of all past Messengers and Religions, this was His destiny, to bear what all of them had borne before Him.

Bahá'u'lláh's loved ones, His followers, whose destiny it was to raise up the *Christ-promised Kingdom of God on earth,* were likewise subjected, for this reason, to all the combined persecutions that had been inflicted upon the people of all past religions.

It is for *this* reason that the followers of the Báb and Bahá'u'lláh have undergone nearly one hundred and fifty years of persecution in Persia (Iran). Their goal, the unity of all nations, religions, races and peoples in that long-awaited, "Christ-promised Kingdom of God on earth," the Day of the "One Fold and One Shepherd," the "Golden Age" of human society, has required a suffering, agony, martyrdom and sacrifice commensurate with that goal. For this reason, their cruel and ruthless persecution and martyrdom has continued, and, will continue until the world, aware at last of Bahá'u'lláh's exalted station, rises up to prevent it.

These Bahá'ís are, indeed, a "new breed of martyrs". They were not just men, women and children who were killed for their Faith because they were Bahá'ís. Quite the opposite. They were killed because they would not deny their Faith. Or recant. They were martyrs by choice. Something quite unique in the annals of the history of religion. All they had to do was speak three words: "I don't believe" and they would be freed, released with honors and rewards.

Their answer was: "No. Never!"

It will always be the same. Because those Bahá'ís are fighting, not for their lives, but for the future of all humanity. Including you. Perhaps some day, soon, the world will hear the "wondrous story" and arise like a tidal wave to help win our common victory.

What is it that makes the martyrdom of these Bahá'í friends of mine in Iran so different? Why should the world care whether they live or die? Apart, that is, from the natural sorrow and sympathy all decent human beings feel who deplore killing, persecution, and violence of any kind.

After all, people are being killed all over the world these days. Violence and murder surround us every day of our lives. It has almost become a way of life. In the newspapers, on radio and television, we see and hear the dreadful things happening to our dearly-loved fellow human beings.

Since six million innocent Jews died so tragically and so wrongly in the murder-chambers of Nazi Germany, martyrdom has become almost an empty phrase.

People, unfortunately, have become inured to killing. They shut themselves off. They are weary of reading, hearing, and being told stories about more killings, more violence and more deaths.

So why should the world be concerned about, or involved in, the martyrdoms of a few thousands of Bahá'ís in Iran over the past one hundred and fifty years?

It is difficult for people to believe when first they hear it, that the real, underlying reason why the murders committed by the terrorists of Iran against the Bahá'ís are not only crimes against the Bahá'í community, but also crimes against society. It is not a local tragedy that is taking place behind that black-bordered death-map of Iran. It is a true world calamity.

Every passing day mankind is becoming one of the most seriously 'endangered species' in the world. His chances of survival are becoming less and less. He is being threatened increasingly from every side.

The nuclear bombs, the multi-warhead intercontinental missiles with their nose-cones of death, plus all the other terrible weapons of war which he, man himself, has devised, might easily vaporize and obliterate both the fashioner and all his cities he is so proud of one of these days. Taking most of the world, including us, with him.

In the face of such an inexcusable, horrifying, self-inflicted genocide, the extermination of a small religious minority in Iran would seem to be of no great significance. In the great picture of destruction before us.

Except for one thing.

It might *not* be so important were it not for the fact that this Bahá'í Faith may be the only available source of spiritual 'fire power' in the world today, which is capable of reversing the trend of destruction, and rescuing mankind from the apparently, inevitable disaster which are now overtaking it.

The Bahá'í Faith has already proved, incredible as it may seem, that it indeed *does* have this spiritual "fire" power. It can mitigate the approaching catastrophe if used properly, and quickly enough. At the very least, it can help some small remnant of society to survive the world-wide devastation which now threatens to engulf us all. Inevitably, unless something marvelous and miraculous happens soon. There is only *one* place for the world to look.

To expect such a fantastic accomplishment from a Faith whose followers are still being killed in Iran right and left at the will and whim of their enemies, sounds a little like setting a *mouse* to drive the formidable elephant from the field.

Yet, this is exactly what this Bahá'í community has been doing for the past century and a half. In spite of the combined forces of the government, the army, the religious leaders, and the people of Persia (Iran), who have tried unsuccessfully to exterminate and obliterate them not only from their own country, but from the face of the earth, the Bahá'ís have not only survived. They have spread their Message of love and unity to over one hundred thousand places in the world.

It all began right there in Persia (Iran), with the Báb and Bahá'u'lláh, and the struggle for survival — not of the Bahá'í community, but of the human race. This spiritual battle for the ultimate freedom of all mankind continues, even as the gallant Bahá'í soldiers fall in battle.

Anyone truly conversant with the sacred Scriptures of the past would not be surprised at all. It is not the plan of man, but the Plan of God. This is exactly what has been promised to the world for this day in all the Holy Books.

I know that such a religious concept of human affair, sometimes puts many people off. They lose all interest. However, when it is the 'last train out of Madrid' for all humanity, perhaps a little patience will bear wondrous fruit. We've tried *man's* answer and solutions. Where has *that* got us? Right where we stand now. On the brink of an awesome abyss.

Why not try God's answer? Or, at least satisfy ourselves whether or not it *is* God's answer? That's one of our "challenges", isn't it?

That's why we're telling the "wondrous story".

The 'spiritual fire power' we are talking about is a down-to-earth, every day, run-of-the-mill miracle.

The *real* pollution the world faces is not in the smog over our cities, not in the mercury, oil spills, and other poisons to be found in our oceans, lakes and streams, not even in the cancer-causing additives in the food we eat, the liquids we drink, the insufficiently tested drugs we take with their terrifying side-effects. All these are nothing compared to the real pollution.

That pollution is in the hearts of men.

The hatreds, the prejudices, the greed, the corruption for material things at any cost, these are the animal-like qualities which have always destroyed individuals, families, states, nations and civilizations. A decadent, overpowering, overwhelming, cancerous materialism now has all mankind in its iron grasp, and will not let go.

It will take a spiritual remedy to cure all that. Nothing else has, or we wouldn't be in all this present trouble.

Fanaticism has no place in the Bahá'í Faith. Bahá'ís are expected to live a full, rich, wonderful life, experiencing and extracting all the joy, wonder and awe in every day of our lives. But always remembering our primary responsibilities to God and to our fellow men.

When mankind forgets these responsibilities, he uses, selfishly and to his own danger, the great material, physical, and scientific gains the human mind has created. The proper use of these blessings depends on the heart and conscience of man. He can use these wonders to heal or to destroy.

That is the crisis.

Until this *real* pollution of hate, prejudice and greed in the heart of man is removed, our civilization will only continue on its downward plunge toward that awesome abyss that lives ahead.

Where can mankind turn for help?

Many thinking people are now beginning to wonder if perhaps we haven't paid too dearly for these material gains of ours, gains which, in one moment of caprice on the part of the world's leaders, could be swept away, leaving the world in ashes.

Visionless and unshepherded on a world scale, man in his plight proclaims his spiritual bankruptcy. So where can he turn for help in this planetary crisis?

Where is his ultimate hope?

In God's Plan, not man's.

In Bahá'u'lláh, the *Prince of Peace*. No one else has the "fire power".

A spiritual power that already has demonstrated its capacity to change the human heart. These are united, vigorously functioning Bahá'í communities of *Arabs and Jews, Irish and British, Black and White, East and West*. In fact, every group of peoples and nations who cannot live together, who kill and maim, are now working with love, harmony, admiration for each other, and loving (really loving) each other in the Bahá'í communities of the world.

Not in places far off from the trouble-spots of the world, but right in the midst of them. There where death is but a breath away: Beirut, Northern Ireland, Southern Africa, the Deep South. Everywhere.

The *Microcosm* is growing slowly, imperceptibly, but irresistibly toward that *Macrocosm* of the *Kingdom of God on earth*.

That is firepower!

You will find it nowhere else.

"As the waters cover the sea."

30.

The Cloudburst

All of the wonderful prophecies associated with the Báb and Bahá'u'lláh, no matter how overwhelming and continuous, are but one drop from the sea of fulfillment you will discover when you study Their lives and Teachings.

For our purposes of discovering if the "wondrous story" has really been *told* to the world, this final outpouring will summarize it all.

It will help us understand why such tremendous numbers of "awakened" and "prepared" souls have already arisen all over the planet in answer to the Call and Summons of Bahá'u'lláh Who they have accepted to be the *Supreme Redeemer of men*.

We need only share this brief but beautiful "Cloudburst" concerning Bahá'u'lláh. The *Glory of God*, the *Promised One of all Ages, Peoples, Races and Religions*, the *King of Kings*, the *Lord of Hosts*.

These "titles of Bahá'u'lláh" alone suggest why so many have already arisen in such a flood of service. Every one of these *titles* are also prophecies which can be proven from the sacred Scriptures.

The following historical account of Bahá'u'lláh's relationship to the other *Religious Systems* of the past, makes Bahá'u'lláh's Station unmistakably clear.

We shall know why the "wondrous story" has been told, and why only the spiritually "blind" and "deaf" could have failed to "Behold" and "Wonder marvelously" as Scripture foretold.

Listen!

Tributes to Bahá'u'lláh

"To Israel He (Bahá'u'lláh) was neither more nor less than the incarnation of the 'Everlasting Father', the 'Lord of Hosts' come down with ten thousands of saints."
To Christendom, Christ returned "in the glory of the Father."
To S̲h̲í'ih Islam, the return of the Imám Ḥusayn.
To Sunní Islam, the descent of the "Spirit of God" (Jesus Christ)
To the Zoroastrians the promised S̲h̲áh Bahrám.
To the Hindus, the reincarnation of Krishna.
To the Buddhists, the fifth Buddha.
To Him, the greatest of the Jewish prophets, *Isaiah,* alluded as the "Glory of the Lord", the "Everlasting Father", the "Prince of Peace", the "Wonderful", the "Counsellor", Who "shall judge among the nations", Who "shall assemble the outcasts of Israel, and gather together the dispersed of Judah from the four corners of the earth".
Of Bahá'u'lláh, *David* sang in his *Psalms,* also acclaiming Him as the "Lord of Hosts" and the "King of Glory" Who will come to 'Akká, the "Strong City".
To Him *Haggai* referred as the "Desire of the Nations".
Zachariah described Bahá'u'lláh as the "Branch" Who "shall build the Temple of the Lord". Bahá'u'lláh wrote a Tablet about this "Temple" of *Zachariah,* a document of great power and beauty.
Joel referred to Bahá'u'lláh's Day as "the day of Jehovah."
Zephaniah called Bahá'u'lláh's Day, a "day of the trumpet and alarm against the fenced cities, and against high towers [Fortified Cities]".
Daniel called Bahá'u'lláh's Day, the "day of the Lord".
Malachi described Bahá'u'lláh's Day as "the great and dreadful day of the Lord" when "the Sun of Righteousness" will "arise", with "healing in His wings".
Habakkuk foretold the day when "the earth shall be filled with the knowledge of the glory of the Lord, as the waters cover the sea".
Zoroaster referred to Him, Bahá'u'lláh, as the One Who would

bring about the advent of "the World-Savior S̲h̲áh-Bahrám Who would usher in an era of blessedness and peace".

Bahá'u'lláh alone is meant by the prophecy attributed to Gautama Buddha Himself that "a Buddha named Maitreya, the Buddha of universal fellowship" would, "in the fullness of time", arise and reveal "His boundless glory".

The Bhagavad-Gita of the Hindus referred to Bahá'u'lláh, as the "Most Great Spirit", the "Tenth Avatar", the "Immaculate Manifestation of Krishna".

To Bahá'u'lláh, Jesus Christ, had referred as the "Comforter", as the "Spirit of truth" Who will "guide men into all truth". He, Who, "shall not speak of himself, but whatsoever He shall hear, that shall he speak".

Christ referred to Bahá'u'lláh as the "Lord of the Vineyard" and the "Son of Man" Who "shall come in the glory of his Father".[1]

Our *Cloudburst* has ended.

At least, from this time forward to the end of "As the waters cover the sea", we shall now know with Whom we are dealing.

'ABDU'L-BAHÁ

"As the waters cover the sea."

31.

The Beloved Master

Our theme now takes up the enthralling story of 'Abdu'l-Bahá, the Succesor of Bahá'u'lláh, His Eldest Son.

The influence of 'Abdu'l-Bahá's life and His Writings had an immediate and tremendous impact upon the world and human society.

Especially in Europe and North America.

The influence which the many travels of 'Abdu'l-Bahá, to Africa, twice to Europe, once for eight months to the United States and Canada, cannot be overemphasized.

We shall put that unique story into the briefest possible capsule, taking but a few ever-green trees and leaving the forest. Regrettable, but surely more than sufficent for our purpose.

The contribution of 'Abdu'l-Bahá to the worldwide spread of the Bahá'í Faith was equally as dramatic and astonishing, if not even more so, than that of the Herald, the Báb, and the Founder, Bahá'u'lláh.

'Abdu'l-Bahá was appointed by Bahá'u'lláh as His Successor. In His, Bahá'u'lláh's, own handwriting.(*) He carried the fame of

(*) Another of the unique and precious distinctions of the Faith of Bahá'u'lláh. Such a written Will and Testament, as part of the Covenant of Bahá'u'lláh, had never before happened in religious history. Every door one opens reveals the majesty and wonder of the Faith of Bahá'u'lláh, and the importance and significance of that Faith to our present day society

His Father's Faith, the Bahá'í Faith, to all parts of the world with both His voluminous correspondence, His books as well as through His travels to Africa and to the West.

It is impossible to overstress the worldwide effect of 'Abdu'l-Bahá's correspondence. While engaged in other activites of a vital nature which helped tremendously with the consolidation and spread of His Father's Faith, such as the construction of Edifices that would add greatly to its glory and fame abroad, as well as in the Holy Land itself, 'Abdu'l-Bahá wrote continuously *to all parts* of the world. Almost uninterruptedly both day and night.

One account declares:

"Nor would He ('Abdu'l-Bahá) allow any obstacle, however formidable, to interfere with the daily flow of Tablets (letters) which poured forth, with prodigious rapidity and ever-increasing volume, from His indefatigable pen, in answer to the vast number of letters, reports, inquiries, prayers, confessions of faith, apologies and eulogies received from countless followers and admirers in both the East and the West."[1]

'Abdu'l-Bahá inspired each soul, whether friend or stranger, to arise and carry the Word of God into every corner of the planet. He did this both in person with the constant flood of Pilgrims, and through His correspondence with the world.

Eyewitnesses have testified:

"... that during an agitated and perilous period of His life, they have known Him ('Abdu'l-Bahá) to pen, with His own Hand, no less than ninety Tablets in a single day, and to pass many a night, from dusk to dawn, alone in His bedchamber, engaged in a correspondence which the pressure of His manifold responsibilities had prevented Him from attending to in the day-time."[2]

During his eight months journey in America, 'Abdu'l-Bahá proclaimed His Father's Faith in schools, universities, churches, synagogues, among the poor and underprivileged as well as among the rich and famous, including the leaders of men: Presidents,

Senators, Legislators, Mayors, Scientists, Inventors, and Scholars.

'Abdu'l-Bahá during His journeys to the West, warned the world of the inevitable coming of the first World War. Following that war, after the failure of mankind to establish a lasting peace, 'Abdu'l-Bahá foretold the inevitable coming of a second and greater world war.

He forewarned mankind of the horrifying persecution of the Jews that would take place on European soil because of the lack of mankind's spiritual progress. 'Abdu'l-Bahá warned the peoples of the earth of that terrible "force" that existed in the earth. An awesome force mentioned earlier by His Father, Bahá'u'lláh, which could poison the atmosphere and cause the burning and destruction of the cities.

The strongest and perhaps most specific of these warnings was delivered in Paris to an Ambassador of Japan, Viscount Tadoka Arakawa, in whose country the first atomic bomb was to be exploded during that more terrible war yet to come as forecast by the *Master,* as 'Abdu'l-Bahá was tenderly called by His loved ones.

'Abdu'l-Bahá said to Ambassador Arakawa:

> "Scientific discoveries have increased material civilization. There is in existence a stupendous force, as yet, happily, undiscovered by man. Let us supplicate God, the Beloved, that this force be not discovered by science until spiritual civilization shall dominate the human mind. In the hands of men of lower material nature, this power would be able to destroy the whole earth."[3]

This section of the book you are now reading, is called "As the waters cover the sea". It is designed to show both the indifference of the world to the greatness of the Day in which they were living, as well as to recount for you the repeated, unending opportunities which the peoples of the world have been given to see, to hear, and to respond to the world-healing Message of Bahá'u'lláh.

It is perhaps necessary to mention at least a few of those leaders and gifted people whom 'Abdu'l-Bahá met on His travels, rather than merely state generally that He was overwhelmed by their numbers.

Wherever 'Abdu'l-Bahá went, countless numbers of visitors gathered around Him. Huge throngs of both friends and seekers followed Him everywhere.

No one was neglected. 'Abdu'l-Bahá willingly and lovingly met them all.

'Abdu'l-Bahá's doors were open to everyone.

To them all He told the "wondrous story" of Bahá'u'lláh's coming in the sweetest words imaginable.

"As the waters cover the sea."

32.

Rising Tide: America

Specifically, 'Abdu'l-Bahá, during the course of His several visits to North Africa, had, according to written accounts: "... more than one interview with the Khedive, 'Abbás Ḥilmí Páshá II, was introduced to Lord Kitchener, met the Muftí Shaykh Muḥammad Bakhít, as well as the Khedive's Imám Shaykh Muḥammad Ráshid, and associated with several 'ulamás, páshás, Persian notables, members of the Turkish Parliament, editors of leading newspapers in Cairo and Alexandria, and other leaders and representatives of well-known institutions, both religious and secular."[1]

The stories of 'Abdu'l-Bahá's visits, as well as the Teachings of His Father, Bahá'u'lláh, which He expounded so brilliantly, were carried in the newspaper reports of those events.

In England, a house in Cadogan Gardens was placed at 'Abdu'l-Bahá's disposal. Immediately His home became a center for great numbers of visitors of all kinds.

"O these pilgrims, these guests, these visitors!" 'Abdu'l-Bahá's hostess cried out, overcome by the ever-increasing numbers.

"Remembering those days," she said, "our ears were filled with the sound of their footsteps — as they came from every country in the world."[2]

The eyewitness account of those hectic and incredible days continues:

"Every day, all day long, a constant stream, an interminable procession! Ministers and missionaries, oriental scholars and occult students, practical men of affairs and mystics, Anglicans,

Catholics, and Non-conformists, Theosophists and Hindus, Christian Scientists and doctors of medicine, Muslims, Buddhists, and Zoroastrians; There also called: politicians, Salvation Army soldiers, and other workers for human good, women suffragists, journalists, and artisans, poor workless people and prosperous merchants, members of the dramatic and musical world, these all came, and none were too lowly, nor too great, to receive the sympathetic consideration of 'Abdu'l-Bahá Who was always 'giving his life for the good of others.' " [3]

'Abdu'l-Bahá addressed an overflowing congregation from the pulpit of the *City Temple* in London. He also spoke at an evening service at *St. John the Divine*, in Westminster, at the request of the Venerable Archdeacon Wilberforce.

'Abdu'l-Bahá breakfasted with the Lord Mayor of London at Mansion House; addressed the Theosophical Society at the request of their President; He was guest in Dr. T.K. Cheyne's home in Oxford, and delivered an address to a "large and deeply interested audience" at Manchester College.[4]

On and on goes the record of 'Abdu'l-Bahá's triumphs of which this is but one leaf from one tree in all of Hyde Park.

Among the huge numbers who called upon him during those memorable days spent in both England and Scotland, were included only this very few who can be mentioned here because of time and space. They were:

Lord Lamington, Sir Michael Sadler, The Jalálu'd-Dawlih, son of Zillu's-Sulṭán, Sir Ameer 'Alí, the late Maharaja of Jalawar, who paid many visits and gave an elaborate dinner and reception in 'Abdu'l-Bahá's honor, Princess Karadfa, Baroness Bernkow, Professor E.G. Browne, Professor Patrick Geddes, Mr. Albert Dawson, Editor of the Christian Commonwealth, Mr. David Graham Pale, Mrs. Annie Besant, Mrs. Parkhurst, and countless others. The same was true in France, Germany, and Austria.

Even greater crowds attended 'Abdu'l-Bahá on His visit to the United States and Canada. He came in contact with, and spoke to, multitudes of people in His journey from the Atlantic to the

Pacific and back, including a visit to Canada.

A true account of those days and all of 'Abdu'l-Bahá's travels which were, all by themselves, a "marvelous work" and "wonder", it would be impossible to do justice to in such a brief narrative as this.

An actual attempt to do so, other than mine, admits:

"A full-account of these diversified activities which crowded His ('Abdu'l-Bahá's) days during no less than eight months, would be beyond the scope of this survey; suffice it to say that in the city of New York alone, 'Abdu'l-Bahá delivered public addresses in, and made formal visits to, no less than fifty-five different places."[5](*)

'Abdu'l-Bahá spoke to large gatherings such as that at the Peace Conference at Lake Mohonk in New York State. Little did his audiences dream that they were looking upon the Successor and Son of the One depicted so clearly in the sacred Scripture as the *Promised One*, the *Counsellor*, the *Everlasting Father*, the *Prince of Peace*.

'Abdu'l-Bahá addressed packed halls and auditoriums at Columbia, Harvard, and New York Universities. Far across the land He gave an illuminating address to eighteen hundred students and one hundred and eighty teachers and professors at Leland Stanford University in Palo Alto, California. The President, Dr. David Starr Jordan, introduced Him, and declared that 'Abdu'l-Bahá "walked the mystic spiritual path with practical feet."[6]

A full front page story of 'Abdu'l-Bahá's visit with a large picture of Himself covers the event in the minutest detail. Copies of that front page have been sent all around the world.

'Abdu'l-Bahá's travels took Him from the bowery Mission in the slums of New York to a brilliant reception in the social life of the capital city in Washington, D.C.

'Abdu'l-Bahá spoke to no less than two thousand in the Temple

---

(*)See *God Passes By*, Shoghi Effendi, pp. 279-294, for a detailed and fascinating account of 'Abdu'l-Bahá's travels and His Proclamation of Bahá'u'lláh's Faith to the Western world. Superbly told, and movingly inspiring.

Emmanu-El in San Francisco. He also participated in the Fourth Annual Conference of the NAACP in Chicago.

Secretaries of State, Ambassadors, Congressmen, distinguished Rabbis and Churchmen, and other people of eminence attained His presence, among whom were such figures as: Professor Jackson of Columbia University, Professor Jack of Oxford University, Rabbi Stephen Wise of New York, Dr Martin A. Meyer, Rabbi Joeph L. Levy, Rabbi Abram Simon, Alexander Graham Bell, Rabindra Nath Tagore, the Honorable Franklin K. Lane, Mrs. William Jennings Bryan, Andrew Carnegie, the Honorable Franklin MacVeagh, Secretary of the United States Treasury, Mr. Roosevelt, Admiral Wainwright, Admiral Peary, the British, Dutch and Swiss Ministers in Washington, the Turkish Ambassador, Thomas Seaton, and many more.

This wholly inadequate account of 'Abdu'l-Bahá's impact on leaders of thought in every field is hardly more than a glimpse. It is but one drop from the surging sea of 'Abdu'l-Bahá's twenty-nine years dedicated to spreading far and wide the news and significance of Bahá'u'lláh's coming and His Message of love and unity.

'Abdu'l-Bahá told everybody about His Father, Bahá'u'lláh wherever He went. No one ever "told" the "wondrous story" of Bahá'u'lláh so beautifully, so convincingly, and so frequently ("as the waters cover the sea").

The North American continent, above all others, bore witness to the "boundless vitality" which 'Abdu'l-Bahá exhibited in the course of these unique and incredible journeys."

An historical account of 'Abdu'l-Bahá's fantastic travels in America, and the unending list of the people He met on these journeys, reports that 'Abdu'l-Bahá had undertaken:

"A visit which entailed a journey of over five thousand miles, which lasted from April to December (1912), which carried Him from the Atlantic to the Pacific Coast and back, which elicited discourses of such numbers as to fill no less than three volumes."[7]

The Guardian of the Bahá'í Faith, Shoghi Effendi, in *God Passes By*, (p. 295), declares:

" 'Abdu'l-Bahá's historic journeys to the West, and in particular His eight-month tour of the United States of America, may be said to have marked the culmination of His ministry whose untold blessings and stupendous achievements only future generations can adequately estimate. As the day-star of Bahá'u'lláh's Revelation had shone forth in its meridian splendor at the hour of the proclamation of His Message to the rulers of the earth in the city of Adrianople, so did the Orb of His Covenant mount its zenith and shed its brightest rays when He Who was its appointed Center ['Abdu'l-Bahá] arose to blaze the glory and greatness of His Father's Faith among the peoples of the West."

Indeed, 'Abdu'l-Bahá's three years of travel, first to Egypt, then to Europe, and later to America, mark, if we would correctly appraise their historic importance, a turning point of the utmost significance in the history of the century."[8]

No one who has tried to follow the footsteps of 'Abdu'l-Bahá, to count His endless correspondence, to read His Books, and special Messages to the world, or to bask in the wonder of His Words and interviews with the renowned and famous, can doubt for a moment that the "wondrous story" had been offered with love, time and again, to the peoples of the world, by the *Master*, 'Abdu'l-Bahá.

Over and above all these wonders, the Writings of 'Abdu'l-Bahá will have an eternal effect upon the peoples of the future Ages. There is no way to measure the impact which His Words as Centre of the Covenant will shed upon the history of the Bahá'í Faith, as well as upon the mankind for ages yet to come. It is far beyond our understanding.

One swift example will throw a brilliant light upon His present and future greatness. His *Will and Testament* is the Document that holds together the Three Ages of the Faith: The Apostalic Age, The Formative Age, in which we now find ourselves, and the Golden Age yet to come. Some five hundred thousand years of history in the Bahá'í Cycle, the Cycle of Bahá'u'lláh, under whose shadow the Messengers of God will come in succession down through the dim ranges of time.

Wouldn't it be wonderful if I had the time and space to tell the story. Look into it with a searching eye yourself. What joy and happiness it will bring you.

However, what is now coming up is in itself just too wonderful for words.

"As the waters cover the sea"

33.

The Kingdom of God on earth, A Beginning

Whoever would have dreamed that you and I would be living in the day of the *Christ-promised Kingdom of God on earth*?
Yet, it is true!
We are.
That is part of the "marvelous work" and "wonder" that God would bring about in the *last days* at the *time of the end*.
It is happening right now! Perhaps even in your own home town!

This is probably one of the most exciting parts of our "wondrous story". When 'Abdu'l-Bahá was in Wilmette, Illinois in 1912, He laid the cornerstone for the Bahá'í House of Worship there. A Temple dedicated to the Oneness of God, the Oneness of His Messengers, the Oneness of the Religions of the world, and Oneness of all the peoples of the world, the "children of God".
All, without exception.

How amazing and wonderful that these Events should happen in our time. So that you and I could become an active part of them.
And not only hear about them as we did in the past ages, but

to see them with our eyes.
Living!
Working!
Imagine!

Bahá'í Houses of Worship (Temples) have already been raised up in each Continent. All are dedicated to the unity of God and the human race, peoples everywhere on earth. Without preference. Without exception. Without doubt. Everyone. Not for the special, the privileged, the leaders, but for all humanity. Every single soul alive upon the planet. Including, with tender love, the welcome presence of those "darling souls, the seething masses" of mankind. This is their Religion, too. If not especially.

The Mother Temple of the West for which 'Abdu'l-Bahá Himself laid the cornerstone, has contributed tremendously to the worldwide spread and fame of the Bahá'í Faith. Not only through the thousands upon thousands of visitors who come in a continuous flood each day from all parts of the world, from all nations, races and religions to visit the House of Worship, but also from the publicity and proclamation about it in all media.

When 'Abdu'l-Bahá laid the cornerstone of this majestic Temple, He Himself predicted that "when the foundation" of that Temple was "laid in America", a most "wonderful and thrilling motion will appear in the world of existence". He foretold that "from that point of light the spirit of teaching, spreading the Cause of God and promoting the teachings of God, will permeate to all parts of the world".[1]

Is that telling the "wondrous story"? Or not?

Even more wonderful, were the Words of 'Abdu'l-Bahá about the significance to mankind of this history-making Event:

"... This mighty Structure," He said, "will mark the inception of the Kingdom of God on earth. This Temple of God shall be built, it will be to the spirit and body of the world what the inrush of the spirit is to the physical body of man, quickening it to its utmost parts, and infusing a new Light and Power."[2]

"... this mighty Structure," He said, "shall be renowned

throughout the world." It will, 'Abdu'l-Bahá said, several times, mark "the inception of the Kingdom of God on earth".

Thousands of other Houses of Worship would be born from it, 'Abdu'l-Bahá promised, but this would be the "Mother Temple".

Why would it "mark the inception of the Kingdom of God on earth"? Over and above the fact that the Promised One of all Ages, the King of Kings, and the Lord of Hosts, had said it was so?

There were many wonderful practical reasons. Here we can touch upon only a few highlights.

Around every one of these Bahá'í Houses of Worship, and they will eventually be raised up in every city, town, village and hamlet, every Indian Reserve, and humble community of the world, there will be:

    A home for the orphans
    A home for the aged
    Hospitals and Medical Institutions
    Schools and Universities
    The National Bahá'í Headquarters
    A Secretariat
    An Archives
    A Library
    A Publishing Office
    An Assembly Hall
    A Council Chamber
    A Treasury
    A Pilgrim's Hostel and Resting Place

They will all be "brought together and made jointly to operate in one spot" so that the work of the Lord is carried out exactly as envisioned by the Messenger of God for today, Bahá'u'lláh, Who is looking out for the welfare of every single human being on the planet, as well as for all the Nations of the world.

These Institutions around the Holy House of Worship, where all the Messengers of God and all His Religions are honored and revered, a thing unique in the religious history of mankind, will "increasingly be regarded as the focus of all Bahá'í activity". They symbolize, in a befitting manner, the ideal of service to humanity which is the spirit that always "animates the Bahá'í Community in relationship to the Faith and to mankind in general".[3]

Those are the words, the magic words, "service and worship". They always go together.

Now we begin to see what a great thing 'Abdu'l-Bahá did when He was in North America, over and above the wonders already described. Not only for the Bahá'ís, but for the whole world.

Imagine!

Never again, anywhere in the world, will there ever be an orphan who is unloved and unwanted! They will be loved and cherished by every member of the Bahá'í Local Assembly and every member of the Bahá'í Community. What a beautiful picture! These children will be loved and educated by their new parents. As the Writings of the Bahá'í Faith say so movingly, the Bahá'ís will be "fathers" and "mothers" to those in need.

Imagine!

Never again will there ever be old people sitting on their forlorn porches, rocking back and forth, unloved and unwanted. Never again! Anywhere on earth! They will not be abandoned to their fate.

They will be loved, cherished, protected and made to feel an important part of the Community again, for as long as they live. I have myself, with my wife Marguerite, already personally visited some of these dear old ones in their special *Home for the Aged*, near to the Bahá'í House of Worship in Wilmette, Illinois, where such a wondrous Institution already exists.

Imagine!

Medical Institutions, hospitals, clinics so the ill may be healed, and the maimed and wounded restored to health. Those in need of physical help are assisted in every way. All returned, as quickly as possible, to work and full activity wherever possible.

Imagine!

Schools and Universities so that every human being in the Community can secure a good education, so that the latent talents of every heart can be fully developed and utilized for the good of mankind, and that precious gift not lost to humanity. If a child cannot afford such an education, the Bahá'ís of that Local Assembly and Community will see that he or she gets one. Without preference, without prejudice, without exception!

Without doubt!

Imagine!

It is not a hope, it is a reality. It is already being built step by step all over the earth, a gradually rising part of that *Kingdom of God on earth*. The beginning of which Kingdom already exists in microcosm. It is growing by leaps and bounds toward that inevitable macrocosm that will capture and hold the loving hearts of all humanity.

Imagine!

A Treasury where all contributions are voluntary. Where every lover of Bahá'u'lláh gives from his heart for the good of all. There is no other way to "give" in the *Kingdom of God*. All that each one of us possesses came from God in the beginning anyway, and all we can do is return some of His countless blessings so that all mankind, every human being, may live without fear for the future.

On and on go the "wonders", but I shall content myself with one final comment. I have said it earlier, but I shall now say it again. I know it will have far more meaning to you now.

The National and Local Administrative Headquarters for this *Kingdom of God on earth* are called in the language of Bahá'u'lláh, *Ḥaẓíratu'l-Quds,* which means in English: "The Sacred Fold".

Every one of these Bahá'í Centers everywhere in the entire world are called: *The Sacred Fold*. There, the sheep of the One Shepherd of all humanity, in this Day of the *One Fold and One Shepherd*, are gathered together with all the peoples of the world in love and unity.

Sorry. I forgot to say:

Imagine!

Now we know what the Beloved Master, 'Abdu'l-Bahá, did

when He laid the cornerstone of that beautiful Temple in Wilmette, the "Holiest House of Worship that will ever be raised to the Name of Bahá'u'lláh. That *Mother Temple* already has children in Kampala, Uganda; Sydney, Australia; Frankfurt, Germany; Panama City, Panama; Apia, Western Samoa; and in New Delhi, India in this very hour, to which this entire book is dedicated.

We, you and I, have been living in the earliest beginnings of that *Kingdom of God on earth*. It began thirty three years ago when that *House of Worship* in Wilmette was dedicated to public service.

Thirty Three Years Already!

Imagine!

The *inception of the Kingdom of God on earth*, a beginning is not surprising at all to the followers of Bahá'u'lláh. Their reasons can be found in those wonderful Words about the Founder of their Faith. To Him, the *Prince of Peace,* the *Wonderful*, the *Counsellor*, the *Supreme Redeemer of men*, nothing would ever be impossible.

He, Bahá'u'lláh, is the One Whom history has described, and the One Whom posterity will acclaim as:

> "... the Judge, the Lawgiver and Redeemer of all mankind, as the Organizer of the entire planet, as the Unifier of the children of men, as the Inaugurator of the long-awaited millenium, as the originator of a new 'Universal Cycle', as the Establisher of the Most Great Peace, as the Fountain of the most Great Justice, as the Proclaimer of the coming of age of the entire human race, as the Creator of a new World Order, and as the Inspirer and founder of a world civilization."[4]

We return now to the Master and share 'Abdu'l-Bahá's final contribution to the fame and glory of the Cause of God, as we follow Him to the Holy Land, and those dramatic, tense, and final hours of His precious life.

But we shall remember His Words about the Bahá'í *House of Worship* and its planetary effect on the World as it carries Bahá'u'lláh's Message of Oneness to the world.

The Master said that when the Bahá'í Temple with its accessory Institutions "is established in the world, aside from its religious or spiritual influence, it will have a tremendous effect upon civilization".[5]

"As the waters cover the sea"

34.

Rising Tide: The Holy Land

No account of the worldwide impact of 'Abdu'l-Bahá's life upon the world, and the planetary spread of His Father's Faith, would be complete without some reference — however brief — to 'Abdu'l-Bahá's days in the Holy Land during World War I.

The wondrous story of which we have been speaking was unquestionably told to mankind over and over by 'Abdu'l-Bahá Himself, and through Him by His followers whom He inspired to arise and cover the earth with the good news. Every pilgrim He met, every letter He wrote carried the good news farther and farther.

'Abdu'l-Bahá had repeatedly foreshadowed the coming of the war of 1914-1918 in His talks in the West. Eight months after His return to the Holy Land, war broke out. The last dark cloud that was to enshroud the closing years of His agitated but glorious Ministry began to surround Him.

The Commander-in-Chief of the Turkish forces in the Holy Land, the "brutal, all powerful and unscrupulous Jamál Páshá" had expressed his intention of "crucifying" 'Abdu'l-Bahá if the Turkish Army was forced to abandon the Holy Land in the face of advancing Allied Forces.

The English believers learned of the dire peril threatening the life of 'Abdu'l-Bahá and took immediate steps to insure His safety. Lord Curzon and others in the British Cabinet were advised of the critical nature of the situation in Haifa.

The prompt intervention of Lord Lamington, who immediately wrote to the Foreign Office, explained the importance of 'Abdu'l-Bahá's position. The dispatch of a letter of General Allenby, instructed him to "extend every protection and consideration to 'Abdu'l-Bahá, His family and His friends". A cablegram subsequently sent by the General, after the capture of Haifa, to London, requested the authorities to "notify the world that 'Abdu'l-Bahá is safe". That same General issued orders to the officer in command of the Haifa operations to insure 'Abdu'l-Bahá's safety, thus frustrating the expressed intention of Jamál Páshá to crucify 'Abdu'l-Bahá and His family on Mount Carmel."[1]

"Notify the world that 'Abdu'l-Bahá is safe."

Such was the breadth of 'Abdu'l-Bahá's influence. He had completely captured the hearts of friends and strangers alike wherever He appeared. Especially the hearts of those loyal believers busily engaged around the world in spreading the Glad Tidings of the coming of Bahá'u'lláh with all that it meant to a disillusioned and suffering humanity.

Some of 'Abdu'l-Bahá's Muslim enemies were perturbed by the name of 'Abdu'l-Bahá's rescuer, General Allenby. In their frustration at 'Abdu'l-Bahá's release, they sought reasons to excuse their own surprising failure to capture 'Abdu'l-Bahá, and their repeated inability to humiliate Him. Eventually, they even stooped to superstition. Allenby's name they said, was all too similar to "Allah Nebi" — God's Prophet. No wonder 'Abdu'l-Bahá had been rescued.

'Abdu'l-Bahá enrolled the famous scientist and entomologist, Dr. Augustus Forel of Switzerland in the Path of Bahá'u'lláh through a weighty letter (Tablet) which the Master, 'Abdu'l-Bahá sent to Dr. Forel.

'Abdu'l-Bahá opened up the far-off continent of Australia to the Bahá'í Faith through the pioneering efforts of the courageous and heroic Hyde Dunn and his wife Clara, who inspired to do so by 'Abdu'l-Bahá's Words to them. Between them, the Dunns carried the Message of Bahá'u'lláh to no less than seven hundred towns throughout the Commonwealth.

During those remarkable days, the "Star Servant" of Bahá'u'lláh's Faith, "the indomitable and immortal" Martha Root, designated by 'Abdu'l-Bahá Himself as a "herald of the Kingdom", embarked upon the first of her historic journeys which were to carry her several times around the world.

It was only a glimmer of what was yet to come, as every corner of the earth was soon to be touched by the "glad tidings" of Bahá'u'lláh's appearance in the world with His Message of love, unity and peace. What "wondrous story" could compare to it.

The news of 'Abdu'l-Bahá's passing, so sudden, so unexpected, spread like wildfire throughout Haifa and 'Akká. It flashed instantly over the wires to distant parts of the globe, stunning with grief the community of the followers of Bahá'u'lláh in east and west. Messages from far and near. From high and low alike, cablegrams and letters, poured into Haifa in an increasing flood from around the world.

No need to list the names of the famous and renowned who attended the funeral of 'Abdu'l-Bahá and those who sent Messages of condolence.(*)

A description of the worldwide effect of that great loss to humanity, reports:

"Many divers newspapers, such as the London Times, the Morning Post, the Daily Mail, the New York World, Le Temp, the Times of India and others, in different languages and countries, paid their tribute to one Who had rendered the Cause of human brotherhood and peace such signal and imperishable services."[2]

The High Commissioner, Sir Hubert Samuel, sent an immediate message to "express my respect for His creed and my regard for His person".

Boy Scouts of Christian and Muslim choristers chanted verses from the Qur'án. The chiefs of the Muslim community headed by the Muftí, and accompanied by a number of Christian priests,

---

(*)The story of the majesty and beauty of that event told in the beautiful booklet "The Passing of 'Abdu'l-Bahá" by Shoghi Effendi and Lady Bloomfield.

Latin, Greek and Anglican walked in front of the coffin. Behind the simple casket walked the members of 'Abdu'l-Bahá's family, the British High Commissioner, Sir Herbert Samuel, the Governor of Jerusalem, Sir Ronald Storrs, the Governor of Phoenicia, Sir Stewart Symes, officials of the government, consuls of various countries resident in Haifa, notables of Palestine, Muslim, Jewish, Christian, Druze, Egyptians, Greeks, Turks, Arabs, Kurds, European and American men, women and children.

The long train of mourners, amid sobs and moans of many a grief-stricken heart, wended its slow way up the slopes of Mt. Carmel to the Mausoleum of the Báb.

At times, among the soft inward sobbing of hearts broken by the tragic losses of that loving Father of all mankind who had left them, the only sound that could be heard in all the countryside was the singing of the birds.

These momentous events marked the earthly conclusion of the contribution made by the three Central Figures of the Faith, the Báb, Bahá'u'lláh, and 'Abdu'l-Bahá to the worldwide spread of the Bahá'í Faith during their lifetimes. This, of course is a pitifully abridged account of an impact and influence which in reality turns all these words to ashes. An influence which increases immeasurably with the passing of time, and will continue to echo in the hearts of men.

The influence and inspiration of their lives greatly increased and intensified the work of telling the "wondrous story" which their followers have continued to do ever since that time.

Indeed it was a "marvelous work" and "wonder" which is slowly, almost imperceptibly at times, but irresistibly and definitely changing the hearts and souls of the human race.

THE GUARDIAN AND THE UNIVERSAL HOUSE OF JUSTICE

"As the waters cover the sea"

35.

Flood Tide

There has already been raised up in the Holy Land, the World Center of the Bahá'í Faith, an International Supreme Body called *The Universal House of Justice*.

It is far more than that, however. As we shall see.

This House of Justice was called for by Bahá'u'lláh Himself in His Writings. It has been mentioned earlier, but its full significance has not yet been explored as an Agent for the world-wide spread of the Faith of Bahá'u'lláh.

That it has been greatly responsible for the recognition of the Bahá'í Faith all over the world can be judged by the title of this chapter: "Flood Tide!"

The most important thing for us to understand at this point is the recognition and appreciation of the station of the *Guardian of the Bahá'í Faith*, Shoghi Effendi Rabbani.

He is the great-grandson of Bahá'u'lláh, a descendent of the Báb, and the grandson of 'Abdu'l-Bahá, the Center of Bahá'u'lláh's Covenant. Like 'Abdu'l-Bahá before Him, Who was appointed by His Father, Bahá'u'lláh, in a special Will and Testament; so, likewise, was Shoghi Effendi appointed by 'Abdu'l-Bahá in His Will and Testament.

All of these Documents are in the Archives of the Bahá'í Faith, signed, sealed, and preserved for posterity. The world of Religion has never seen its like before. The uniqueness of it all has been mentioned before in this book, and needs no amplification here. It stands unparalleled in religious history, and its importance is immediately self-evident.

Every word from this page onward is a tribute to the Guardian of the Faith, Shoghi Effendi. His spirit and his genius breathe from every page. It is he who raised up that Mother Temple which the Beloved Master dedicated. It is he who has guided and supervised the raising up of Bahá'í Houses of Worship everywhere in the world.

The beloved Guardian's *First* and *Second Seven Year Plan* laid the Foundation for the launching in every part of the world his breath-taking *World Crusade*, his *Ten Year Plan*, for the beginning of the "spiritual conquest of the planet".

Every victory, every accomplishment, revolves around him, Shoghi Effendi, whether it is teaching, raising up new Local Assemblies, National Assemblies, or building Temples, Schools, and other Structures that redound to the glory of the Faith for which he gave his life.

It was his words you first heard when our theme "As the waters cover the sea." began, remember?

> "... in the jungles of the Amazon, scale the mountain-fastnesses of Tibet, establish direct contact with the teeming and hapless multitudes in the interior of China, Mongolia and Japan, sit with the leprous, consort with the outcasts ...."

On and on goes the rhythm of his spiritual conquest of the planet. Love. Speed. Perseverance. Hurry, the time is short.

This is Shoghi Effendi, the beloved Guardian of the Bahá'í Faith.

It was through his guidance that the *Universal House of Justice* was established in 1963 on the one hundredth Anniversary of the *Declaration* of Bahá'u'lláh. The beautiful words you hear in this chapter about this August Body were from the pen of the Sign of God on earth, Shoghi Effendi, Guardian of the Bahá'í Faith. His inspiring Words will be heard throughout all of the remaining chapters of "As the waters cover the sea."

Bahá'u'lláh, at the end of His four grievous Exiles, stood on the side of Mount Carmel, and proclaimed the coming of the Universal House of Justice.

The Universal House of Justice inspires and guides, all over the world, the countless number of Bahá'ís who support these worldwide Institutions.

The significance of this Supreme Body to the world, and the work it is already doing, can be found in these Words from the Writings of the Guardian of the Bahá'í Faith, Shoghi Effendi:

> "When the Universal House of Justice shall have stepped forth from the realm of hope into that of visible fulfillment and its fame be established in every corner and clime of the world, then that August Body, solidly grounded and founded on the firm and unshakable foundation of the entire Bahá'í Community of East and West, and the recipient of the bounties of God and His divine inspiration, will proceed to devise and carry out important undertakings, worldwide activities and the establishment of glorious Institutions. By this means the renown of the Cause of God will become worldwide and its light will illuminate the whole earth."[1]

As an important part of demonstrating to the world that the "wondrous" story of Bahá'u'lláh and His Faith has indeed been "told" to the peoples of the earth, nothing has been more significant than the raising up of this Mighty Institution, the Universal House of Justice.

As is almost invariably the case, whenever we search deeper and deeper into the Bahá'í Faith, we uncover additional, marvelous things about this "wondrous story".

The *Universal House of Justice* is far more than the Supreme Administrative Body of the Bahá'í Faith. It is, in reality, the House of the Lord of Hosts, its establishment was foretold ages ago in the pages of ancient Scripture.

Let us begin with *Isaiah*, whose famous Yuletide Prophecy of the *Prince of Peace* is the main theme of this book.

> *ISAIAH:* "And it shall come to pass in the *last days*, that the mountain of the Lord's house shall be established in the top of the mountains, and shall be exalted above the hills; and all nations shall flow unto it. (*Isaiah, 2:2*)

The Old Testament prophet, *Haggai*, in the first chapter of his book, quotes the Lord of hosts, saying:

> *HAGGAI:* "Go up to the mountain, and bring wood and build the house; and I will take pleasure in it, and I will be glorified, saith the Lord." (*Haggai, 1:14*)

And again in that same chapter:

> *HAGGAI:* "... and the spirit of all the remnant of the people ... came and did work in the house of the Lord of hosts, their God." (*Haggai, 1:14*)

And finally on this theme, the "Amazing Micah" as I described him in *Thief in the Night!*(*)

> *MICAH:* "But in the *last days* it shall come to pass, that the mountain of the house of the Lord shall be established in the top of the mountains, and it shall be exalted above the hills; and people shall flow unto it." (*Micah, 4:1*)

Micah continues his words of praise.

> "And many nations shall come, and say, come, and let us go up to the mountain of the Lord ... and he will teach us of his ways, and we will walk in his paths." *(Micah, 4:2)*

(*)George Ronald, Publisher, 46 High Street, Kidlington, Oxford OX5 2DN. Nearly three hundred pages of prophecies fulfilled by the appearance of Bahá'u'lláh in the world.

The nations have come. They have already held five great World Conventions to establish and re-elect that "House of the Lord of Hosts", *the Universal House of Justice*, called for by the Pen of Bahá'u'lláh.

I call attention to these words of *Micah*, who was speaking of the *Lord of his Salvation*. Micah promised the Lord would come in those *last days* and bring about the resurrection and rescue of human hearts.

Micah promised that this great Figure would be shown "marvelous things" by the Almighty for exactly *"forty years"*.

Bahá'u'lláh's earthly Mission began in 1852 when He was cast into the Black Pit prison in Ṭihrán. It ended with His death in the Mansion of Bahjí in 1892 — exactly *forty years* later.

During those *forty years,* Bahá'u'lláh wrote over one hundred volumes, each revealing some parts of those "marvelous things" which were shown unto Him by God.(*)

We must return at once to our theme "As the waters cover the sea", or there will be no end to it. As we have already warned you. The *wonders* and *marvels* of this glorious tale are endless.

This Supreme Organ of the Bahá'í Faith, *the Universal House of Justice*, was established in 1963. It was elected by the worldwide Bahá'í Community through the many National Spiritual Assemblies of the entire Bahá'í World, its electorate.

The Universal House of Justice as mentioned earlier, has already been elected five times, and this election is renewed once every five years at the present time.

The Universal House of Justice has, as foretold, "devised important undertakings"; they have carried out "worldwide activities"; and have "established glorious Institutions" — Local, Continental and International — All of which are already functioning vigorously in nearly every part of the planet.

(*)This story is told in beauty and detail elsewhere. See *Half-Inch Prophecy,* a charming and delightful story of these unique and incredible events. Ask any Bahá'í

The guidance and healing of the world is implicit in these Words from the Bahá'í Writings about the Universal House of Justice:

> "... the mighty Edifice, the Universal House of Justice will be erected, raising high its noble frame above the world of existence. The unity of the followers of Bahá'u'lláh will thus be realized and fulfilled from one end of the earth to the other ... and the living waters of ever-lasting life will stream forth from that fountain-head of God's World Order upon all the warring nations and peoples of the world to wash away the evils and iniquities of the realm of dust, and heal man's age-old ills and ailments."[2]

The Universal House of Justice not only has the power to change human hearts through its guidance, but is already busily engaged in doing so across the face of the world.

This work of human "transformation" increases daily. Every Bahá'í everywhere in the world is not only committed to telling the "wondrous story" to everybody on the planet, but even more important, they are dedicated to helping their fellowman, and living that story in their daily improved personal lives.

It is the greatest "Operation Befriend" in the history of the world. Bahá'ís are not only their brother's-keeper, they are their brother's brother and sister. Wherever and whenever they arrive on the scene, the people in that part of the world are immediately the better for it.

The Bahá'ís teach by the example of their lives. The entire purpose of their teaching is to raise up the *Kingdom of God on earth*. That means they must, every one of them, become better people, finer human beings. Otherwise, their words are meaningless. And they are not suited themselves to be a part of that Kingdom.

This is the guidance and instruction of their sacred writings, the Words of Bahá'u'lláh Himself, the Báb, 'Abdu'l-Bahá, and the beloved Guardian.

Any map of the world we might print for you, to show you

where the Bahá'í Faith has established its Centers in less than one hundred and fifty years, in more than one hundred thousand places, would already be obsolete before you saw it. So rapidly is the Faith of Bahá'u'lláh spreading its healing wings into more and more parts of the earth, none too crowded, none too primitive.

This religion of love and unity is growing with such speed in the hearts of men, women and children of every class, country, race and religious belief, that even the printing-presses of the world have difficulty keeping pace.

Whatever statistics I give to you for the growth of the Bahá'í Faith tody, are obsolete tomorrow. This world-healing, world-redeeming Faith of Bahá'u'lláh has put down its wholesome roots into the thirsty soil of human hearts everywhere. More each day.

It will become even more difficult for the map-makers with each passing day. The Message of love, unity and the oneness of the human race, as taught by Bahá'u'lláh, will grow by leaps and bounds in the hearts of men everywhere.

That's Scripture.

It is also a fact of life.

Our purpose here is to show how widespread across the world the knowledge of the Bahá'í Faith has become in less than one hundred and fifty years.

Above all, our purpose has been to show that anyone who doesn't know about the Bahá'í Faith today, must be "totally out of it", as they say. They themselves are in danger of becoming victims of that "sleep like unto death" foretold by the Prophets of old. This book was designed to make certain that you and all your friends, now my friends, are not numbered among them.

The Bahá'ís and their Bahá'í Communities are alive and growing. They are active. All else is wrapt in that spiritual death, and is on the decline.

That, too, is the promise of Scripture.

These Bahá'ís, that living miniscule minority, are coloring and shaping the spiritual life of the planet.

They move ever closer to the *Christ-promised Kingdom of God on earth.* To raise up that glorious spiritual Kingdom is the ultimate objective of Bahá'u'lláh and His Faith. So that the peace, prosperity and happiness of all mankind can be assured. For all time. And never again be lost.

All of this, of course, is the natural work of the *Prince of Peace*, Bahá'u'lláh. It should give you a very clear and distinct picture as to whether the Bahá'í Faith, and Bahá'u'lláh's "radiant spiritual Army", have told the "wondrous story" or not.

THE BAHÁ'ÍS OF THE WORLD

"As the waters cover the sea."

36.

Flood Tide: Continued

As I examine these pages, I feel ashamed that I have so unskillfully unrolled the scroll of this world-transforming story. Everything I mention leaves ten greater stories untold. Perhaps the unsung song might be the very one that would most effectively appeal to you.

Since the days of the Báb, Bahá'u'lláh, and 'Abdu'l-Bahá, the Bahá'í Faith has been proclaimed far and wide on an ever greater scale, carrying its fame into the four corners of the earth by press, radio, journeys by Bahá'í traveling teachers, wherever planes, boats, trains, buses, cars, horses, donkeys, and feet could take them — into every part of the world.

There are now well over one hundred thousand Bahá'í Centers in all parts of the world, all telling the "wondrous story", and carrying on the "great work".

There are thousands and thousands of Bahá'í Local Spiritual Assemblies in all corners of the planet, representing the cities, towns, villages, reserves and hamlets of the world in more than three hundred countries, territories and islands of the seven seas.

In every one of them, the active, enthusiastic followers of Bahá'u'lláh are all doing the same "great work". The Faith comes first in their lives.

In Israel, the Holy Land, there has already been established an

International Body, the Universal House of Justice, dedicated to the peace, prosperity and happiness of all the peoples of the planet.

All.

Without exception. Without preference. Without prejudice.

An International Bahá'í Teaching Center has been raised up in the Holy Land, and it is linked to every continent on the planet through a special body of Bahá'í Counsellors, who with their Auxiliary Board members and Assistants, have launched repeated teaching plans so that no spot on earth shall fail to hear and be moved by the news of the coming of Bahá'u'lláh. These Bahá'ís are all on the move everyday, everywhere, to touch every receptive heart.

How different the viewpoint now appears when you ask yourself, "Has the world really had a proper chance to hear this wondrous Story?"

Furthermore, the Bahá'í Faith has launched and completed two Seven-Year Plans of teaching, followed by a Ten Year Plan, a Nine Year Plan, a Five Year Plan, and Bahá'í pioneers and teachers are now all busily engaged in the closing stages of a third Seven Year Plan which will soon come to an end. It will be followed immediately by a Six Year Plan, with still others to follow, until, as the Writings of the Bahá'í Faith say so clearly: The entire planet is suffused with the light of Bahá'u'lláh's Message of love, unity and cooperation.

Primary target: The peace of the world.

Worldwide and enduring.

It is well on its way.

During the course of these various Teaching Plans designed to achieve the spiritual conquest of the planet, nearly thirty huge Intercontinental, International, Oceanic, and Continental Bahá'í Conferences have been held in all parts of the world.

A downpour of National and Regional Conferences followed in their wake. Far too many to mention. International, National and Regional Youth conferences in ever-increasing numbers have added greatly to the total each year.

In every case, these gala events were surrounded by coverage in the various media: press, radio, television, and magazines. Both international and local.

Five great World Conventions have been held in the Holy Land, at the World Center of the Bahá'í Faith, for the purpose of electing the Supreme Administrative body of the Bahá'í Faith, the Universal House of Justice.

The author of this book, was blessed with the privilege of attending all five World Conventions. He can testify to the joy, excitement and eagerness of every delegate — Black, Yellow, Brown, Red and White — from the four corners of the earth. Each Convention was an International Festival of love such as the Holy Land and the World has never before seen.

A joyous heaven on earth for all who attended.

Hundreds and hundreds of elected Delegates from the five races of mankind, and from the various nations of the world, participate in ever-increasing numbers in each one of these great World Elections. There will be another in 1988.

Each World Convention received international publicity, plus a far greater flood of national and local publicity and attention in the participating Countries and Regions of the world. This publicity took place generously both before and after these World Conventions. Covered both in color and black-and-white photographs, films and videos.

Those Bahá'ís who attended either the World Conventions, or the many other International, Continental, and Oceanic gatherings, invariably visited city after city, both going and coming from these Conferences. Their visits to the masses of mankind were designed to teach the world about the Bahá'í Faith, and to tell the "wondrous story" of love and unity.

There has never been such a planetary plan of teaching the *Word of God* in the religious history of the world. Ten times around the planet, coming and going from five World Conventions. The Sixth to come, followed by a Seventh, Eighth, Ninth,

... Coming and going sixty times around the World from thirty International, Intercontinental and Oceanic Conferences. Hundreds of thousands of cities, towns, villages, hamlets and reserves personally visited by the followers of Bahá'u'lláh.

This same worldwide proclamation, teaching, public meetings, media coverage in the press, on the radio and on television, happens on a State, Province and Regional basis throughout every month every week of every year, all over the world in every Bahá'í Local and Regional Area. This same eager enthusiasm takes place to as great a degree as is possible in those well-over one hundred thousand Bahá'í Centers around the planet, as well.

It never stops; it only increases in intensity as the numbers of Bahá'ís grow, a process of excitement and victory such as this weary old world of ours has never before known. No wonder they welcome the fresh "water of life" everywhere.

All of this is no doubt happening this very moment as you read these words; perhaps in your own hometown; somewhere today the skies are lighting up with the happy news of the appearance of Bahá'u'lláh. Maybe your next door neighbor is hearing it for the first time. These Bahá'ís, peaceful, law-abiding, non-violent, tell the "wondrous story" only when they are asked to. They are eager to bring hope and encouragement to a disillusioned and discouraged world, but await your willing and welcoming ears.

Fortunately the world need not be discouraged and disillusioned any longer.

"As the waters cover the sea."

37.

Hip! Hip! Hooray!

No account of the planetary spread of the Bahá'í Faith would be complete without an understanding of what effect this "flood tide" has already had on the hearts of those "prepared souls" who were "waiting" and were "ready" and "awake" as Scripture urged them to be.

They have arisen spontaneously in this the day of the coming of the Promised One of all ages, peoples and nations, the *Prince of Peace*, the Supreme Redeemer of men, to do work of the Lord.

These willing and eager followers of Bahá'u'lláh have been "set on fire" by the inspiration of their Faith. They are working industriously all over the planet, teaching every moment of their lives, whenever it is possible.

These Bahá'ís are determined to become the finest doctors, merchants, mothers, fathers, educators, lawyers, scientists, architects, engineers, whatever their profession might be. They are committed to bringing integrity and skill back into every profession trade or job with which they become associated.

In their personal lives, the goal for each one of them is to become a better human being, a finer person, one who will set an example not only for their own families, but for all the peoples of the world.

This is why the news of even one person entering the Bahá'í Faith, means immediately the whole world is that much better.

No matter how infinitesimal that act may at first appear, it means that world is steadily improving, making progress. It is an integrating force in a world of disintegration.

The numbers of new believers, Bahá'ís, will increase more rapidly with each passing year. In many places in the world, it is no longer a slow process. Molasses has become syrup, and the turtle has become the Jack-rabbit.

This is all good news for the world.

This transforming of human souls that inspires them to change their lives, and behave in a more lofty and noble manner is too worldwide in the Bahá'í Faith not to have been noticed by the peoples of the world, friends and neighbors alike who have witnessed these transformations.

Perhaps a few glimpses into what has been happening, will help us to realize the impact which the Words of Bahá'u'lláh, the Supreme Redeemer of men, has had on the hearts of those who have discovered His Teachings.

Viscount Samuel, High Commissioner for Palestine under the British Mandate, wrote of the Faith of Bahá'u'lláh in August, 1959, saying that the Bahá'ís "were generally regarded as a valuable element in the population, intelligent, well-educated, and above all, trustworthy. In Government service and in commercial employment service and in commercial employment they were much esteemed as being free from corruptibility ...well behaved, courteous to others."

"The Bahá'í Faith," Samuel said, "commands the respect and goodwill of its neighbors."

The Christian scholar and author, Charles Baudouin, in his *Contemporary Studies,* says that the Bahá'í Teachings "may serve, amid our present chaos, to open for us a road leading to solace, to comfort; may restore our confidence" in the "spiritual destiny of man."

Boudouin says further of Bahá'u'lláh's Teachings that this Bahá'í "ethical code is dominated by the law of love taught by Jesus and by all the prophets. In the thousand and one details of practical life, this law is subject to manifold interpretations. That of Bahá'u'lláh is unquestionably one of the most comprehensive of these, one of the most exalted, one of the most satisfactory to the modern mind ..."[1]

It is this spirit that has transformed the lives of those who have become Bahá'ís, and is gradually changing the lives of their neighbors and friends. It is moving even closer, littly by little, toward that *Christ-promised Kingdom of God on earth.*

This spirit of justice and uprightness has been praised by Supreme Court Justice William O. Douglas in his book *West of the Indus.* Douglas speaks of his visit to Iran, the land of the birth of Bahá'u'lláh and His Faith. Of the followers of Bahá'u'lláh in that land, Douglas says:

"The Bahá'ís have many businessmen among their numbers. They enjoy a fine reputation as merchants. The reason is that they maintain a high ethical standard in all their dealings. Merchants in the bazaars are quick to take advantage; they will cheat and palm off false or inferior goods. Never the Bahá'ís. They are scrupulous in their dealings; and as a result, they grow in prestige."

The renowned Christian Horticulturalist, Luther Burbank, states that he is "heartily in accord" with the Bahá'í Faith. "I have been interested for several years. The religion of peace is the religion we need and have always needed, and in this Bahá'í is more truly the religion of peace than any other."[2]

Ex-Governor, William Sulzer, in *Roycroft Magazine,* says the Bahá'í Faith is "growing by leaps and bounds", and tells us why. "It is a world movement — and is destined to spread the effulgent rays of enlightment throughout the earth until every mind is free and every fear is banished ... the day of Truth, of Justice, of Liberty, of Magnanimity, of Universal Peace, and of International Brotherhood ..."[3]

Not only for the *West,* but for the *East* as well. Y.S. Tsao, former President of the University of Shanghai, after studying deeply in the Bahá'í Teachings, and translating the book,

Bahá'u'lláh and New Era, declared:

"Not China alone, but the whole world needs these teachings".[4]

The Reverend K.T. Chung, Christian clergyman and scholar, referred to this translation by his senior, Mr. Y.S. Tsao. The Reverend Chung, also Chinese, after reading it carefully, was delighted by the Teachings of Bahá'u'lláh, and expressed his "profound appreciation".

K.T. Chung went on to say:

"Should the Truth of the Bahá'í Faith be widely disseminated among the Chinese people, it will naturally lead to the coming of the Kingdom of Heaven. Should everybody again exert his efforts towards the extension of this beneficient influence throughout the world, it will then bring about world peace and the general welfare of humanity."[5]

And finally upon this theme, although time and space force me to set aside great numbers of similar tributes, these, to me, were among the most intriguing.

The Reverend J. Tyssul Davis, a Christian, not a Bahá'í, in his book *A League of Religions* has spoken of the pattern of individual life set by Bahá'u'lláh. He writes:

"The Bahá'í religion has made its way ... because it meets the needs of its day. It fits the larger outlook of our time better than the rigid exclusive older faiths. A characteristic is its unexpected liberality and toleration. It accepts all the great religions as true and their scriptures as inspired ... Their ethical ideal is very high and is of the type we Westerners have learned to designate 'Christ-like'. 'What does he do to his enemies that he makes them his friends?' was asked concerning the late leader. What astonishes the student is not anything in the ethics or philosophy of this movement, but extraordinary response its ideal has awakened in such numbers of people, the powerful influence this standard actually exerts on conduct ... 'By their fruits shall ye know them!' We cannot but address to this youthful religion an All Hail! of welcome. We cannot fail to see in its activity another proof of the living witness in our own day of the working of the sleepless spirit of God in the hearts of men ..."⁶

Already the face of the earth is being "transformed" to the degree that "prepared souls" have arisen to raise up the *Kingdom of God on earth.* The Plan of God is going forward with gradual but ever-increasing speed and intensity toward that better world, while the old blind, deaf and unresponsive, uncaring society, sinks steadily deeper into its own quicksand of decadent materialism. Slowly it is approaching the point of no return.

As the world becomes worse, the Bahá'í World Community becomes better. As we have quite obviously seen.

Wherever in this vast world of ours, a member of the "radiant spiritual Army" of Bahá'u'lláh, the *Prince of Peace,* resides, he or she has before them at all times clear Words of guidance from the Sacred Writings of their Faith to guide their daily lives. The Words are not suggestions or hints concerning a suitable behavior. They are direct and inescapable instructions. They are not suggestions, but commands. This behavior is not optional. It is obligatory.

To every Bahá'í everywhere in the world.

These instructions on personal behavior, are to be obeyed implicitly, without exception, by every Bahá'í. With willingness, eagerness and joy. And so it is wherever you meet these "radiant Bahá'í souls". Their attraction is love: For all people, friends and strangers alike.

No wonder people feel better in their presence.

The reason can be found in these unmistakable Words from the Sacred Writings of their Faith which guide them each day of their lives:

> "The most vital duty in this day is to purify your characters, to correct your manners, and improve your conduct. The beloved of the Merciful must show forth such character and conduct among His creatures, that the fragrance of their holiness may be shed upon the whole world, and may quicken the spiritually dead, inasmuch as the purpose of the Manifestation, (Messenger of God) ... is to educate the souls of men and refine the character of every living man."⁷

Bahá'u'lláh made it plain to all of his followers what was

expected of them in their daily life.

"Let truthfulness and courtesy be your adorning".

"Beware, O people of Bahá, lest ye walk in the ways of them whose words differ from their deeds."

Be a "breath of life to the body of mankind, an ensign of the basts of justice ... it is through your deeds that ye can distinguish yourselves from others. Through them [your deeds] the brightness of your light can be shed upon the whole earth."[8]

The Sacred Writings of the Bahá'í Faith explain clearly how every Bahá'í must behave wherever they travel from city to city, from place to place:

> "Should any one of you enter a city, he should become a center of attraction by reason of his sincerity, his faithfulness and love, his honesty and fidelity, his truthfulness and loving-kindness towards all the people of the world, so that the people of the city may cry out and say: 'This man is unquestionably a Bahá'í, for his manners, his behavior, and disposition reflect the attributes of the Bahá'ís. Not until ye attain this station can ye be said to have been faithful to the Covenant and Testament of God.'"[9]

Ask yourself: Would you welcome such a new neighbor to your village or town? Or invite them to help you with your problems? With your family troubles? Or your business? Above all, with your precious children?

Do you know anywhere else in the world today where you can find such men, women, youth and families who are living and teaching in such a loving spirit? Whose doors are open, *always,* to friends and strangers alike? Under the direct command of a Messenger of God so that their homes and their lives — and yours because of them — are filled with that same wonder people felt in the Presence of Christ, *the Son,* and now in the Presence of Bahá'u'lláh, *the Father?* One Who speaks with the same authority with which Moses, Christ and the Prophets of old spoke? Who brings a Message of love and unity. A gift to you. From people who want nothing from you. Whether you become a Bahá'í or don't become a Bahá'í will never change their love for you. They love you because you are one of the children of God, and therefore a member of the family of man.

Do you know anyone anywhere like that?

Well, *now* you do!

They are called Bahá'ís.

Every Bahá'í Center in the world, is one of those "dots of decency", as I call them. They indicate Bahá'ís who are devoting (no, consecrating) their lives to befriending their neighbors, to serving their fellowman, to becoming a useful part of the local community, as they labor to reform the world into the pattern of that *Christ-promised Kingdom of God on earth.*

By example, not by preaching. By deeds, not words.

You might call the Bahá'ís in their more than one hundred thousand Centers around the world the "spiritual mutants" of this age, for they have already demonstrated their ability to change hate into love, prejudice into admiration, indifference into enthusiasm, and neglect into involvement. Through the Spirit with which Bahá'u'lláh, the Founder of their Faith, has imbued them, they have been able to change the hearts of men. Something far more difficult to do than changing copper into gold.

The need to change the hearts of mankind is devastatingly apparent everywhere. The Bahá'ís are working that very miracle every day of their lives all over the planet. The world could find no more hopeful or encouraging example anywhere than that offered every day by the Bahá'í communities around the world.

Already, in their growing microcosm of a world community, the Bahá'ís have won victories which humanity is still desperately and unsuccessfully struggling to achieve. Already they have resolved devastating racial differences, desolating religious prejudices, and have conquered those seemingly unconquerable hatreds, all of which now threaten the entire macrocosm of the world.

Where else can mankind find another such proof that these

things *can* be done?

But just how effective is this "transforming spirit" of Bahá'u'lláh?

A world in despair might think about this important and incredible fact, as I repeat it once again.

Bahá'ís already have Arabs and Jews working together side by side in their local communities, not necessarily in Chicago or London or Buenos Aires where it might be safe, but in those very areas of the world where members of these races who are *not* Bahá'ís stand ready, poised, and prepared to kill and annihilate each other.

Bahá'ís of Christian and Muslim backgrounds now live together in peace and in active participation in the Bahá'í communities of Lebanon.

Irish and British Bahá'ís in Northern Ireland, once Catholic and Protestant, are now one in spirit and love for each other. They serve together harmoniously, with genuine affection and co-operation, in their Bahá'í local communities in that land.

The same holds true of the black and the white in Africa, and in the southern States of the United States.

The *Spirit* of the Bahá'í Faith has captured their hearts, and transformed their former hatreds and antagonisms into love and unity, genuine and sincere. They work together happily, with laughter, and a new-found joy, in enthusiastic co-operation.

This also holds true of capitalist and communist, East and West, rich and poor, old and young, passive and dominant — They have all forsaken their former limited and defensive isolated positions in order to allow the *Spirit* of Bahá'u'lláh to take over and transform their lives.

They are indeed a "new race" of men and women.

They are only too happy to give up everything in life to be a part of this wonderful, healing, hope-restoring *Kingdom of God on earth*. Not tomorrow, or in some far-off day. But *now*, today, when the world needs it.

This is a new kind of world entirely, one in which every person on earth will be motivated, for a change, by his *human*, his *moral*, his *ethical*, and his *spiritual* virtues. Not by his animal nature, as we see happening so grossly in the darkened world around us.

This will be a world in which every man, woman and child will be able to develop the latent talents and gifts with which God has so generously endowed them. Where education will be for all on the planet who wish it, *really* for all. Where *have* and *have-not* people, and *have* and *have-not* nations will no longer exist.

We have become a pleasure-seeking society, now we shall become a truth-seeking society. We *should* be both. We have become a profit-making, rather than a welfare-producing society. We should be both. And so we shall be now.

We should be balanced. Mature human beings living full, rich, useful lives of happiness and service, surrounded by the warming love and comfort of our families, our friends, and our neighbors.

It is *this* world the Bahá'í community wants everyone to enjoy. This is the world for which every Bahá'í martyr in Iran, and all Bahá'ís everywhere on the planet, are sacrificing their time, their resources, their energies, and if necessary, their lives to raise up here on earth.

It is the long-awaited, and universally foretold, *Kingdom of God on earth*.

That's *worth* dying for, isn't it!

Every single new Bahá'í in the world is a reinforcement against the forces of darkness, the despoilers. They are "the forces of Light" facing, advancing, and never retreating before "the forces of darkness".

It means that God is winning at last. Exactly as promised. Every Bahá'í everywhere is spreading this glorious "decency virus". It is "catching", fortunately for all mankind. And sooner or later, will be victorious over all, and *the Christ-promised Kingdom of God on earth* will become a reality in all our lives.

Violence, terrorism, corruption, graft, dishonesty, drug abuse, child-abuse, alcoholism, and all deceitfulness will be relegated to the place they belong: The abyss of sorrow. Never again to raise their evil faces.

Joy and singing, peace and happiness, safety and security, will once again be the normal way of life. As promised by God and His Messenger, the *Prince of Peace*.

There is no excitement to compare with this excitement: The raising up of "the Kingdom of God on earth!"

That is the destiny for which each one of us was born. As we improve ourselves, we improve the world.

That's a winner, not a loser. It keeps getting better every day.

So every time a new "dot of decency" appears on the map of the world, and you hear there is a new Bahá'í *anywhere,* anytime, rejoice!

Everybody, stand up on your feet, and shout aloud:
"Hip! Hip! Hooray!"

"UNION OF NATIONS"

"Evidences of worldwide regeneration"

38.

The First Attempt

It is one of the most fascinating but ironic twists in the history of mankind that the very information which the present nations of the world on two separate occasions needed to assure their safety and survival on the planet, information which would have enabled them to create a World Body capable of establishing and maintaining World Peace, had been given to the Leaders of all their countries by Bahá'u'lláh, the *Prince of Peace*. Nearly a century before that information for their survival was needed, Bahá'u'lláh supplied it.

What a unique and remarkable occurrence!

Does that sound as though a "marvelous work" and "wonder" had been offered to mankind, and to the world, one which its leaders did not "believe" even when it was being "told" to them? And explained to them "right before their very eyes."

You decide.

It was a veritable "mother-lode" of Truth. An assistance which these countries had received in clear and unmistakable language. They were given a spiritual "force" from Bahá'u'lláh which would have enabled them to meet head-on, and completely resolve, the terrifying and paralyzing problems of peace which were even then weighing down the world.

As they still do today.

Unwittingly, blissfully ignorant of the Source that drove them on to their destiny, completely unaware of the direct *written* guidance which their own leaders had received from Bahá'u'lláh, the *Prince of Peace*, one hundred years or more before; guidance which could not only have made their path to peace possible, but inevitable.

The nations of the world twice, without even considering the "Counsels" which the "Wonderful!", the "Counsellor!" of *Isaiah* had offered them, made a gallant and courageous effort to establish just such a World Peace through a special "Union of Nations".

Just such a world body had actually been described in the sacred Writings of Bahá'u'lláh's Faith long before. It had even given the name "Union of Nations."

The first attempt by mankind was the *League of Nations*. The second was the *United Nations*.

The great World Body envisioned by Bahá'u'lláh would be composed of all the nations of the world, both great and small. Every nation on earth without exception. This Body would usher in a worldwide lasting Peace and would rule with justice the entire earth upon an invincible enduring foundation.

The Writings of Bahá'u'lláh's Faith say clearly that such a World Body:

Would exercise unchallengeable authority over unimaginable vast resources of the world, blending and embodying the details of both the East and the West, liberated from the curse of war and its miseries, and bent on the exploitation of all the available sources of energy on the surface of the planet, for the welfare of all humanity. It would be a system in which Force would be made the servant of Justice, a world dedicated to the safety, security and happiness of all the peoples on the planet, without preference, without prejudice, without exception.[1]

So unique is this intertwined story of the *League of Nations*, the *United Nations*, the Bahá'í Faith and Bahá'u'lláh; so interwoven are their destinies with each other and the world, that it seemed imperative to share with you this "marvelous work" and "wonder" before returning to *Isaiah* and his Yuletide Prophecy.

If we had been able to record the impact of Christ, and the other great Messengers of God upon the world using all the modern tools of communications at our command, what a blessing that would have been for mankind.

It is too late to achieve that blessing now, but it is not too late to record the background of both the Herald of the Bahá'í Faith, the Báb, and its Founder Bahá'u'lláh. Their relationship to the world is a veritable catalogue of stories that touch and uplift the heart of mankind with hope and assurance, and steadily build toward that inevitable "Union of Nations" destined by God for a mature human society.

George Townshend, who has been described as the greatest Bahá'í writer in the West, has said that all the tremendous advancements in the world, in every area of human endeavor, which have resulted in fostering the welfare and well-being of mankind; in fact, every great advancement in the progress of the peoples of the world, have merely been "ringing the changes" on the guidance and Teachings which Bahá'u'lláh brought to the world and offered to its peoples a century ago.

Bahá'u'lláh Himself, expatiating upon the "forces" latent in His Faith for the benefit of humanity, declared:

> "Through the movement of Our Pen of glory We have, at the bidding of the Omnipotent Ordainer, breathed a new life into every human frame and instilled into every word a fresh potency. All created things proclaim the evidences of this worldwide regeneration."[2]

The world should not be surprised that the Messenger of God for today would have such a deep and abiding effect upon all phases of human life, moving, motivating, and inspiring even those who are unaware of the spiritual power that sends them even unwittingly on their way. This power which the *Word of God* breathed into every human frame has the same overwhelming effect on the growth and the sudden bursting into a whole new world with "all things made new", as does the coming of Spring to the body of nature. This new Springtime in the outer world is accomplished with such ease with the help of nature. It is the same in the inner world of the spirit with the coming of each new Messenger of God and His contact with human society. The people are "reborn", changed, transformed, until they themselves become eager willing instruments of the Lord.

Bahá'u'lláh like the Messengers of God before Him, also announced this wonderful "awakening" of the world and its peoples in this new day.

Bahá'u'lláh proclaims:

> "Every word that proceedeth out of the mouth of God is endowed with such potency as can instill new life into every human frame, if ye be of them that comprehend this truth. All the wondrous works ye behold in this world have been manifested through the operation of His supreme and most exalted Will, His wondrous and inflexible Purpose. Through the mere revelation of the word 'Fashioner', issuing forth from His lips and proclaiming His attributes to mankind, such power is released as can generate, through successive ages, all the manifold arts which the hands of man can produce."[3]

The Bahá'ís of the world, moved and motivated by this Spirit, have been thus enabled to make such remarkable strides in such a short time everywhere in the world in raising up the *Christ-promised Kingdom of God on earth*. It is easy for us to see why as we listen to these Words from the Pen of the *Prince of Peace*.

Bahá'u'lláh continues His theme:

> "No sooner is this resplendent word uttered, than its animating energies, stirring within all created things, give birth to the means and instruments whereby such arts can be produced and perfected. All the wondrous achievements ye now witness are the direct consequences of the Revelation of this Name. In the days to come, ye will, verily, behold things of which ye have never heard before. Thus hath it been decreed in the Tablets of God..."[4]

We have already beheld many of them, haven't we? And "wondered marvelously".

It is indeed a new spiritual Springtime in the hearts of humanity.

You may wish to read the entire explanation of this remarkable transformation of human society in Bahá'u'lláh's own Words at your leisure.(*)

After all, Bahá'u'lláh wrote over one hundred volumes, how can we do more here than catch the ocean in a cup. The ocean, however, remains for you to immerse yourself in at your own pace.

The astonishing material story we are about to recount concerning the Bahá'í Faith, Bahá'u'lláh, and the United Nations will become even more exciting and understandable to you now that you have this background of spiritual information about Bahá'u'lláh, the Supreme Redeemer of men, the Promised One of all past ages.

The story will seem less magical and incredible when it is viewed in the light of these Words of Bahá'u'lláh.

This is, in general, true of all the seemingly astonishing things you have already experienced, and will yet experience in these pages. The more you deepen yourself in the Words and Teachings of Bahá'u'lláh, the more you will see that what the world looks upon as astonishing, are merely "run of the mill" miracles that happen every day, as the world is warmed by the Springtime *Sun of Truth*, Bahá'u'lláh, and is put in touch with both the *work* and the *Word* of God.

Much detail about the *First Attempt* to establish this World Body, one able to cope with the problems of peace, the *League of Nations*, following World War I, can be found in the books of history. No need to dwell upon the background here.

Several of the *Fourteen Points* which President Woodrow Wilson presented in launching his concept of the *League of Nations* fairly breathed the Spirit of Bahá'u'lláh's Teachings on world

---

(*)See *Gleanings from the Writings of Bahá'u'lláh*, pp 141-142. Bahá'í Publishing Trust, Wilmette, Illinois.

unity. President Wilson was familiar with the Writings of Bahá'u'lláh, but the Source remained unrecognized and unmentioned. That source, alone, could deliver the spiritual "fire power" absolutely essential to the success of the entire venture.

The League struggled and failed in its primary task of securing world peace. It was unable to heal the wounds kept fresh in the minds of its members by suspicion and fear. Each nation trying to establish its own position and prestige by using for "doctrines, the commandments of men" and "laying aside the commandments of God."*(Mark 7:7,8)*

How could it succeed when it had by-passed the one and only Source of power and Spirit capable of accomplishing such a herculean task. It was the Plan of God that was needed, not the plan of man.

Bahá'u'lláh, the *Prince of Peace,* the Source of those world-healing principles and Teachings which could have come to the rescue of mankind, was never accepted, never acknowledged, or even mentioned.

Bahá'u'lláh's planetary plan for the Peace of the world, a Mission given Him by God to achieve with the willing support of mankind, was never put into effect.

Or even considered.

Only the most fragmentary part of Bahá'u'lláh's Peace Plan was ever attempted. Without realizing or recognizing the Source from whence came these marvelous concepts that were in the air in those days. Stirring up the hopes of mankind.

Although the *League of Nations* accomplished many useful and remarkable things, and laid the foundations of important world agencies, in the most vital area of establishing and maintaining World Peace, it was ultimately a conspicuous failure. It could not prevent the militarism which finally lead to World War II.

Peace was shattered.

Man's fondest hopes dashed yet another time.

"Zoom! A cat again!"

39.

Second Attempt

The United Nations

It chills the heart to think that even this marvelous accomplishment of the human race, the United Nations, may not in the end be able to save us. We had counted on it so strongly in the hour of its birth. The hopes of every human being rode triumphantly with it. The spirit of the peoples of the world were "high" and "happy".

The United Nations was at once the "darling of all our hearts".

No fair-minded man would ever deny the wonderful victories of the United Nations in so many fields. Who can fail to appreciate the fires it has put out, the threats it has averted, or the ominous catastrophies it has delayed? And in some cases totally prevented.

BRAVO!

The great services of the United Nations in Peace-Keeping. Its remarkable victories in World Health, World Bank, UNESCO, UNICEF Catastrophe Relief, Economic Assistance, and in so many other splendid areas of human services are brilliant and unquestioned.

Mankind has never seen such a genuinely concerned world-protecting instrument up until this present time.

Yet, in the most vital area of all, the important political realm, which determines the survival of nearly every human being on the planet, our old friend *Partisan Prejudice* — National, Hemisphere, Group, and Block-of-Nations Politics — eats remorselessly away at the framework day by day.

There is no need to catalogue the various conflicts, divisions, and tactics which now threaten the ultimate survival of this slowly-fading hope of the world. Its lack of united, unified action, and cohesive oneness in challenging, meeting and overcoming the problems facing a slowly disintegrating society are all too plain to see. A mighty giant redwood of unequalled beauty and magnificence can feel the inward tremors as the world's nations chop at whichever part of the root that most displeases them.

Everyone has been, reluctantly and gradually, forced to admit the danger. But no one seems to know what to do about it. Many threaten to withdraw their support. Others agitate to move the United Nations Headquarters to a new location in some other part of the world, perhaps more favorable to them. Still others, quite obviously, quite openly, quite blatantly try to use the troubles, prejudices, and divisions now troubling the United Nations for their own ends, forgetful of the purpose for which that potentially wonderful Body was created in the beginning. They are mindful only of their own gain, whatever the cost, whether confessedly so or not.

The lustre of those 'golden days' in San Francisco is long forgotten. The worldwide joy and rapture of those happy hours, when the Charter was first written, and the interlinked chains of unity on that blue-and-white *Flag of World Peace,* were first fashioned, and flown, have dimmed.

There is no longer that exciting "spell" of World-Oneness that once brightened our hopes and cheered our hearts the world over in those early days. Gone is the sense of world solidarity against War. Gone is that world unity and planetary determination to sacrifice whatever needs to be sacrificed in order to survive and make progress toward world peace in spite of grave basic national differences.

Gone is the wonderful oratory and rhetoric at San Francisco which, to thunderous applause, assured the peoples of the world that even though the relationship between the participating nations was tenuous, it appeared that all were willing to give up something so that our planet would be in safe hands for the future.

We all felt that we could confidently put aside the haunting spectre of a Third World War.

What days they were!(*)

(*)See *A Cry from the Heart,* same author. Publisher: George Ronald, 46 High Street, Kidlington, Oxford, England OX 2DN pp. 186-191

Gradually, the United Nations has become like the Cat in Aesopès Fable. The Cat was permitted to attend the great Banquet Table dressed as a beautiful damsel, provided it would remember to behave properly.

So, in like manner, do the leaders of the world's nations now attend critical summit conference tables. Some, like the "Cat", are masqueraded as lovers of all mankind. They express concern for the welfare of all nations and all peoples as well as for their own. They acknowledge that no one nation can be considered greater or more important than the whole, including their own. Until, suddenly, the *'Mouse of Spoils'* — Power, Prestige, Position, Advantage — runs across the banquet table in front of them.

Zoom! A Cat again!

It is beginning to appear that the printer, who made the unfortunate typographical error with his linotype machine at San Francisco in those early days was accidentally prophetic.

On the day of the signing of the United Nations Charter, he misplaced the letter "I" in one of the newspaper headlines. Instead of writing: THE UNITED NATIONS, he typed: THE UNTIED NATIONS.

It was laughable that day because we were all in such high spirits, confident of unity, even in diversity. We were tied together however loosely against the awesome spectre of a third world war which the participating Nations assured us would never be permitted to raise its ugly head.

Sad to say, that great world-protecting *knot* has been slipping, little by little, more and more, since those early beginning days of great expectancy. Now, more than forty years later, the life-saving knot has slowly but surely been loosened by the increasing hostility of the contending member nations. Growing suspicion, mistrust and hostility have eaten remorselessly at the foundation. The looser the knot becomes, the greater looms the danger for our planet.

Most of the peoples of the world still rest their hopes on, and support of, the United Nations. They are still willing to sacrifice generously to assure its survival. The United Nations remains the very best of all the hopes we have.

Optimistic, as sincere lovers usually are, mankind is gradually becoming aware that the United Nations probably cannot save us. Not until the "pollution" in the hearts of its member nations has been replaced by the wholesome selfless virtues needed to put the *world,* not their own country, first in all deliberations. Only then will the United Nations be successful. The way it was in spirit during those earliest beginning days.

It is, after all, the United *Nations,* not the United Nation.

That wonderful Body can still delay, it can mitigate, it can soften threatening disasters. It can win precious time for us. Yet increasingly it appears that the United Nations in the political area is helpless to prevent the inevitable, all consuming flood of disasters that are slowly and resistlessly drawing ever nearer in spite of all we can do to stem the terror of the tide.

What is true of the leaders of men and nations, is equally true of the peoples of the world. What the world has to learn sooner or later is an important Truth from the *Spirit of Truth,* Bahá'u'lláh, the *Prince of Peace,* concerning world unity and the oneness of mankind.

The Writings of Bahá'u'lláh's Faith say that this truth must be upheld in its entirety. This is a truth that is obligatory, not optional.

There are no more uplifting and hopeful words in the English language than the following as we face a world on fire with lesser wars, border disputes, terrorism, endless hijackings, drug-abuse, child-abuse, alcoholism, the brutal slaying of civilians including children — all increasing, not diminishing.

Bahá'u'lláh clearly explained to the leaders and peoples of the world what they must do if they sincerely wished for world peace. There was no other way.

The Writings of His Faith declare:

"The different nations of the world will never attain peace except after recognizing the significance of the Teachings [of Bahá'u'lláh, the *Prince of Peace,* the *Spirit of Truth*] and whole-heartedly upholding them, for through these precepts, all international problems will be solved and every man will secure the spiritual atmosphere in which his soul can evolve and produce its highest "fruit."(*)

In those Words is found yet another tremendous promise in the Writings of the Bahá'í Faith. Not only the solution to all our "international problems" if we adopt the "precepts" and "teachings" of Bahá'u'lláh; but perhaps even more significant, the establishing of "a spiritual atmosphere" in the world, and atmosphere in which every human being will have the peace and tranquillity to develop the full latent talents of the heart, the soul and the creative mind.

Thus, every person will be enabled to extract the full potential of his or her opportunities to become the very best they can become at their chosen profession or job, and at the same time have the freedom to become a finer person and a better human being, the true reason for their existence on the planet.

They can, as you will see, accomplish this through the power and spirit of love breathed into each human frame by Bahá'u'lláh, Who came to achieve that very miracle, so mankind might have "the best of both worlds"

(*)The fascinating story of Bahá'u'lláh's Letters to the leaders of those countries which were involved in trying so earnestly to establish both the *League of Nations* and the *United Nations;* and the offer of His, Bahá'u'lláh's, healing solutions for resolving their problems, can be found in rich abundance in *The Promised Day Is Come,* by Shoghi Effendi, Guardian of the Bahá'í Faith, Bahá'í Publishing Trust Wilmette, Illinois, and in *The Proclamation of Bahá'u'lláh,* Bahá'u'lláh's actual Letters, (Bahá'í World Center, Haifa, Israel). They both describe this thrilling and dramatic story of Bahá'u'lláh's *Call to the Nations,* which is yet another book for your study.

Hopes rose high and hearts rejoiced everywhere in the world when the nations met in San Francisco. Time has dimmed those fond hopes. Renewed hostility and suspicion have turned rejoicing into fear and doubt.

The same old terrifying questions are back again, blacker and more desperate than ever.

Once again, as in the story book of old, mankind waits in fear, eyes glued to the summit doors, never knowing who will come out: The Lady or the Tiger.

Two times mankind launched itself forward with brilliant plans for the Peace of the world. Both were closely linked with the spirit of the Teachings of Bahá'u'lláh, the *Prince of Peace!*

Both attempts, however gallant and sincere, failed to achieve their goal, especially in the all important political arena.

There was no recognition or even awareness of the Source or Spirit from whence sprung these heroic calls for peace in our time, the so-called "last days".

If one were to read carefully the Teachings of Bahá'u'lláh, then compare them to the United Nations Charter and the Declaration of Human Rights, one would see how powerful was the influence of Bahá'u'lláh and His Teachings upon those Documents.

It would appear as though a ghost-writer familiar with all that Bahá'u'lláh had said to the leaders and rulers of men, and what the Bahá'í Faith itself stood for, had helped pen those promising and hopeful historical documents.(*)

The Bahá'í World Community at the United Nations, is a member of the Non-Governmental Organizations associated with UNESCO. A consultative member. The Bahá'í World Community works diligently and industriously each year to help carry out the world-unifying programs of the United Nations. Whatever will enhance the prestige of that great World Body, the Bahá'í Faith endorses and works energetically to achieve.

(*)Or as my son, William, sacrilegiously but aptly said, some "Holy Ghost Writer" must have guided their destiny. The Bahá'ís of the world know exactly who it was. It is long past time the world knew and recognized the truth — For their own protection and survival.

Under the direction of the Bahá'í World Community at the United Nations, the Bahá'ís the world over support the special U.N. programs. They repeatedly call the attention of the world to the work which the United Nations is constantly carrying out for the benefit of mankind.

No other Organization associated with the Non-Governmental Bodies of the United Nations does more to celebrate and praise *United Nations Day* than the Bahá'ís of the world. The Faith of Bahá'u'lláh will continue to do so.

Could the Children of the *Prince of Peace* do less?

They patiently await that day when the world and everybody in it will at last recognize Who Bahá'u'lláh really is, what He stands for, so that He can lead them to their true hearts-desire: And enduring World Peace, serenity, and happiness; and an end to war and all fear of it.

Forever.

We stood on the threshold of golden moments in those early hours, days, and weeks of both *The League of Nations* and *The United Nations*.

What a tragedy.

We were so close!

"A better world for all men"

40.

Summon the Nations unto God

Now we come to the part for which you have been waiting.

What a pity the leaders and rulers of men didn't listen a century ago to the story you are now reading.

It is one of the most fascinating and intriguing parts of this entire drama of the *PRINCE OF PEACE* given to the world by Bahá'u'lláh. His little-known yet vital and urgent link with the United Nations, now becomes the heart of our story.

It can be found in all its intriguing, fascinating wonder, in the story of the development of the first *Security Council*.

Among the Letters which Bahá'u'lláh addressed to the Rulers and Leaders of mankind nearly a century earlier, were four very special Letters. Four astonishing historic documents which issued from Bahá'u'lláh's Supreme Pen.

To whom did Bahá'u'lláh write these four famous Letters?

He wrote to the Rulers of the four countries who were later to be designated *four out of the five* "Permanent Members" of the first Security Council of the United Nations!

Imagine!

The rulers of Britain, France, Russia and the United States received special messages from Bahá'u'lláh concerning the responsibilities of their nations toward the vital needs of the emerging world society in this present day. And above all: The urgent necessity to establish and maintain World Peace.

China was the fifth member of that first Security Council of the United Nations. That Nation, China, as well, received special attention on this same score from Bahá'u'lláh's Successor, 'Abdu'l-Bahá, the Center of Bahá'u'lláh's Covenant with all mankind.

UNION OF NATIONS

It would be hard to imagine a more intriguing story than this: *The Bahá'í Faith* and *The United Nations*.
What a pity the world knows so little about it.
It is astonishing that the world did not trumpet it to the four corners of the earth.

In His letter to Queen Victoria of England, Bahá'u'lláh called upon the rulers of the earth to be reconciled among themselves, to reduce their armaments, and to be united so that their peoples might "find rest".
Bahá'u'lláh advised them to take counsel together:

> "... let your concern be only for that which profiteth mankind, and bettereth the condition thereof..."[1]

His Mission, Bahá'u'lláh told them, was "to regenerate and unify mankind".
This certainly was the primary work of the *Prince of Peace*, wouldn't you say? As well as that of the United Nations.
Bahá'u'lláh wrote over one hundred volumes dealing directly with the various problems and dilemmas now affecting both individuals and our modern society collectively.
Some of Bahá'u'lláh's most moving and significant Words on Peace were addressed to those four nations who would later become the Charter Members of the first *Security Council* of the United Nations.
Repeat: How odd, how tragic, that the world still knows so little about these exciting, dramatic events which are so unique and soul-stirring. They surely must be a part of that "marvelous work" and "wonder" which Scripture promised would take place in our day.
While it is true that Scripture warned us that the majority of the peoples of the world would not "believe" this "marvelous work" and "wonder" even when it was being "told" to them, not even when it was actually taking place before their very eyes, as we see happening today; still, shouldn't the religious leaders who professed to be so familiar with the Scriptures and their own Books, have warned and alerted their flocks?

"Watch" and "pray" and be "ready" Christ Himself had warned, for "ye know not" the "time" and the hour. It was imperative for them to be "alert" if they, and their flocks, were to survive. There was no special exemption for them. They were surely included in the Words of Christ:

What I say unto you, I say unto all." (*Mark 13:37*)

Perhaps even more strange and peculiar is the fact that scholars, historians, particularly those from these four nations should have been so totally unaware and ill-informed concerning one of the greatest dramas and stories associated with their own time, their own land, and their own future.

There is not sufficient time to deal properly here with this fascinating drama in full detail. How I deplore that. However, it is the stuff that epic films are made of, filled with suspense and drama on a world scale. It is exciting, intriguing and reassuring, as is almost every facet of the world-redeeming story about Bahá'u'lláh and the nations of the world.

With a little effort on your part, you can have it all, the entire story, and study it at your leisure. It will be captivating, stimulating, but most of all satisfying and rewarding. These words from the Writings of Bahá'u'lláh's Faith will testify to the depth and excitement of such a search on your part.

"If you read the utterances of Bahá'u'lláh and 'Abdu'l-Bahá with selflessness and care and concentrate upon them, you will discover truths unknown to you before, and will obtain an insight into the problems that have baffled the great thinkers of the world."[2]

UNION OF NATIONS

That's only to be expected when we are dealing with the *Promised One* of all ages, peoples, religions and nations. Sometimes we lose sight of that.

This story of the Bahá'í Faith and the United Nations is only one of the "wonders" that will reward your own personal search into the life and teachings of Bahá'u'lláh, the *Prince of Peace*.

His many volumes, as well as those of His Successor, 'Abdu'l-Bahá are available to you whenever you choose to dip into that great ocean. Both Bahá'u'lláh and 'Abdu'l-Bahá had a direct and important part in this United Nations story.

However, so that you may know it is fact, and not fancy, we shall share with you one extremely brief excerpt from the Letters of Bahá'u'lláh, the *Prince of Peace*, to each one of those four nations: Russia, the United States, Britain and France, all members of the first *Security Council* of the United Nations. We shall also share with you the Words of Bahá'u'lláh's Successor, 'Abdu'l-Bahá, concerning the fifth member of that first *Security Council* to come, China.

The purpose is to let you know there were such letters. That the whole incredible, fantastic story is fact not fiction.

Amazing as it is, it is truth not legend.

We have taken but one leaf from one tree, and left the forest for you to explore at your leisure. We have spooned out one drop from one sea, and left the vast depths of the mighty ocean with its "pearls" of wisdom for your personal research.

The "waters of life" which Bahá'u'lláh has poured out upon the planet are yours to examine at your own pace.

Warning: You may never again be the same.

We recommend to you *The Proclamation of Bahá'u'lláh* which contains long excerpts taken from Bahá'u'lláh's most important Letters to the rulers and leaders of men, both secular and religious. As well as Bahá'u'lláh's Letters to the peoples of the world. This will include His Letters to Russia, the USA, Britain and France.

Bahá'u'lláh said to Czar Alexander Nicolaevitch II:

RUSSIA
"I am the One Whom the tongue of Isaiah hath extolled..."
"Arise thou amongst men in the name of this all-compelling Cause and Summon, them, the nations unto God..."[3]

To President Ulysses S. Grant:

UNITED STATES OF AMERICA
"The Promised One hath appeared... Verily, to meet Him is better for you than all that whereon the sun shineth... Bind ye the broken with the hands of justice, and crush the oppressor who flourisheth with the rod of the commandments of your Lord..."[4]

To Queen Victoria of England:

BRITAIN
"It behooveth them, [these leaders of men] however, to be Trustworthy among His servants, and to regard themselves as the representatives of all that dwell on earth."[5]

To Louis Napoleon of France, Napolean III:

FRANCE
"Know of a truth that your subjects are God's trust amongst you. Watch ye, therefore, over them as ye watch over your own selves. Beware that ye allow not wolves to become shepherds of the fold, or pride and conceit to deter you from turning unto the poor and the desolate."[6]

These have been but the briefest of excerpts, a phrase that conveys the spirit, a leaf in the stream that shows the direction of the current. This world-engulfing tide of Guidance from the *Spirit of Truth*, Bahá'u'lláh, consists of more than one hundred volumes.

What better place for the *Prince of Peace* to begin than with these four governors of human society? The Messages in full were rich with the wholesome flavor of world peace and justice.(*)

(*)I know.
What you want are more quotations and details about Bahá'u'lláh's Words to England, Russia, the U.S.A., and France; and everything about China to be found in the Bahá'í Writings.

But that's really your job, isn't it?

I've put you onto a good thing here, haven't I? No one's told you a story like it before. Right? So you should have enough curiosity and stamina to follow it to the end, and do your own research. There's still much to tell about the Bahá'í Faith and the United Nations, and I want to get on with it.

Still, I can understand your viewpoint, so here's what I'm going to do. I suggest you immediately get hold of *The World Order Of Bahá'u'lláh* and study it. It will more than suffice to answer your questions about what Bahá'u'lláh said to all nations, countries, leaders of men and Heads of State concerning this better world of the future, that *World Civilization* and *Golden Age* we can all look forward to as the ultimate destiny of the entire human race. No one could ask more than that.

"A bright candle of guidance to the world."

41.

"Look Chinaward!"

CHINA

The great significance of the nation that was to become the fifth member of that first *Security Council* of the United Nations, China, was not overlooked. The importance and value of that part of the world, China, to the future of humanity, were highly extolled in the Writings of the Bahá'í Faith. The call that went out to awaken and touch the hearts of this vast and wonderful region of the planet, for the sake of the peace, security and happiness of the peoples of the world, was loud and clear.

'Abdu'l-Bahá, the Successor of Bahá'u'lláh, and the Center of His Covenant with all the peoples and nations of the world, as far back as 1917, in a significant Pilgrim's Note, is reported to have announced, unmistakably that "China" was one of the great countries "of the future."

'Abdu'l-Bahá encouraged the followers of Bahá'u'lláh and the teachers of the Bahá'í Faith to look China-ward.

"China," 'Abdu'l-Bahá said, "has most great capacity."

He praised the people as being "truth-seeking".

'Abdu'l-Bahá was eager for the right kind of Bahá'í teachers to journey to China, and in "that vast empire to lay the foundation of the Kingdom of God, to promote the principles of divine civilization" and "unfurl" the Banner of Bahá'u'lláh.

'Abdu'l-Bahá was eager for the Bahá'í teachers to invite all of that multitude of praiseworthy Chinese souls "to the banquet of the Lord".

Many of those souls, 'Abdu'l-Bahá said, had the potential of being a "bright candle" of guidance to "the world of humanity."

So important and significant did 'Abdu'l-Bahá, the Center of Bahá'u'lláh's Covenant, feel about China and its place in the scheme of things, that He Himself is reported to have declared that if health had permitted:

> "I would have taken a journey to China myself."[1]

Special attention has been called to China by Bahá'u'lláh's *Universal House of Justice* in these very days. It cannot be overlooked. Bahá'ís are constantly being encouraged to arise and journey to this vast and worthy part of the world.

Have you ever heard a more intriguing story than this story of the *Prince of Peace*? And the five nations who were later to make up the *Charter Members* of the First Security Council of the United Nations?

The hope of the world!

What Bahá'u'lláh offered to do for them, makes the story even more remarkable. Bahá'u'lláh did far more than merely *Call* for the establishment of this great World Body, He offered, in writing, the laws, principles, institutions, agencies and the guidance which would enable the nations of the world to raise up, preserve, and perpetuate this great world peace. Above all, Bahá'u'lláh brought the spirit to make it all work. The spirit was capable of winning the enthusiastic cooperation and united efforts of all the peoples of the world. This "spirit" would assure the victory, if their leaders would arise to show the way.

One would hardly think there could possibly be more to this utterly astonishing story.

But there is.

Much more.

Some of the most startling events of all.
As we so repeatedly are forced to say:
The very best is yet to come.
Even in this astonishing link between the *Bahá'í Faith* and the *United Nations*.

California, the site of the first Great United Nations Conference, where the united Nations Charter was written, and where its brilliant blue-and-white interlinked flag of world peace was born, had already been designed for this honor in the Writings of the Bahá'í Faith.
Long before that event took place.
Did you know that?
I didn't think so.
Neither did the world.
Although the story had been printed in the important papers of America where these very events were later to take place.
Bahá'u'lláh appointed 'Abdu'l-Bahá, His eldest Son, as His Successor. Bahá'u'lláh gave to 'Abdu'l-Bahá the responsibility and authority to deal with the problems of mankind after His own passing. 'Abdu'l-Bahá visited the Western World, and in the shadow of San Francisco uttered these prophetic words:

"May the first flag of International Peace be upraised in this State..."[2]

It was!

The magic of our story races to new heights when we find that 'Abdu'l-Bahá also visited New York City. He addressed many people, high and low alike, in that city, in more than fifty-five separate meetings.
Since 'Abdu'l-Bahá's journey to New York, that city has been

designated in the history of the Bahá'í Faith as the *City of the Covenant*.

The City of the Covenant of Bahá'u'lláh with all the nations and peoples of the world. A Covenant which linked the planet with the Power on high, as Noah's rainbow, the eternal symbol of that Covenant, unites heaven and earth, notifying mankind that God will never forget or abandon them.

This Covenant of Bahá'u'lláh is above all, a Covenant with all His followers that they will recognize, accept, and serve Him as the Messenger of God for this day, the Supreme Redeemer of men. That they will arise like *lions* of this Covenant, so that the *Christ-promised Kingdom of God on earth* may be established in all parts of the world, a harbinger of the coming of that "Most Great Peace".

That work of Peace, and *The Kingdom of God* is already begun in more than one hundred thousand places all over the earth.

That, without doubt, is all part of the "marvelous work" and "wonder" which God said He would "work" in the world in "the last days" so all mankind might "Behold" and "wonder marvelously".

This Mighty and Everlasting Covenant of Bahá'u'lláh was explained to mankind by 'Abdu'l-Bahá Himself, the Center of that Covenant, appointed by His Father, Bahá'u'lláh. 'Abdu'l-Bahá explained that Covenant for the very first time, with all its planetary significance, during His visit to New York City in 1912.

Where?

New York City!

New York City which was, such a short time later, to be chosen by the nations of the world as the first International Headquarters of the United Nations!

This has been a richly rewarding part of "As the waters cover the sea". We have seen the world has indeed been inundated with the glorious news of the coming of Bahá'u'lláh. His influence and love have changed the hearts of men and women in all parts of the planet. they have spontaneously arisen, in their turn, to change the hearts of all mankind with the sweet music of Bahá'u'lláh.

We shall now return to the mainstream of our story, and to *Isaiah's* Yuletide prophecy. These side journeys, however, have been very beneficial. Even wonderful.

Who would dare to say that the "wondrous story" had not been "told" to the world.

Told, and retold, time and time again.

If anyone hasn't heard it, it would be wise to check in with their spiritual eye-doctors, and spiritual ear-specialists.

I can't think of a kinder way to say it.

Except: The best is yet to come.

This time I think you'll believe me.

And be ready for it.

RETURN TO:
"WONDERFUL! COUNSELLOR!"

"Rivers of mercy have flowed."

42.

Wonderful! Counsellor!

We come now to the final *Counsels* of Bahá'u'lláh for the betterment of human society. He tells us how every individual can best serve his fellowman, and at the same time fulfill their own true human destiny.

Bahá'u'lláh declared that His "counsels and admonitions have compassed the world" and that no human being would ever be deprived if he or she would arise to aid their fellowmen and serve humanity.[1]

Bahá'u'lláh counselled:

> "Address yourselves to the promotion of the well-being and tranquillity of the children of men. Bend your minds and wills to the education of the peoples and kindreds of the earth, that haply the dissensions that divide it may, through the power of the Most Great Name [Bahá'u'lláh], be blotted out from its face, and all mankind become the upholders of one Order and the inhabitants of one City. Illumine and hallow your hearts; let them not be profaned by the thorns of hate or the thistles of malice. Ye dwell in one world, and have been created through the operation of one Will. Blessed is he who mingleth with all men in a spirit of kindliness and love."[2]

Bahá'u'lláh's Counsels were simple and direct:

> "We exhort the men of the House of Justice and command them to ensure the protection and safeguarding of men,

women and children. It is incumbent upon them to have the utmost regard for the interests of the people at all times and under all conditions. Blessed is the ruler who succoureth the captive, and the rich one who careth for the poor, and the just one who secureth from the wrong doer the rights of the downtrodden, and happy the trustee who observeth that which the Ordainer, the Ancient of Days hath prescribed unto him."[3]

And again. Bahá'u'lláh instructs his loved ones:

"Do not busy yourselves in your own concerns, let your thoughts be fixed upon that which will rehabilitate the fortunes of mankind and sanctify the hearts and souls of men. This can best be achieved through pure and holy deeds, through a virtuous life and goodly behavior. Valiant acts will assure the triumph of this Cause, and a saintly character will reinforce its power."[4]

Bahá'u'lláh throughout His voluminous Writings, each one of which has been described as a treatise on the moral and material betterment of the world and its peoples, constantly called attention to the healing power of His Counsels:

"O people of God! Give ear unto that which, if heeded, will ensure the freedom, the well-being, tranquillity, exaltation and the advancement of all men."[5]

Bahá'u'lláh said further of these Counsels, that they had been directed to all humanity. They were, He said, a veritable flood of world-healing remedies:

"Moreover We counsel them to observe justice, equity, honesty, piety and that whereby both the Word of God and their own station will be exalted amongst men... Unto this beareth witness He from Whose Pen rivers of mercy have flowed and from Whose utterance fountains of living waters have streamed forth unto all created things."[6]

Perhaps we have dwelled in too much detail upon both the planetary spreads of the Bahá'í Faith in such a short time, completely unique in the history of religion, and upon the Niagara of Bahá'u'lláh's Counsels that have flowed like a river into every corner of the earth.

Yet, there seemed to be no other way to demonstrate that it was indeed a "marvelous work" and "wonder" which God had wrought in this day through Bahá'u'lláh and His Faith, exactly as foretold in the sacred Scripture.

There appeared to be no other way to prove that the world, in general, still did not "believe" in spite of being surrounded every day of their lives by the "great work".

Above all, we wanted to make sure that you, yourself, were aware that you, too, were in danger of being caught up in this planetary spiritual deprivation. However inadvertently, innocently, or unwittingly. It was always my hope that, together, we could take the steps necessary to prevent that from happening to you.

In some ways, this has been the story of Father Abraham told all over again. Told, this time, today, on a planetary scale, involving most of the peoples of the world.

Hopefully, we have made sure that you are no longer numbered among them.

The story of Father Abraham is described in the Book of *Luke* (16:23-31).

A rich man dies, and descends into hell. He now knows that all is lost for himself because of his evil ways on earth, and his complete indifference to the words of guidance given to him by Messengers and Prophets of God. He had remained deaf and blind to Their Message all the days of his life when he was on earth. He was much too busy with material success to pay any attention to, or bother with, something so unessential as to what a Prophet of God had to say.

Unfortunately, because of "business as usual", he died and went to hell. Unexpectedly. He now had quite a different viewpoint. He had an eternity to think it over. And over. He realized that on earth he had put his trust in all the wrong things. That rich man now begged Father Abraham to send an urgent message to his five brothers who were still living on earth so that they might not make the same terrible mistake he had made. The rich man wanted his brothers to be warned about their desperate state and danger. They were trusting in all the wrong things. Even though they didn't suspect it. He wanted his brothers to heed the Words of truth and the good Counsel of God's Messenger.

Father Abraham said, "They have Moses and the prophets; let them hear them."

The rich man replied, "No, Father Abraham."

He knew only too well from his own experience on earth, that it would take far more than that to awaken his brothers. He remembered his own paralyzed spiritual state on earth only too well.

He entreated Father Abraham again, saying: "If you send one from the dead, then perhaps my brothers will repent."

And Abraham said to the rich man: "If they hear not Moses and the prophets, they will not be persuaded even though one rose from the dead to warn them:

Such is also the Irane state of our present-day material society.
According to Scripture.
Hopefully, it no longer applies to you, yourself.

In the Words of Bahá'u'lláh, Who has come to awaken a similarly spiritually dead society in an even more dangerous state of deprivation and loss:

"So blind hath become the human heart that neither the disruption of the city, nor the reduction of the mountain in dust, nor even the cleaving of the earth, can shake off its torpor. The allusions made in the Scriptures have been unfolded, and the signs recorded therein have been revealed, and the prophetic cry is continually being raised. And yet all, except such as God was pleased to guide, are bewildered in the drunkenness of their heedlessness!"[7]

And again:

"If ye pay no heed unto the counsels which, in peerless and unequivocal language, We have revealed in this Tablet [Letter], Divine chastisement shall assail you from every direction, and the sentence of His justice shall be pronounced against you. On that day ye shall have no power to resist Him, and shall recognize your own impotence."[8]

Such is the state of the world today. It's condition is evident to every unprejudiced and discerning eye. Bahá'u'lláh, the Divine Physician, has prescribed the Remedy. The world has refused it.

It is with sorrow that Bahá'u'lláh diagnoses the approaching terminal state of human society, both spiritually and physically:

"Witness how the world is being afflicted with a fresh calamity every day. Its tribulation is continually deepening... Its sickness is approaching the stage of utter hopelessness, inasmuch as the true Physician is debarred from administering the remedy, whilst unskilled practitioners are regarded with favor, and are accorded full freedom to act... Erelong, they will perceive the consequences of what their hands have wrought in the Day of God."[9]

There is no place for mankind to turn, except to this "Ark of human salvation" as the Teachings of Bahá'u'lláh have been described. The Writings of Bahá'u'lláh's Faith point out that the sole remedy for the ills of the world are the *Counsels* of Bahá'u'lláh.

These *Counsels* alone, if merely listed, would make an entire book.

This account of the Teachings and *Counsels* of Bahá'u'lláh, in spite of its length, has been only a fleeting glimpse. Still, it can assure the reader why *Isaiah* in his Yuletide Prophecy called Bahá'u'lláh not only the "Counsellor" but also "Wonderful".

The following *Counsels* of Bahá'u'lláh should indeed confirm that title. They should touch every receptive heart. They are all taken from the sacred Writings of the Bahá'í Faith and from the *Supreme Pen* of the Blessed Beauty, Bahá'u'lláh.

They are among the additional words of guidance given to the rulers of *Britain, Russia, France* and *America,* and the leaders of mankind in all parts of the world.

Weigh them carefully in your own heart.

FINAL COUNSELS

> "Summon ye then, the people to God, and invite humanity to follow the example ... Be ye loving fathers to the orphan, and a refuge to the helpless, and a treasury for the poor, and a cure for the ailing. Be ye helpers of every victim of oppression, the patrons of the disadvantaged."[10]

And even more movingly:

> "Be ye sincerely kind, not in appearance only. Let each one of God's loved ones center his attention on this: to be the Lord's mercy to man, to be the Lord's grace. Let him do some good to every person whose path he crosseth, and be of some benefit to him. Let him improve the character of each and all, and reorient the minds of men."[11]

And yet again:

> "Think ye at all times of rendering some service to every

member of the human race."[12]

In view of all you have reviewed in these chapters about the *Wonderful*, the *Counsellor*, although this is but the smallest sample imaginable from Bahá'u'lláh's vast ocean, with many others perhaps even more beautiful remaining untouched and unexplained, you should now appreciate more fully Bahá'u'lláh's own Words concerning His Counsels:

> "Every man of insight will, in this day, readily admit that the counsels which the Pen of this Wronged One hath revealed constitute the supreme animating power for the advancement of the World and the exaltation of its peoples. ... We cherish the hope that the Hand of divine power may lend its assistance to mankind and deliver it from its state of grievous abasement."[13]

Thus we see that the second part of that astonishing prophecy of *Isaiah* from the *ninth chapter* of his Book concerning the "Wonderful", the "Counsellor", applies far more to Bahá'u'lláh than to Christ.

Beyond a shadow of a doubt.

"THE EVERLASTING FATHER"

"A Truth that none can refute"

43.

The Pure Mirrors

The prophecy of *Isaiah* in the *ninth chapter* of his Book continues:

> "... And his name shall be called ...the mighty God, the everlasting Father ..." (*Isaiah 9:6*)

Christ emphatically disclaimed being the "Mighty God" when He called Himself the *Son of God*. He differentiated clearly between Himself and God when He said:

> "Why callest thou Me good? There is none good but one, that is God..." (*Matthew 19:17*)

Bahá'u'lláh, in like manner, made it clear that God was exalted above all His Messengers and far beyond the comprehension of mankind.

In Bahá'u'lláh's own Words:

> "To every discerning and illuminated heart it is evident that God, the unknowable Essence, the Divine Being, is immensely exalted beyond every human attribute ..."[1]

And further, Bahá'u'lláh declares:

"Far be it from His [God's] glory that human tongue should adequately recount His praise, or that human heart comprehend His fathomless mystery. He is, and hath ever been, veiled in the ancient eternity of His Essence, and will remain in His Reality everlastingly hidden from the sight of men."[2]

In another place, Christ said:

"I and my Father are one." (*John 10:30*)

He was stoned for blasphemy for making such a statement. On yet another occasion, Christ uttered a similar statement:

"... the Father is in me, and I in Him." (*John 10:38*)

They tried to sieze Jesus to punish Him for such blasphemy, but he escaped to safety.

Bahá'u'lláh makes it unmistakably clear that Christ was not guilty of blasphemy. In His *Book of Certitude* Bahá'u'lláh points out that Christ was absolutely right to say "the Father is in me, and I in Him". It was a true and beautiful eternal truth. One which every man should understand and believe.

This truth which He, Christ, spoke on that occasion was self-evident to those with "eyes to see" and "ears to hear". Bahá'u'lláh's Words explain that fundamental truth in simple, unmistakable terms, exactly as Christ had foretold He would do.

Christ prophesied that He, the *Spirit of Truth:*

"... shall take of mine, and shall shew it unto you."
(*John 16:15*)

Bahá'u'lláh did exactly that.

Bahá'u'lláh explained that God is like the Sun. Christ was a perfect Mirror of that Sun. The sun in the heavens and the sun in the mirror are indeed one and the same. Identical, though separate.

Such was Bahá'u'lláh's simple, clear, beautiful explanation of Christ's Words. Bahá'u'lláh continued His explanation.

It is always thus with the infinite, unknowable God and His Messengers. They are perfect Mirrors of His Light. They reflect God's attributes to mankind exactly as a mirror reflects the physical sun to the eyes of the peoples on earth. Even while God, like the physical sun itself, remains single, alone, and indivisible in the Heavens above.

Thus, all the Messengers of God might well and truly say, as did Christ:

"... the Father is in me, and I in Him". (*John 10:38*)

Bahá'u'lláh, for His clear, courageous, but unwelcome explanations, suffered the same harsh treatment from the clergy and people of His Day that Christ had suffered before Him. The people mistook this spiritual truth for the same blasphemy of which they had accused Christ.

Fearing that such a doctrine endangered their own prestige and position, these religious leaders in Christ's day closed both their ears and eyes to the truth. They were thus tragically deprived themselves and, as a result, they deprived their followers and the world. That same tragic mistake has been repeated today, in Bahá'u'lláh's time.

These so-called spiritual leaders of men saw and heard the "wondrous story", but refused to believe it. Even when it was happening before their very eyes.

So said *St. Paul*. So said *Isaiah*. So said *Habakkuk*.

Bahá'u'lláh, *the Father,* as Christ, *the Son,* before Him, tried to reopen the eyes of the people to this fundamental and beautiful Truth about all Religion.

Bahá'u'lláh explained to the world, plainly and simply, the symbolic meaning behind those true and beautiful Words spoken by Christ. He took of Christ's teachings and showed them to the world, exactly as Jesus had foretold He would.

Christ said:

"... he shall take of mine and shew it unto you."
(*John 16:15*)

Bahá'u'lláh declared:

"No man's understanding shall ever gain access unto His [God's] holy court. As a token of His mercy, however, and as a proof of His loving-kindness, He hath manifested unto men the Day-Stars of His divine unity, and hath ordained the knowledge of these sanctified Beings to be identical with the Knowledge of His own Self. Whoso recognizeth them hath recognized God..."[3]

There was no Blasphemy in it.
It was a clear, eternal, heart-inspiring truth from the *Spirit of Truth*, Bahá'u'lláh.

Bahá'u'lláh makes it clear that this truth applied in exactly the same manner to the Founders of all the great revealed Religions: Krishna, Moses, Zoroaster, Buddha, Christ, Muḥammad, the Báb and Bahá'u'lláh. It applies to them all, without exception, without preference, without prejudice.

It would also apply with equal truth to the Messengers of God Who were yet to come in the distant ages that lay ahead.

The Words of love and unity which are shed upon the world by all of these Messengers of God are as inseparable from God, the Originator, as are the rays of sunlight in the Mirror inseparable from the sun in the physical heavens.

This truth applies to all the Messengers of God, to every "Pure Mirror" of God's Light, both in the past and in the future.

No Words ever spoken were more true than those simple beautiful Words of Christ:

"The Father is in me, and I in Him." (*John 10:38*)

The Words were eternal.
Bahá'u'lláh declares that this is a truth that no man with an open mind and understanding heart can ever refuse or refute.

"Hearken unto the Counsels"

44.

The Lightning Flash

If there is any one thing that is clear in the *New Testament*, it is this: Christ was not the *Everlasting Father*.

He never pretended to be. In fact, Christ categorically denied it. Christ Himself explained clearly and emphatically that there was a clear distinction between Himself and the Father.

Christ said:

"... my Father is greater than I." (*John 14:28*)

The Words of Christ concerning this difference between Himself and the Father were too frequent to miss. Words such as "I go to the Father", and "I will pray the Father", and "Him that sent Me", and "I do nothing of myself, but as my Father hath taught me..." (*John 14:28; 14:16; 8:29; 8:28*)

Bahá'u'lláh, in His turn, also made it unmistakably clear that many of those thrilling references which Christ made to *"the Father"* referred not to Him, Bahá'u'lláh, Who came in the station of *the Father* as Christ came in the station of *the Son*, but referred directly to Almighty God, and to no one else.

Christ said that he would return to earth, not in the "glory" of Himself, *the Son*, but in the "glory" of *the Father*.

In this instance, Christ was referring to Bahá'u'lláh.

It was always clear to those with *spiritual eyes* and *spiritual ears* that when Christ returned in *"the glory of the Father"*, it would not be God Himself Who came down to earth. Such an earthly concept of infinite, unknowable God is both unacceptable and sacrilegious. Not to mention totally impossible. It needs no elaboration here.

Instead, Christ's promise means that some great Figure would come in the station of *the Father*, exactly as He, Christ Himself, had come in the station of *the Son*.

That Figure is Bahá'u'lláh.

Your research into the Life and Teachings of Bahá'u'lláh will prove this to you beyond all question or doubt.(*)

God, the Unknowable, the Infinite, is beyond all definition and description. He never could and never would appear on earth other than symbolically, or the entire planet would be consumed away. Obviously, Christ referred to another Great Figure like unto Himself.

Bahá'u'lláh has declared that God, the Divine Being and Unknowable Essence, is exalted beyond every human attribute such as "corporeal existence, ascent and descent, egress and regress."

In the *sixteenth chapter* of *John* which is so filled with the promise of Christ's return as *the Comforter* and the *Spirit of Truth,* Jesus says yet again:

> "... but the time cometh, when I shall no more speak unto you in proverbs, but I shall shew you plainly of the Father."
> *(John 16:25)*

Thus we see that the reference in *Isaiah's* prophecy to "The Everlasting Father" could not, according to Jesus' own testimony, be applied to Him, Christ, *the Son*.

(*)A careful examination of *Thief in the Night!* will also be of benefit to you because of its more detailed answers. George Ronald, Publisher, 46 High Street, Kidlington, Oxford, England OX5 2DN. Same author.

A study of Bahá'u'lláh's Life and Teachings will make it equally apparent that these references can and do apply, time and again, to none other than Bahá'u'lláh, Who came in the station of *the Father*.

One of the tributes written of Bahá'u'lláh declares:

> "To Israel He [Bahá'u'lláh] was neither more nor less than the incarnation of the 'Everlasting Father', the 'Lord of Hosts' come down 'with ten thousands of saints'; to Christendom Christ returned 'in the glory of the Father',..."[1]

The Son, Christ, had indeed Returned in the glory of *the Father*, Bahá'u'lláh.

The "lightning" had flashed "out of the east" and had "shined" even "unto the west" as foreseen by Christ, the *Son of Man*, for the day of His Return. (*Mathew 24:27*)

The time had come for the world to hearken unto the Counsels of the *Wonderful*, the *Counsellor*, the *Everlasting Father*, the *Prince of Peace*.

If the peoples of the world continued their neglect of the *Counsels* given by the Representative of God on earth in this day, as shown in the preceding chapters, mankind would ultimately have to pay the consequences.

The story of the "*Everlasting Father*" of *Isaiah* continues.

> *"And they came and did work in the House of the Lord of Hosts."*

45.

The Sacred Fold of the Father

It is essential that we never lose sight of one fundamental fact: In the same way in which the title of "Christ" as *the Son* of God is symbolical of His spiritual station, in like manner the title of Bahá'u'lláh as *the Father* is also symbolical.

This cannot be repeated too often if we are to avoid misunderstandings in our quest for the *Everlasting Father*.

This spiritual truth has been explained in greater detail with many references in some thirty pages of the book, *The Wine of Astonishment*.(*)

Repeat: Bahá'u'lláh made it unmistakably clear that many of the thrilling references which Christ made to "the Father" did not refer to Him, Bahá'u'lláh, but referred only to Almighty God, and no one else.

This distinction was always clear from the context, and showed unmistakably which Words referred to God and which referred to that great Figure yet to come in the station of *the Father*; in Whose "glory" the Spirit of Christ would make His promised Return to earth.

For example: In explaining the Words of Christ in Matthew 24:26:

> "But of that day and hour knoweth no man, no, not the

(*) See *The Wine of Astonishment*, pp. 83-96, "In the glory of the Father". William Sears author, George Ronald, Publisher, 46 High Street, Kidlington, Oxford England, OX5 2DN.

angels of heaven, but my Father only." (*Matthew 24:36*)

Bahá'u'lláh says:

> "By Father in this connection is meant God — exalted be His glory. He, verily, is the True Educator, and the Spiritual Teacher."[1]

Many of the other references to *the Father*, on the other hand, *do* refer to Bahá'u'lláh. It is these references with which we are concerned here in reviewing that *ninth chapter* of *Isaiah*.

The Son and *the Father*, as mentioned in Scripture, when referring to Christ and Bahá'u'lláh, are both figurative.

Jesus is not to be thought of as God because He is called *the Son*. Bahá'u'lláh is not to be thought of as God because he is called *the Father*.(*)

In *chapter forty* of his Book, *Isaiah* says:

> "Behold, the Lord God will come ... He shall feed his flock like a shepherd..." (*Isaiah 40:10,11*)

One of the lovely prayers of the Bahá'í Faith which refers to its Founder, Bahá'u'lláh, declares:

> "O Thou real shepherd! Educate and train thy sheep in thy green and verdant pastures ...
>
> "Verily they are all thy flock, and thou art the one shepherd of all."[2]

Bahá'u'lláh, *the Father*, has already begun to gather together all

---

(*) See *Wine of Astonishment*, pp. 66-81, Chapter Six: "The Meaning of Jesus, Son of God."

THE EVERLASTING FATHER

of the religions, nations and peoples of the world, as a good Father and Shepherd of the flock gathers together all of his children. This Yuletide drama will demonstrate that to you quite clearly before it draws to a close.

How delightful and significant it is to learn that the Bahá'í Administrative Centers the world over are called the "*Sacred Fold*".(*)

It is yet another of those "marvelous" things which were destined by sacred Scripture to be revealed to our eyes in this wondrous day.

No language is too strong when speaking of the astonishing events now taking place in the world around us, in more than one hundred thousand Bahá'í Centers all over the planet.

The "*Sacred Fold*" of God is welcoming the "Sheep of the Lord" everywhere. Exactly as Christ foretold. They will "hear" and "know" His "voice" in the day of the "One fold and one shepherd." (*Mathew 24:27*)

There, the "sheep" of the Lord those "herds" of the Lord referred to by this same *Isaiah*, will find shelter. These "sheep", he said, would "lie down" in "safety" on that coming day if they had "sought" for the Lord.

Even those who were *not* seeking for Him would be attracted to Him, and they, too, might be numbered with the "Elect" in that day. If they were sincere and their hearts were pure. That is the hope of all of us who arise to serve.

These are the very "sheep" who, *Isaiah* promises, will be called by "a new name" in that day. They are being gathered together by *The Everlasting Father*, Bahá'u'lláh, as a Father gathers together His flock, and His family of nations.

His "sheep" who Christ said would recognize His "voice" are now finding refuge within His "Sacred Fold". The seeds and the early beginnings of that "marvelous work" and "wonder" which

---

(*) See *Bahá'í Glossary*, p. 19.

Isaiah and the prophets of old had spoken about so glowing, have now been planted in well over one hundred thousand places in all parts of the world.(*)

Exciting?
Isaiah thought so long ago.

(*) See *Isaiah 62:2; 65:1, 9, 10*

"Human speech can never unfold their mystery."

46.

Reborn

The Bahá'í Faith, claiming as it does to be the culmination of a prophetic cycle, and the fulfillment of the Promises of all ages and all past Religions, does not attempt in any way to belittle or whittle down the greatness and glory of those Religions that have preceded it.

Instead, it honors them. The God-given authority vested in each one of them, the Bahá'í Faith recognizes, praises, and firmly defends.

The Faith of Bahá'u'lláh regards all of these great revealed Religions as different stages in the eternal history and constant evolution of one religion. A Religion that is Divine and indivisible, of which it, the Bahá'í Faith, forms but one fundamental progressive part.

The Bahá'í Faith does not seek to obscure the Divine origin of any one of the beautiful Religions that have preceded it. It does not attempt in any way to "dwarf the admitted magnitude of their colossal achievements."[1]

The Teachings of the Bahá'í Faith, far from aiming at the overthrow of the spiritual foundations of the world's Religions, instead seeks to restate their fundamentals, to reconcile their aims, to reinvigorate their life, to demonstrate their oneness, to restore the pristine purity of their Teachings, and to assist in the realization of their highest aspirations, and to weave them into the One great pattern of Religion devised by God for the continuous protection, inspiration and upliftment of the human race.

Each part, each Religion, is equally important, every bit as necessary, and unquestionably as Holy and God-sent, as any other part, any other Religion.

These divinely-revealed Religions, as one close observer has graphically expressed it:

"... are doomed not to die, but to be reborn ... 'Does not the child succumb in the youth and the youth in the man; yet neither child nor youth perishes?"[2]

This great "gathering together" is the work of the *Everlasting Father*, the *Prince of Peace*, Bahá'u'lláh. There is no other work accomplished by the *Prince of Peace* that is more important than assuring the Oneness of all the children of the *Everlasting Father*.

The Voice is One, though the Speakers are many.

Bahá'u'lláh proclaims:

> "They [the Messengers of God] Who are the Luminaries of Truth and the Mirrors reflecting the Light of Divine Unity, in whatever age or cycle they are sent down from the invisible habitations of ancient glory unto this world to educate the souls of men and endue with grace all created things, are invariably endowed with an all-compelling power and invested with an invisible sovereignty... Human tongue can never befittingly sing their praise, and human speech can never unfold their mystery."[3]

God sends His Messengers, these pure Mirrors, to reflect the Truth and Beauty of His Words of guidance to mankind. These Messengers or Prophets are like the rays of the sun. They are the Light and Guidance of the world.

You can thus see how true and beautiful the Words of Christ were when He said:

> "I am the way, the truth, and the life: no man cometh unto the Father, but by me." (*John 14:6*)

Absolutely true. For the wonderful Day of God in which Christ appeared.

It is equally true of every other Messenger of God in the Day of His appearance, whatever time that may be in the history of the world. In the past, the present, or in the future. It was true of Christ, *the Son.* It is true of Bahá'u'lláh, *the Father.*

It is equally true of the Founders of all the great Religions. It is true of each One without exception, without preference, without prejudice. They are, one and all, progressive stages in the one Grand Redemptive Scheme of God for mankind. Each Religion plays a basic and fundamental part. Including yours.

We have now come to the stage of "The Everlasting Father". This is the day of fulfillment. These are the last days, the time of the end, the day of the *One Fold and One Shepherd*, the Day of Bahá'u'lláh, the supreme Redeemer of men, the "Spirit of truth", the *Prince of Peace*.

There has never been another day such as this day in the entire history of religion on the planet.

Even so, and no matter how great this Day appears, or the majesty and wonder of the Day of your own Prophet, if we love any one of these Lights, these Mirrors, or Messengers of God, more than we love another, or all the others, it has to be prejudice on our part.

For all the reasons already given.

It is the time in history that determines the greatness of the outpouring of love and unity and guidance from the Messenger of God. It is the capacity and receptivity of the world to receive the Message that is important. It is always the Light not the Lamp that reveals it.

This mistake on the part of the peoples of the world has been made time and again. Almost invariably with the coming of each Messenger of God. It means that man has given his allegiance to the Name on the Mirror, not to the Light within it. Mankind, too often, unfortunately, remembers the Messenger, but forgets the *Message*.

No mistake could be more tragic.

It is this same inexcusable state of self-deception into which the world has fallen once again in this day, in the day of the *Prince of Peace*.

Let us hear again from Bahá'u'lláh, the *Everlasting Father* , the "gatherer" of nations and peoples. Bahá'u'lláh echoes the Truth and vital importance of recognizing and supporting all of these Mirrors. These Nightingales of God, Whose melody is designed to capture, sooner or later, even the hostile hearts of antagonistic men and women, so that a worldwide and endurable Peace may be established upon the earth.

First, They must transform the hearts of men, and then transform the world. They can do it because they bring the Plan of God, not the plan of man. They have and control the Power and Spirit of God, not man.

Bahá'u'lláh declares:

> "Whoso hearkeneth to their call, [the Teachings of these Messengers of God] hath hearkened to the Voice of God, and Whoso testifieth to the truth of their Revelation, hath testified to the truth of God Himself. Whoso turneth away from them, hath turned away from God, and whoso disbelieveth in them, hath disbelieved in God."[4]

Bahá'u'lláh adds:

> "Everyone of them [without exception] is the Way of God that connecteth this world with the realms above, and the Standard of His truth unto every one in the kingdoms of earth and heaven. They are the Manifestations of God... and the signs of His glory."[5]

We have shared with you Bahá'u'lláh's insight into the beautiful, inseparable oneness of all the Messengers of God, and especially the Oneness of Christ, *the Son*, with that of Bahá'u'lláh, *the Father*.

Let us delve even deeper into the significance of that prophecy found in *Isaiah* (9:6) in which *Isaiah* foretells:

> "... and his name shall be called ... The Everlasting Father." (*Isaiah 9:6*)

> *"Behold me! Standing ready and defenseless before you."*

47.

The Thrust of the Spear

Bahá'u'lláh left nothing to chance.

He spoke clearly and categorically to the religious leaders of Christianity. He announced to them plainly and unmistakably that He, none other, was the promised *Father*.

Bahá'u'lláh used the very words of *Isaiah* in His so-called Christmas-prophecy from the *ninth chapter* of his, *Isaiah's*, Book when addressing them.

Bahá'u'lláh proclaimed:

> "He Who is the *Everlasting Father* calleth aloud between earth and heaven."[1]

To the head of all Roman Catholic Christianity, Pope Pius IX, Bahá'u'lláh declared:

> "O Pope! Rend the veils asunder .... The Word which the Son [Christ] concealed is made manifest. It hath been sent down in the form of the human temple in this day. Blessed be the Lord Who is the Father! He, verily, is come unto the nations in His most great majesty. Turn your faces towards Him, O concourse of the righteous!"[2]

Bahá'u'lláh addressed the "Supreme Pontiff" in a most forthright manner. He reminded that secular leader of hundreds of millions of Christians, exactly to what lengths He, Bahá'u'lláh, was prepared to go in order to sacrifice Himself, exactly as Christ before Him had been sacrificed, for the salvation and redemption of all mankind.

If that was the only way to awaken a world in a "sleep like unto death", so be it.

Bahá'u'lláh proclaimed:

> "O Pope! ... My body longeth for the cross, and Mine head waiteth for the thrust of the spear, in the path of the All-Merciful, that the world may be purged of its transgressions..."[3]

Perhaps no Words of Bahá'u'lláh's show more clearly the tender love that linked His heart with that of Christ, than those Words found throughout Bahá'u'lláh's "glorious tributes" to Jesus.

It was exactly what He, Christ, had foretold that the *Spirit of truth* would do.

In the *Gospel of John*, Christ had promised:

> "He shall glorify me..." (*John 16:14*)

The Words of Bahá'u'lláh's many tributes to Christ stand as sufficient testimony to the Truth of Christ's own Words quoted above.

Bahá'u'lláh did more than "glorify" Christ. He extolled and praised Christ before the eyes of all mankind. In a far more exalted and wonderful manner than any tribute ever made to Christ by His own followers.

Some of the Beautiful Words of Bahá'u'lláh showing His tender love for Christ, have already been shared with you in our earlier Dialogues.

There is no end to it. There are many more.

When we look into everything with that "searching eye of truth," as instructed by Bahá'u'lláh, we immediately recognize and accept the complete oneness of the Mission of Christ, *the Son*, with the Mission of Bahá'u'lláh, *the Father*. We realize in a very special symbolical way how many of these prophecies of *Isaiah* refer to both Christ and Bahá'u'lláh.

Without exception. Without preference. Without prejudice. Without doubt(*) The *Father* and *Son* are one in spirit.

No one could have made this more plain to us than Bahá'u'lláh Himself. How tender, how confident, are His Words. How poignant and sweet to our ears are those expressions of love from Bahá'u'lláh demonstrating His own love for Christ, and His complete dedication and consecration to the oneness of Their common efforts exerted for the good of the human race.

Bahá'u'lláh, as had Christ before Him, was prepared to sacrifice everything — everything! — for the sake of the salvation and redemption of the peoples of the world.

> *BAHÁ'U'LLÁH:* "If ye be intent on crucifying once again Jesus, the Spirit of God, put Me to death, for He hath once more, in My person, been made manifest unto you. Deal with me as ye wish, for I have vowed to lay down My life in the path of God."[4]

And again:

> "If ye have resolved to shed the blood of Him Whose coming... Jesus Christ Himself hath announced, behold Me standing ready and defenseless, before you."[5]

Surely the Christian world, among the people of all other Religions, should have understood the Call of Bahá'u'lláh. In particular, the leaders of the Christian clergy from the Pope to the humblest lay preacher, including every branch and denomination of the Christian church, however fragmented.

Bahá'u'lláh directed special messages to each and every segment of them, as we shall see in our next and closing chapter of this engrossing theme of Isaiah's "The Everlasting Father."

Bahá'u'lláh, *the Father*, did exactly what Christ, *the Son*, had promised He would do in that *sixteenth chapter* of *the Gospel of*

---

*Yes, it is true, I do like that phrase, but can anything say it better?

THE EVERLASTING FATHER

John. Bahá'u'lláh "reproved" and castigated the world for not "believing" in Christ. Bahá'u'lláh admonished them for not understanding the *greatness* and the *glory* of His, Christ's, exalted Station.

He, Bahá'u'lláh, tried in every way possible to awaken every Christian heart to arise and help Him, the *Everlasting Father*, the *Prince of Peace,* to raise up their own *Christ-promised Kingdom of God on earth,* which would add so greatly to the glory of Christ. It has been the hope of Jesus Who longed to see this Kingdom become a reality here on earth.

Bahá'ís everywhere are trying to make that vision of Christ come true every day of their lives, everywhere in the world.

It is really *your* job.

Wouldn't you like to become a part of it at long last?

He, Bahá'u'lláh, "glorified" Christ time and again. He did indeed "testify" to the greatness and wonder of Christ. He exalted Christ's Holy Name in page after page of the Writings of His Faith.

As we have already seen.

In abundance.(*)

For *the Son* and *the Father* were one in their purpose: To assure the redemption, the security, the tranquillity and the happiness of all the peoples of the world in an atmosphere of "peace without end."

Who else could mankind call upon in this day?

If not the "Everlasting Father" of *Isaiah*, the "Prince of Peace."

(*) See *Chapter nine* of this book: "He hath testified of Me, and I do testify of Him." This will remove any doubt that **Bahá'u'lláh** did indeed testify of Christ and more, far more. And yet even to this day, how many sincere and loving Christian hearts are still not even aware of the surprising beauty of these tributes of Bahá'u'lláh, *the Father*, to Christ, *the Son?*

"Here am I! Here am I! Oh, Lord, My God!"

48.

The Everlasting Father

Bahá'u'lláh continued His forceful and all-inclusive Call to the highly placed among the hierarchy of the Christian Catholic Church: The Pope, the Patriarchs, the Archbishops, the Bishops, the clergy, the lay-preachers, priests, monks, nuns, and to all the peoples of Christianity. Every denomination, every hierarchy, the followers of all sects and all divisions.

No one was left out.

To them all Bahá'u'lláh called out once more. He repeated the very words of Isaiah's so-called Yuletide Prophecy:

"... He Who is the Everlasting Father calleth aloud between earth and heaven."[1]

Bahá'u'lláh announced to every Christian heart that the Day of the fulfillment of the promises made to them by Christ had at long last arrived. He left no doubt in their minds, nor in ours, that He, Bahá'u'lláh, was indeed the "Everlasting Father" foretold by *Isaiah*.

Bahá'u'lláh proclaimed to the Christian world, to the entire Christian world:

"Lo! The Father is come, and that which ye were promised in the Kingdom is fulfilled!"[2]

Bahá'u'lláh addressed one of His most powerful Messages to a famous Christian King.

He made it unmistakably clear that He, Bahá'u'lláh, was the Father referred to by *Isaiah* in his prophecy, and that Christ Himself had confirmed this truth that They were one and the same in Spirit.

Once again Bahá'u'lláh linked the Mission of Christ, *the Son*, with that of Himself, Bahá'u'lláh, *the Father*.

Bahá'u'lláh wrote to the Czar of Russia, saying:

> "O King ... He, Who is the Father is come, and the Son, (Jesus), in the holy vale crieth out: 'Here am I, here am I. O Lord, My God!' "[3]

Time and space prevent our citing each Message of Bahá'u'lláh to the leaders of the Christian world in full, or His Messages to the followers of the Gospels. The following excerpts will make it unmistakably clear that the Christians had indeed been told the "wondrous story".

Time and again.

Bahá'u'lláh, the *Everlasting Father,* wrote to the religious leaders of Judaism, Zoroastrianism, Islam, and to the people of all Faiths. After all, His Message was for the world, for the peoples of all Religions, as He, Himself, had repeated so often.

Still, Bahá'u'lláh did address unique and special Messages to the entire hierarchy of Christianity, those lovers of *the Son*. There can be no doubt of that.

As a kindly and loving *Father* would do, Bahá'u'lláh entreated them to turn to the One Whom Christ Himself had promised them so clearly.

Bahá'u'lláh did His best to awaken their hearts and souls with tender, moving Messages of love. His appeal to them, however, was direct, majestic and powerful.

There could be no mistaking His Words:

"*O Pope!*
"Lo, the Father is come!"[4]

"*O concourse of Patriarchs!*
"He Whom ye were promised in the Tablets is come!"[5]

"*O concourse of Archbishops!*
"He Who is the Lord of all men hath appeared."[6]

"*O concourse of Bishops!*
"He Who is the *Everlasting Father* calleth aloud between earth and heaven ... Ye are the stars of the heaven of My knowledge. My mercy desireth not that ye should fall upon the earth. My justice, however, declareth: 'This is that which the Son (Jesus) hath decreed!' And whatsoever hath proceeded out of His blameless, His truth-speaking, trustworthy mouth, can never be altered."[7]

"*O concourse of Priests!*
"Prefer ye to be silent whilst every stone and every tree shouteth aloud: 'The Lord is come in His great glory! ... He, verily, is the One Whom ye were promised in the Books of God ... How long will ye wander in the wilderness of heedlessness and superstition? Turn with your hearts in the direction of your Lord, the Forgiving, the Generous."[8]

"*O concourse of Christians!*
"Verily, He (Jesus) said: 'Come ye after Me, and I will make you to become fishers of men.' In this day, however, We say: 'Come ye after Me, that We may make you to become quickeners of mankind.' "[9]

"*O people of the Gospel!*
"They who were not in the Kingdom have now entered it, whilst We behold you, in this day, tarrying at the gate. Rend the veils asunder by the power of your Lord, the Almighty,

the All-Bountiful, and enter, then, in My Name My Kingdom. Thus biddeth you He Who desireth for you everlasting life."[10]

To all Christianity — man, woman, youth, and child — Bahá'u'lláh proclaimed those profound Words which now echo from the past throughout the entire Christian world. They resound with even greater momentum and power today. The Words of Bahá'u'lláh said simply and clearly to every Christian heart exactly Who it was that was calling out to them:

> "... He Who is the *Everlasting Father* calleth aloud between earth and heaven."[11]

There can be no question in the minds of the sincere seeker after truth that the references in the *ninth chapter* of *Isaiah, verse six*, concerning the *Everlasting Father*, refer not to Christ but to Bahá'u'lláh.

This has been but a trickle of the flood of confirmations available to us from the outpouring ocean of Bahá'u'lláh's Pen. The limitations of time and space have prevented our sharing all of them with you here. You will be able to read, study and meditate upon them at your leisure in the libraries of the world, as you make your own personal search into this uplifting and delightful story of the *Prince of Peace*.

Should you encounter any difficulty in securing the books you need for your study, ask any Bahá'í. They are all over the planet and only too eager to tell the "wondrous story" over and over again.

I envy you.

I remember my own early days of search. And the joy and excitement it generated in my heart as wonder after wonder unrolled before my eyes.

"THE PRINCE OF PEACE"

> *"There is no greater glory than service in the cause of peace."*

49.

The Bahá'í Peace Program

The prophecy of *Isaiah* continues:

> "... and His name shall be called the Prince of Peace."
> *(Isaiah 9:6)*

This is the most fascinating and perhaps the most significant of all the phrases used by *Isaiah* in his famous prophecy. It should be. This entire book is ultimately centered around that one phrase: *The Prince of Peace.*

Christ's own Words inform us categorically that this prophecy could not possibly refer to Him. It was not His Mission to bring peace to the world.

Christ Himself said so.

In the light of Christ's Words, it is difficult to understand why the Christian world would have ever attributed this title to Christ, let alone insisted upon it.

Christ said:

> "Think not that I am come to send peace on earth: I came not to send peace, but a sword." *(Mathew 10:34)*

Nothing could be more plain than that. Unless it would be these further Words of Christ cited in the *Gospel of Luke* where even stronger language is used.

Christ unmistakably renounced any such title as *the Prince of Peace.*

"Suppose ye that I am come to give peace on earth? I tell you, Nay; but rather division!" (*Luke 12:51*)

Christ, *the Son*, emphasized unmistakably that He did not "come" to establish "peace on earth".

Bahá'u'lláh, *the Father*, on the other hand, announced plainly to all the world that he *had* come to do that very thing. One of the most fundamental purposes of Bahá'u'lláh's entire Mission was to establish peace on earth.

Bahá'u'lláh makes the urgent need and absolute necessity of this great Peace effort unmistakably clear. In His own Words, Bahá'u'lláh declared that God's purpose in sending his Messenger to earth in this day was two-fold:

ONE
"The *first* is to liberate the children of men from the darkness of ignorance, and guide them to the light of true understanding."[1]

TWO
"The *second* is to ensure the peace and tranquillity of mankind, and provide all the means by which they can be established."[2]

Let me repeat part of *number two* once again, in case we didn't quite hear those astonishing words:

"... and provide all the means by which [the peace and tranquillity of mankind] can be established."

That's quite an offer.

Especially when it comes from One Who has presented concrete evidence that He truly is the *"Spirit of Truth"* foretold by Christ. The One Who will lead mankind into all truth. The *Prince of Peace* Who has come offering convincing proofs that he is indeed

THE PRINCE OF PEACE

the One *Isaiah* envisioned for this very day. The One Who has come to do that very exciting thing: Establish Peace on Earth under His Heavenly Franchise as the *Wonderful*, the *Counsellor*, the *Everlasting Father* and the *Prince of Peace*.

The Writings of the Faith of Bahá'u'lláh go on to say:

> "Today there is no greater glory for man than that of service in the cause of the 'Most Great Peace.' "[3]

In fact, one entire publication of excerpts taken from the Writings of Bahá'u'lláh and His Faith is devoted exclusively to this very subject: World Peace. It includes many inspirational and informative passages from the Bahá'í Writings on this vital, all-important subject of world peace.

It is called: *The Bahá'í Peace Program*.

"Shield mankind from the onslaught of tyranny."

50.

The Promised Day is Come!

Bahá'u'lláh declared:

> "The Great Being, wishing to reveal the prerequisites of the peace and tranquillity of the world and the advancement of its peoples, hath written: The time must come when the imperative necessity for the holding of a vast, an all-embracing assemblage of men will be universally realized. The rulers and kings of earth must needs attend it, and, participating in its deliberations, must consider such ways and means as will lay the foundations of the world's Great Peace amongst men."[1]

Bahá'u'lláh laid down the specific requirements for such a great gathering of the world's nations. Both great and small nations must attend, including the Heads of State from every corner of the globe.

Bahá'u'lláh explained clearly:

> "Such a peace demandeth that the Great Powers should resolve, for the sake of the tranquillity of the peoples of the earth, to be fully reconciled among themselves. Should any king take up arms against another, all should unitedly arise and prevent him. If this be done, the nations of the world will no longer require any armaments, except for the purpose of preserving the security of their realms and of maintaining internal order within their territories. This will ensure the

peace and composure of every people, government and nation."[2]

These *Counsels* were given long before disarmament became a pressing issue in our time.
Bahá'u'lláh continued:

> "We fain would hope that the kings and rulers of the earth, the mirrors of the gracious and almighty name of God, may attain unto this station, and shield mankind from the onslaught of tyranny."[3]

Bahá'u'lláh brought that particular passage to a conclusion with these Words:

> "That one indeed is a man, who, today, dedicateth himself to the service of the entire human race. The Great Being saith: Blessed and happy is he that ariseth to promote the best interests of the peoples and kindreds of the earth. In another passage He hath proclaimed: It is not for him to pride himself who loveth his country, but rather for him who loveth the whole world. The earth is one country, and mankind its citizens."[4]

Bahá'u'lláh, speaking with the Voice of the *Wonderful*, the *Counsellor,* said plainly:

> "O rulers of the earth! Be reconciled among yourselves, that ye may need no more armaments save in a measure to safeguard your territories and dominions. Beware lest ye disregard the counsels of the All-Knowing, the Faithful."[5]

And again:

> "Be united, O kings of the earth, for thereby will the tempest of discord be stilled amongst you, and your peoples find

rest, if ye be of them that comprehend. Should any one among you take up arms against another, rise ye all against him, for this is naught but manifest justice."[6]

Bahá'u'lláh said to a renowned European visitor who came to see Him in the Holy Land:

> "Yet do we see your kings and rulers lavishing their treasures more freely on means for the destruction of the human race than on that which would conduce to the happiness of mankind ... These strifes and this bloodshed and discord must cease, and all men be as one kindred and one family ... Let not a man glory in this that he loves his country; let him rather glory in this: that he loves his kind."[7]

Bahá'u'lláh stated His purpose clearly. It was to breathe a new spirit of hope and confidence into the hearts of human beings residing everywhere on the planet.

His promise was simple, direct and clear. But it would take firmness and courage on the part of the peoples of the world and their leaders. Most of all it would take unity. Complete, enthusiastic and spontaneous.

All of Bahá'u'lláh's Teachings must be put into effect, not some, or a few. A partial application would result only in a partial healing and cure. The Writings of the Faith of Bahá'u'lláh say specifically and forcefully:

> "At so critical an hour in the history of civilization it behooves the leaders of all the nations in the world, great and small, whether in the East or in the West ... to give heed to the clarion call of Bahá'u'lláh and, thoroughly imbued with a sense of world solidarity ... arise manfully to carry out in its entirety the one remedial scheme He, the Divine Physician, has prescribed for an ailing humanity."[8]

For all humanity. Every human being living upon the planet.

THE PRINCE OF PEACE

Bahá'u'lláh's own Words could not be more plain:

> "The summons and the message which We gave were not intended to reach or to benefit one land or one people only. Mankind in its entirety must firmly adhere to whatsoever hath been revealed and vouchsafed unto it."[9]

Bahá'u'lláh made it unmistakably clear to the leaders and rulers of men, to all their supporters and to His own followers as well, what was their first, their primary duty and responsibility.

> *BAHÁ'U'LLÁH:* "By Him Who holdeth in His grasp the kingdom of the entire creation! Nowhere doth your true and abiding glory reside except in your firm adherence unto the precepts of God, your wholehearted observance of His laws, your resolution to see that they do not remain unenforced..."[10]

The astounding joy and rapture that would be bestowed upon the peoples of the world when these *Counsels* were "enforced" in their entirety is an exciting part of our next chapter.

The most incredible, overwhelming promise of unparalled *Peace on earth* is promised (more than promised, assured) to every human being living today. If they will carry out in their entirety the guidance given by the *Prince of Peace*, the world in which all of us live will never be the same again.

Mankind is guaranteed that this "Peace beyond compare" is totally within its reach, entirely in its own hands, and requires no superhuman effort on the part of anyone. Only faith and confidence. And perseverance.

There are two redeeming factors in our favor which make the outcome unquestioned, and the winning of such a glorious, guaranteed Peace inevitable. If we will only arise nobly to play our part.

ONE

The time of waiting is over. It is said that there is nothing more potent in the world than a "dream" whose time has come.

That time is now. For man's dream of Peace.

Now is the time. History and Scripture both say so. Not a cease-fire, not a temporary cessation of hostilities, or a temporary peace between wars, but a bona-fide Peace, worldwide and enduring.

Habakkuk, who once said mankind would "behold" and "wonder marvelously" but would still not "believe" the *wondrous story* even when it was being "told" to them, has also promised that the world would have another chance in those last days when:

> *HABAKKUK:* "... the earth shall be filled with the knowledge of the glory of the Lord, as the waters cover the sea."
> (*Habakkuk 2:14*)

Our thrilling and dramatic chapters of the section called "As the waters cover the sea" proved beyond the slightest doubt that Bahá'u'lláh, Whose Name means, "the Glory of the Lord," is the One foretold.

It is all happening now.

Today.

In our time.

This is the day *Isaiah* envisioned when everyone could "behold" and "wonder marvelously" and "see" and "hear" and cry out in new-found joy.

Isaiah says:

> "In that day shall the deaf hear the words of the book, and the eyes of the blind shall see out of obscurity, and out of darkness." (*Isaiah 29:18,19, 24*)

Just to make sure it meant everyone in that day, both the willing and the rebellious, *Isaiah* added:

> "They also that erred in spirit shall come to understanding, and they that murmured shall learn doctrine." (*Isaiah, 29:24*)

Bahá'u'lláh declares:

> "This is the Day which the Pen of the Most High hath glorified in all the holy Scriptures. There is no verse in them that doth not declare the glory of His holy Name [Bahá'u'lláh], and no book that doth not testify unto the loftiness of this most exalted theme."[11]

Speaking of the ocean of proof now available to the peoples of the earth in this day to inspire and encourage them to arise and carry His "truth" to the four corners of the world, so "the whole earth be enveloped with the morning light" of His Faith, Bahá'u'lláh proclaims:

> "Were We to make mention of all that hath been revealed in these heavenly Books and holy Scriptures concerning this Revelation, this Tablet would assume impossible dimensions."[12]

One thing is certain: *This* is the day.(*)

TWO

The motive power to make such a Peace possible was at last being offered to the peoples of the earth. They now had a Source capable of accomplishing the "great work" and of inspiring the human heart with eagerness to arise and try. For God, not man. It was an entirely new feeling.

It was not a king, a legislator, a military leader, a scholar, a philosopher, a President or Head of State who proffered this advice and *Counsel* to the nations of the world and to their leaders and to their peoples.

It was the *Prince of Peace*, the Messenger of God for today, the *Spirit of Truth* foretold by Christ. The eyes of men had never seen His like before. But they had expected Him, and dreamed about

---

(*) There is an entire Bahá'í book written on this theme. It is called: *The Promised Day Is Come*. Ask any Bahá'í.

Him for countless centuries.

Bahá'u'lláh offered these "God-given" Truths. More important, they were guaranteed to work. If followed, they would "lead men into all truth". Christ Himself had said so. This included a *Peace* of such wonder and delight as would last forever.

As a Guarantor for His credentials, if such were needed, Bahá'u'lláh could offer the many Words of Christ. Together, Christ, *the Son*, and Bahá'u'lláh, *the Father,* had made this *Kingdom of God on earth* a reality. Peace was always a vital, important front-running part of it.

Bahá'u'lláh promised the peoples of the world that if His *Counsels* and guidance were followed and enforced in their entirety, this planet would become a world where the talents and gifts of every human being would be developed and used for the good of all mankind. They would not be squandered and wasted on war.

It would be quite a different world.

In the Words of Bahá'u'lláh, the *Prince of Peace:*

"*O ye peoples of the world!*

"Address yourselves to the promotion of the well-being and tranquillity of the children of men. Bend your minds and wills to the education of the peoples and kindreds of the earth, that haply the dissentions that divide it may ... be blotted out from its face, and all mankind become the upholders of one Order, and the inhabitants of one City. Illumine and hallow your hearts; let them not be profaned by the thorns of hate or the thistles of malice. Ye dwell in one world, and have been created through the operation of one Will. Blessed is he who mingleth with all men in a spirit of utmost kindliness and love." [13]

"The Children of the Prince of Peace"

51.

Administer the Infallible Remedy

The Bahá'ís, conscious of their purpose in life, keenly aware of their potential, carry on their work in every part of the world. They are confident in the society-building power which their Faith possesses. They press forward undeterred and never discouraged or dismayed by whatever happens in the world. They know that, as followers of Bahá'u'lláh, the *Prince of Peace,* they are fashioning the instruments that will inevitably win that final victory of World Peace and World Unity.

All Bahá'ís have before them that enthralling, glorious promise of an unequalled World Peace which was mentioned in the last chapter. They know that their day-to-day work is to touch the hearts of the masses of humanity, and to quicken their enthusiasm and desire to bring that wondrous day ever closer. They know that they are the foundation stones for that *Christ-promised Kingdom of God on earth* which they are raising up in every corner of the earth. It's all a fundamental part of the coming incredible Peace.

Let us now examine that unique, unprecedented promise of World Peace with no further delay. I am sure that none of us have heard a promise of Peace like it.

Ever.

The sacred Writings of Bahá'u'lláh's Faith tell us clearly, and without qualification of any kind, exactly what will happen in the world if Bahá'u'lláh's Teachings, in their entirety, are applied to the problems of mankind. Prepare yourself for the wonder. After all, the quotation calls it "the greatest of all remedies."

THE PROMISE
"Should this greatest of all remedies be applied to the sick body of the world, it will assuredly recover from its ills and will remain eternally safe and secure."[1]

That should be on echo chamber!
And be repeated over and over again.
It is such a wonderful statement on the kind of Peace the world needs. Let's hear it a second time ourselves. Right now.
Best of all, it tells us there *is* a "Remedy" and that we *should* apply it.
Immediately.
If we do, what will happen?

"Should this greatest of all remedies be applied to the sick body of the world, it will assuredly recover from its ills and will remain eternally safe and secure."

Of course, there is still work to be done by the Bahá'ís, and by those of you who join in the great crusade for Peace.
The Teachings of Bahá'u'lláh cannot be applied in their entirety by a world that probably still knows far too little about them.
As an example, how about yourself? Be honest. Have you read Bahá'u'lláh's Teachings in their entirety? Lately? Or ever? Or half of them? Or is your knowledge mostly hearsay?
You can readily see why the Bahá'ís of the world are so busy sharing the good news and glad tidings. And loaning Bahá'u'lláh's Books to everyone who asks. I'm lucky I had time enough to write this book. To be honest, I figured this might be the easiest way to reach you. Write a book.
There are special steps which the leaders and rulers of men must take in order to achieve that wondrous Peace. But, once again, Bahá'u'lláh has spelled it out. He has made it clear and unmistakable.
The Bahá'í Writings state plainly everything that the present-day leaders of men must do in order to start this special matchless "Peace" on its way.

For example:

> "They must make the Cause of Peace the object of general consultation, and seek by every means in their power to establish a Union of nations of the world. They must conclude a binding treaty and establish a covenant, the provisions of which shall be sound, inviolable and definite. They must proclaim it to all the World and obtain for it the sanction of all the human race. This supreme and noble undertaking — the real source of the peace and well-being of all the world — should be regarded as sacred by all that dwell on earth. All the forces of humanity must be mobilized to ensure the stability and permanence of this Most Great Covenant."[2]

And again, on the theme of peace:

> "The well-being of mankind, its peace and security, are unattainable unless and until its unity is firmly established. This unity can never be achieved so long as the counsels which [Bahá'u'lláh] the Pen of the Most High hath revealed are suffered to pass unheeded."[3]

And yet another time:

> "Through the power of the words He [Bahá'u'lláh] hath uttered the whole of the human race can be illumined with the light of unity, and the remembrance of His Name is able to set on fire the hearts of all men, and burn away the veils that intervene between them and His glory."[4]

Bahá'u'lláh repeatedly called out to those whose hearts had not yet been set ablaze:

> "The Word of God hath set the heart of the world afire; how regrettable if ye fail to be kindled with its flame!"[5]

Bahá'u'lláh conferred upon His loved ones all the power and strength needed to complete His spiritual conquest of the planet.

He repeatedly extolled the devotion and courage of His "radiant spiritual Army" as it moved out into every spiritual "front" to attract and win the hearts of the waiting peoples of the world. With love, not force. Attract the hearts, do not enforce the mind, was the instruction given to His loved ones in their spiritual conquest of the planet.

Bahá'u'lláh applauded them, saying:

> "Should anyone arise for the triumph of our Cause, him will God render victorious though tens of thousands of enemies be leagued against him. And if his love for Me wax stronger, God will establish his ascendancy over all the powers of earth and heaven. Thus have we breathed the spirit of power into all regions."[6]

All regions! Every part of the planet where Peace was being waged.

Bahá'u'lláh wrote:

> "He that summoneth men in My Name is, verily, of Me, and he will show forth that which is beyond the power of all that are on earth."[7]

That's a beginning.

There is quite a bit more to it, of course. The Bahá'í Writings speak further on this theme, outlining every step that still remains to be taken.

These sacred Writings say:

> "In this all embracing Pact the limits and frontiers of each and every nation should be clearly fixed, the principles underlying the relations of governments toward one another definitely laid down, and all international agreements and obligations ascertained. In like manner, the size of the armaments of every government should be strictly limited, for if the preparations for war and the military forces of any nation

should be allowed to increase, they will arouse the suspicion of others. The fundamental principle underlying this solemn Pact should be so fixed that if any government later violate any of its provisions, all governments of the world should act to reduce it to utter submission, nay the human race as a whole should resolve, with every power at its disposal, to destroy that government." (*)

Those same Writings declare:

> "He [Bahá'u'lláh], is the One to Whom none can compare. Whose utterance mortal man can never rival ... He from Whose lips have gone out counsels that can satisfy the needs of the whole of mankind, and admonitions that can profit them ... My object is none other than the betterment of the world and the tranquillity of its peoples."[9]

Bahá'u'lláh always made it clear that these wondrous *Counsels* were not from Him, but from One Who was Almighty, All-Knowing, God. As Christ had foretold, He, Bahá'u'lláh, did not speak from Himself, but whatsoever He heard from on High, that did He speak.

All of these *Counsels* and Words about Peace were from on High.

Man now had a clear choice.

He could put all of his hope and trust for the future on the record of what his fellowman had done in the past: Summit Conference, the Dow-Jones Averages, hostile nations; or, he could put his trust in the *Prince of Peace* Who had been sent to accomplish this very miraculous task.

What a wonderful day to be living in! Each one of us can be part of the fulfillment of a dream thousands of years old and help

---

(*) There is a place for force in the Bahá'í Faith. If it is the servant of Justice, and is applied fairly with the agreement of all member nations.

apply the "remedy" for the ills of this afflicted world today as prescribed from on High by the Divine Physician, Bahá'u'lláh.

So staggering, so fantastic, is the promise of world peace held out to the nations and peoples of the world by Bahá'u'lláh and the Bahá'í Faith, that we repeat it once more so it can sink into our consciousness and into our hearts. It is truly a *GIFT OF PEACE* from the *Prince of Peace*.

Everybody on their feet!

Ready? one more time:

THE PROMISE

"Should this greatest of all remedies be applied to the sick body of the world, it will assuredly recover from its ills and will remain eternally safe and secure."

Shouldn't we have that divine little paragraph printed on a small card? So we could all carry a copy in our wallets and purses? Until we really believe it? And join shoulder to shoulder to lend our share in making every wonderful word of that promise come true? Immediately?

I know a remarkable printer in Pima County, Arizona, where we can get enough cards printed for the entire planet at the right price. Certainly at a cost much less than we spend for doctors, chiropractors, masseuses, psychic healers, whirlpools and backrubs. We're always worrying about the future and our own personal daily suffering. We spend a fortune on our aching bodies. Always asking:

"What's going to happen to us?"

Because we just haven't known where to go to get help before.

Now, we do!

"Be the Lord's mercy to men."

52.

Sing out the Song of the Kingdom

We have come to the final chapters of our story about *Isaiah's* famous Yuletide prophecy.

The followers of Bahá'u'lláh have put down deep roots in well over one hundred thousand Centers around the world. More by the time you read these words because these Bahá'ís everywhere are still arising in large numbers so they can consecrate their lives and all they hold dear to raising up that precious *Christ-promised Kingdom of God on earth.*

The "children of the Prince of Peace", as their own Writings call them, are on the move! Many of their friends are also flocking to Bahá'u'lláh's pioneering Banner with each passing day.

Do you know any people anywhere in the world who are living and serving their fellowman in such a glorious selfless manner? And loving it! Devoting their lives and energies to being of service to their neighbors, their friends, their communities? Serving them and loving them whether they are Bahá'ís or not? Whether they will ever be Bahá'ís or not?

Be sure that the love the Bahá'ís feel for you will never change whatever your response to them may be. Their lives are consecrated to Bahá'u'lláh, the *Wonderful*, the *Counsellor*, the *Everlasting Father,* the *Prince of Peace*.

They not only love their neighbor as themselves, they love their neighbor more than themselves because of Him, Bahá'u'lláh.

They prove it every day of their lives.

Do you know any other people on earth, anywhere, who have before them, as a total commitment to *your* welfare, Words such as these from the sacred Writings of their Faith?

It is as though Moses, Christ or the Founder of *your* religion had written these words especially for you.

Listen:

> "Lift up your voices and sing out the song of the Kingdom. Spread far and wide the precepts and counsels of the loving Lord, so that this world will change into another world..."[1]

Do you know any people like that, Anywhere on earth?
Well, *now* you do.

They are called Bahá'ís, they are the children of the *Prince of Peace*.

Do you know anyone in your city, town or village who is doing the Lord's work as their first priority? With no hope or desire for any personal reward? People who have dedicated their lives to their fellowman because of the guidance found in these Words from the sacred Writings of their Faith?

> "Summon ye, then, the people to God, and invite humanity to follow ... Be ye loving fathers to the orphan, and a refuge to the helpless, and a treasury for the poor, and a cure for the ailing. Be ye helpers of every victim of oppression, the patrons of the disadvantaged." [2]

Do you know any other people on the face of the earth today who motivate their entire lives on Words revealed for them to act upon. Every day of their lives?

Prayer and meditation are fine. Wonderful. Use them. But act,

too.
   Immediately.
   Today.
   Move forward on all the problems afflicting your fellowman.
   Now.
   In our time.
   Remember Who stands behind you.
   These Words of guidance from the sacred Writings of the Bahá'í Faith are not optional, but obligatory. They are not suggestions. They are commands. Words that carry all the authority with which Moses, Christ and all the Prophets of old spoke:

> "Thus saith the Lord!"

These Words are directed to every "dot of decency" you can find on that map of the world where Bahá'ís reside. These *Children of the Prince of Peace* have consecrated themselves to carrying out Words such as these from the sacred Bahá'í Writings, on your behalf:

> "Let [each Bahá'í] do some good to every person whose path he crosseth, and be of some benefit to him. Let him improve the character of each and all, and reorient the minds of men. In this way, the light of divine guidance will shine forth, and the blessings of God will cradle all mankind..." [3]

Do you know anyone else, anywhere, who is not only prepared to accept suffering and humiliation for your sake — you, a total stranger — and welcome it? Because of Bahá'u'lláh, the Supreme Redeemer of men? Because the sacred Writings of their Faith tell them to do so, in these Words:

> "Pay no heed to aversion and rejection, to disdain, hostility, injustice: act ye in the opposite way. Be ye sincerely kind, not in appearance only ... Be the Lord's Mercy to man." [4]

Do you know anyone, anywhere, who lives and breathes a life of service to their fellowman? In all their actions? Do you know even one person, not a Bahá'í, who is guided by sacred Words that encourage every Bahá'í man, woman, youth and child every morning of their lives, to:

> "Think you at all times of rendering some service to every member of the human race." [5]

Now you do!
They are called Bahá'ís.
These heroines and heroes of God are devoting their time, their energies, their resources, their very lives if necessary, so that every human being living on earth today, yourself included, may have the chance to become a "better person" and a "finer human being".

They stand ready to sacrifice their all, so that you and they both may be numbered, at long last, among the *Elect* and the *Chosen*.

They are building the Kingdom of God on earth where everyone can live in the midst of a world at peace surrounded by the joy, happiness, security and serenity of their families and friends. And know in their heart as the *Prince of Peace* and Scriptures of old have promised, that this *Peace* will endure forever, and the world "will assuredly recover from its ills and will remain eternally safe and secure."[6]

'Abdu'l-Bahá, Bahá'u'lláh's Successor, and the Center of His Covenant with all mankind, adds this tribute to you and to all the other "Children" of the *Prince of Peace* everywhere on earth.

> "O thou who are carried away by the love of God! The Sun of Truth [Bahá'u'lláh] hath risen above the horizon of

this world and cast down the beams of guidance. Eternal grace is never interrupted, and a fruit of that everlasting grace is universal peace. Rest thou assured that in this era of the spirit, the Kingdom of Peace will raise up its tabernacle on the summits of the world, and the commandments of the Prince of Peace will so dominate the arteries and nerves of every people as to draw into His sheltering shade all the nations on earth." [7]

Bahá'u'lláh Himself declares that not only were the *Old* and the *New Testament* "adorned" with His "Name", but, more explicitly, He has told the world:

"I am the One Whom the tongue of Isaiah hath extolled..." [8]

There can be no doubt about that.

This is the conclusion of our phrase by phrase review of *Isaiah's* prophecy *chapter nine, verse six*, as read on Sunday morning in so many Christian churches of the West during the Yuletide season.

Surely no sincere reader, scholar or seeker after truth would question that the references in *chapter nine, verse six* of the prophecy of *Isaiah* concerning the *Prince of Peace* could possibly refer to anyone else but Bahá'u'lláh.

That brings us to the end of our Yuletide Drama.

It is only fitting that we should conclude with the loving Words of Bahá'u'lláh, the *Prince of Peace*, on behalf of all the peoples of the world:

"We have commanded the Most Great Peace, which is the greatest means for the protection of mankind. The rulers of the world must, in one accord, adhere to this command which is the main cause for the security and tranquillity of the world ... Blessed are those who act accordingly."[9]

And finally:

"Ye are the stars of the heaven of understanding, the breeze that stirreth at the break of day, the soft flowing waters upon which must depend the very life of all men... through you the countenance of the world hath been wreathed in smiles..."[10]

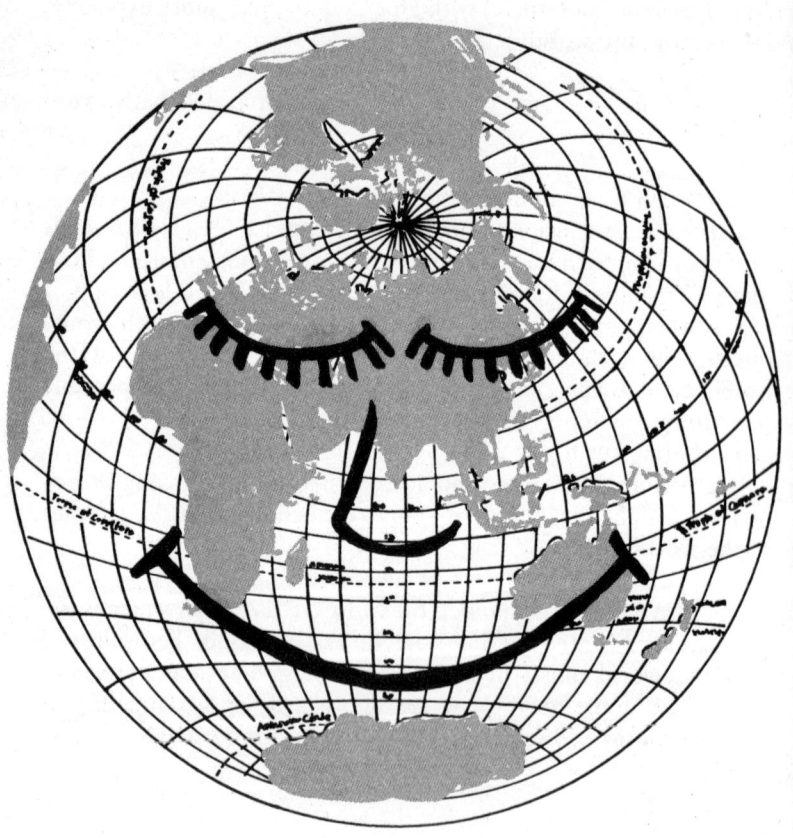

EPILOGUE

TWO GARDENS

"Rejoice with exceeding gladness."

1.

Two Gardens

We have experienced the might and majesty of Bahá'u'lláh as the *Prince of Peace,* we shall now taste of a few quiet, tender moments in the Holy Land. Scenes that unite Christ and Bahá'u'lláh for all eternity. Pictures of poignant and surpassing beauty.

When Bahá'u'lláh arrived in the Holy Land at the end of His four cruel successive Exiles, He addressed tender expressions of love to Bethlehem, the Birth-place of Jesus.

His Words take on a special sweetness as they recall to our mind the promise in the book of *Matthew* about the Return of *the Son* in the "power" and "glory" of *the Father.* *(See Matthew 24:30)*

Bahá'u'lláh wrote:

> "Bethlehem is astir with the Breeze of God. We hear her voice saying: 'O most glorious Lord: Where is Thy great glory established? The sweet savors of Thy Presence have quickened me, after I melted in My separation from Thee. Praised be Thou in that Thou has raised the veils, and come with Power in evident glory ...' "[1]

Bahá'u'lláh spoke of the sorrows and grief of Jesus in the Garden of Gethsemane during the last hours of His Precious life as He approached the agony of the "crown of thorns" and crucifixion.

Bahá'u'lláh called out in prayer to the Almighty:

> "He Who was Thy Spirit [Jesus], O my God, withdrew all

alone in the darkness of the night preceding his last day on earth, and falling on His face to the ground besought Thee saying, 'If it be Thy will, O Thou my Lord, my Well-Beloved, let this cup, through Thy grace and bounty, pass from me.' "[2]

Bahá'u'lláh's prayer continued:

"By Thy beauty, O Thou Who art the Lord of all names and the Creator of the heavens! I can smell the fragrance of the words which in His love for Thee, His [Christ's] lips have uttered and can feel the glow of the fire that had inflamed his soul in its longing to behold Thy face and in its yearning after the Day-Spring of the light of Thy oneness, and the Dawning-Place of Thy transcendent unity."[3]

When Christ, *the Son,* first came to that garden of sorrows, He said to His disciples:

"Sit ye here, while I go and pray yonder."
(Matthew, 26:36)

Each time Christ returned from His prayers in the Garden of Gethsemane, he found His followers asleep.

When Bahá'u'lláh, *the Father,* issued forth from His tent to chant the verses of God during those highly significant hours of His own earthly life in the Garden of Riḍván outside Baghdád, He, too, found some of His followers asleep upon the benches.

Those moments of inexpressible beauty and tender sadness have been recorded for posterity by the pen of the Bahá'í historian, Nabíl, who was "awake" and "watching".

"One night," Nabíl related, "the ninth night of the waxing moon, I happened to be one of those who watched beside His blessed tent. As the hour of midnight approached I saw Him (Bahá'u'lláh) issue from His tent, pass by the places where some of His companions were sleeping. He began to pace up and down the moonlit, flower-bordered avenue of the garden."[5]

Nabíl described the singing of the nightingales which was so loud on every side, that the voice of Bahá'u'lláh would be swallowed up in the sound of their melodious cry, as they sang of the love they felt for the fragrance that emanated from the heart of the roses.

As Bahá'u'lláh passed further down the avenue of fragrant flowers, His voice would vanish into the love-song of the nightingales. Bahá'u'lláh's beautiful chant would be heard again as He returned out of that magnificent chorus. When Bahá'u'lláh approached closer those nearby could once again follow the beautiful Words of His prayer and the heavenly magic of His Voice.

Bahá'u'lláh continued to pray and to walk among them.

Suddenly, He stopped before His companions sleeping on the benches.

Bahá'u'lláh observed:

> "Consider these nightingales. So great is their love for these roses, that sleepless from dusk till dawn, they warble their melodies and commune with burning passion with the object of their adoration."[6]

Bahá'u'lláh turned and looked upon those companions asleep upon the benches and unaware of what was taking place in that magical Garden.

Bahá'u'lláh said:

> "How then can those who claim to be alive with the rose-like beauty of the Beloved choose to sleep?"[7]

It was in that same Riḍván Garden that Bahá'u'lláh later made His Declaration to His companions, and through them, to the world, announcing that all of the promises recorded in the sacred Scriptures of the past had at last been fulfilled.

Bahá'u'lláh has characterized the Day of that Great Announcement as the Day whereon "all created things were immersed in the sea of purification". The Day when "the breezes of forgiveness were wafted over the entire creation."

"Rejoice with exceeding gladness," Bahá'u'lláh proclaimed.[8](*)

(*) The greatness and majesty of that mighty *Declaration*, is told with power and beauty in *God Passes By*, (pp. 151-162) entitled: *"The Declaration of Bahá'u'lláh."*

O LITTLE TOWN OF BETHLEHEM

"O Little Town of Bethlehem!"

2.

The Father and the Son

So glorious and overpowering was the Spirit in the Garden of Riḍván (Paradise) on the Day of Bahá'u'lláh's *Declaration,* that Bahá'u'lláh Himself, in trying to capture its beauty and majesty, and to reveal its import and significance to all humanity, has written:

> "Such is the inebriating effect of the Words of God upon the Revealer of His undoubted proofs that His pen can move no longer."[1]

Another of the touching and tender stories that forever bind together the Names of Christ and Bahá'u'lláh can be found in the Writings of the Bahá'í Faith concerning the "properties" along the Sea of Galilee which were associated with the ministry of Christ, *the Son.*

Bahá'u'lláh, *the Father,* instructed that these properties be purchased. They were designed to be consecrated to the glory of His Faith. They would be "forerunners" of those "noble and imposing structures" to be raised up "throughout the length and breadth" of the Holy Land.

It is hoped that this book *PRINCE OF PEACE* will inspire you to go to the Holy Land, to make your own pilgrim's visit so you may gaze upon the "imposing structures already raised up there: The Shrine of Bahá'u'lláh; the Shrine of His Herald, the Báb; the magnificent Archives Building; and the noble Edifice, the Seat of the Universal House of Justice, with others yet to come.

These final Words from the Pen of Bahá'u'lláh link together yet another time the Mission of Christ, *the Son,* with that of Bahá'u'lláh, *the Father.*
The Words are filled with both joy and sadness.
Their intermediary this time?
The little town of Bethlehem.

Bahá'u'lláh always felt a special love for the Birthplace of Christ and for the One, Jesus, Who was born there. Bahá'u'lláh often expressed a warmth and tenderness for the One Who had announced so bravely and positively that wondrous *Kingdom of God* which some day would be "on earth as it is in heaven".

Bahá'u'lláh had pledged Himself to achieve it, and to redeem that God-given Promise of Christ. It was a favorite theme of the Blessed Beauty, Bahá'u'lláh.

His love for Christ is evident in these tender Words.

For all time, for eternity, these Words of the *Wonderful,* the *Counsellor,* the *Everlasting Father,* the *Prince of Peace* unite together the hearts of Christ and Himself.

Bahá'u'lláh refers to His own journey from East to West as foretold by Christ. Then He asks the Birthplace of Jesus this poignant question:

> "O Bethlehem! This Light hath risen in the Orient, and travelled toward the Occident, until it reached thee in the evening of its life. Tell me then: Do the sons recognize the Father, and acknowledge Him, or do they deny Him even as the people aforetime denied Him (Jesus) the Son?"[1](*)

(*) These tender Words of love which Bahá'u'lláh directs to the Birthplace of Christ, remind us again of His loving tribute to Jesus: "Whatsoever hath proceeded out of His [Christ's] blameless, His truth speaking trustworthy mouth, can never be altered."

THE PRINCE OF PEACE

"This is His Gift of Peace."

3.

The Prince of Peace

Remember all these things next Christmas morning when your clergyman walks to the pulpit, mounts the stairs, opens the Bible, and begins to read aloud to you from the *ninth chapter* of *Isaiah*.

Listen with new ears to those beautiful words about the *Prince of Peace*:

> "... and his name shall be called Wonderful, Counsellor, the mighty God, the Everlasting Father, the Prince of Peace."

It has been.
He is Bahá'u'lláh, the Founder of the Bahá'í Faith.
It is He, Bahá'u'lláh, Who is the Source of that gradual transformation of human society which is now taking place across the face of the planet. This changing of human hearts shall continue until, at last, it *will* become "The Kingdom of God" on this earth of ours, "it is in heaven".

Isaiah said:

> "... he shall be called the Everlasting Father."

He has been.
The Father Who would "glorify" *the Son*.
Bahá'u'lláh has done just that.
In Bahá'u'lláh's own Words:

> "Verily the *Spirit of Truth* is come to guide you into all

truth ... He is the One Who glorified the Son [Christ] and exalted His Cause." [1]

Bahá'u'lláh has opened both His heart and His arms to the "followers of the Gospel", these Christians of all denominations across the surface of the earth, saying:

> "Followers of the Gospel, behold the gates of heaven are flung open. He [Christ] that had ascended unto it is now come."[2]

It is true.
He is no one else.
Bahá'u'lláh is the Return of *the Son*, Christ in the "glory" of *the Father*, Bahá'u'lláh. Their common *Kingdom of God on earth* will endure forever.
As promised.
Announced by *the Son*, Christ, in His *Lord's Prayer*; fulfilled by *the Father*, Bahá'u'lláh, through his "radiant spiritual Army" of love and unity which have already covered the face of the earth.
Their common *Kingdom* will be bathed in "justice" and in "peace", forevermore, exactly as foretold by that same *Isaiah* in that same famous *ninth chapter* of his book, *verse seven*.
If you are a Christian, pray about it to Christ. Ask Him about Bahá'u'lláh, *Prince of Peace*. Ask Him if you have found the truth at last! Beseech Jesus to enlighten your mind and touch your soul. Trust in whatever He, Christ, tells your secret heart.
The Son and *the Father* are one in spirit.
They will both help you.
Be sure.
The final decision shall always be yours. No matter what your decision may be, you will always have the friendship, the love and the trust of your Bahá'í friends.
Nothing will ever change that.

Perhaps this year, you will have a *real* Christmas. A Christmas that even His Holiness Christ would be happy to witness and share with you.

A new life, a new world, a new beginning, a new reason for living!
All gift-wrapped for you on this special Christmas day.
Don't thank me.
Thank Bahá'u'lláh, the *Prince of Peace.*
This is His loving *GIFT OF PEACE* to you.
His gift of peace, serenity, and security for you, your family, your friends, and for all the peoples of the world.

William Sears
Christmas Day
December 25

REFERENCES AND BIBLIOGRAPHY

REFERENCES

Chapter 2 — ON COURSE!
1. *Tablets of Bahá'u'lláh*, p. 157
2. *Hidden Words*, Arabic #2

Chapter 4 — THE PRINCE OF PEACE
1. *Appreciations of the Bahá'í Faith*, p. 18
2. Ibid.
3. Ibid., p. 10
4. Ibid.
5. Ibid., p. 16
6. David R. Williams, *World Religion and Hope for Peace*
7. Joseph Klausner, *The Messianic Idea in Israel*
8. *Appreciations*, p. 62
9. Ibid., p. 16

Chapter 6 — BLESSED DETOUR
1. *The Promised Day Is Come*, pp. 26-27
2. Ibid., pp. 27-28

Chapter 7 — GATEWAY TO THE PRINCE OF PEACE
1. *Appreciations*, p. 27-28
2. George Washington Carver, cited p. 10, *Convincing Answers*
3. Dr. Raymond Frank Piper, *Release the Sun*, p. 230
4. *Appreciations*, p. 56
5. *Appreciations*, p. 45
6. *The Proclamation of Bahá'u'lláh*, p. 91

Chapter 8 — DRAMA OF THE KINGDOM
1. *The World Order of Bahá'u'lláh*, pp. 104-105
2. Ibid., p. 104
3. Ibid.
4. *The Promised Day Is Come*, p. 30
5. *The Proclamation of Bahá'u'lláh*, p. 96
6. *Gleanings*, p. 85
7. Ibid., pp. 85-86

8. *World Order of Bahá'u'lláh*, p. 104

Chapter 9 — THE INSEPARABLE LINK

1. *Gleanings*, p. 86
2. Ibid.
3. *Tablets of Bahá'u'lláh*, pp. 9-10
4. Ibid., pp. 9-10
5. Ibid., p. 12
6. Ibid., p. 11
7. *The Promised Day Is Come*, p. 105
8. *Tablets of Bahá'u'lláh*. p. 11

Chapter 10 — LO, HE IS COME WITH CONCLUSIVE PROOF

1. *Tablets of Bahá'u'lláh*, p. 12
2. Ibid.
3. *Epistle to the Son of the Wolf*, pp. 147-148
4. *Gleanings*, p. 58

Chapter 11 — FULFILLED!

1. *The World Order of Bahá'u'lláh*, p. 201

Chapter 13 — WELL-WISHERS OF THE GOVERNMENT OF THE WORLD

1. *Epistle to the Son of the Wolf*, p. 69
2. *Bahá'í World Faith*, p. 440
3. *Gleanings*, pp. 94-95
4. Ibid., p. 248
5. *Gleanings*, pp. 249-250
6. Ibid., p. 250
7. *Gleanings*, p. 250

Chapter 14 — THE ALL-POWERFUL PHYSICIAN

1. *Gleanings*, p. 254
2. Ibid., p. 254-255
3. Ibid., p. 255
4. Ibid.
5. Ibid., p. 285
6. *Gleanings*, p. 255
7. *God Passes By*, p. 137

Chapter 15 — THE STRONG FORTRESS

1. *Bahá'í World Faith*, p. 38
2. *Tablets of Bahá'u'lláh*, p. 86
3. Ibid., p. 163
4. *Gleanings*, p. 297
5. Ibid., p. 95
6. *Bahá'í World Faith*, p. 184
7. Ibid., p. 183

Chapter 16 — HEARKEN, O YE THAT DWELL ON EARTH!

1. *Gleanings*, p. 286
2. Ibid.
3. Ibid., pp. 198-199
4. *The Promised Day Is Come*, p. 85
5. *Tablets of Bahá'u'lláh*, p. 7
6. *Gleanings*, pp. 93-94
7. Ibid., pp. 96-97
8. Ibid.
9. Ibid., p. 97

Chapter 17 — THE ALL-KNOWING PHYSICIAN

1. *Tablets of Bahá'u'lláh*, p. 69
2. *Gleanings*, p. 286
3. Ibid., p. 218
4. *Gleanings*, p. 213

Chapter 18 — BEAUTIFY YOUR TONGUES

1. *Gleanings*, p. 213
2. Ibid., pp. 92-93
3. Ibid., p. 97
4. Ibid., p. 297
5. Ibid.

Chapter 19 — PRELUDE

1. *God Passes By*, p. 212
2. *Gleanings*, p. 38
3. Ibid.

Chapter 21 — INCOMING TIDE

1. *Messages to the Bahá'í World*, 1950-57, pp. 37-38
2. *Gleanings*, p. 316

Chapter 22 — THE GREAT PARALLEL

1. *God Passes By*, p. 80
2. Ibid.
3. *Release the Sun*, p. 168
4. Dr. T.K. Cheyne, *The Reconciliation of Races and Religions*, p. 185
5. *Release the Sun*, p. 172
6. Ibid., pp. 173-174
7. M.C. Huart, *Le Religion de Báb*, pp. 143-144
8. A.L.M. Nicolas, *Siyyid 'Alí-Muḥammad, dit le Báb*, p. 375
9. *Release the Sun*, pp. 176-177
10. Ibid., p. 177
11. *God Passes By*, pp. 56-57

Chapter 23 — THE DOWNPOUR BEGINS

1. *Some Answered Questions*, pp. 30-31; Cited by Cheyne, p. 18 of *Appreciations of the Bahá'í Faith*
2. *God Passes By*, p. 56
3. Ibid.
4. M. Balteau, *Le Babismé*, p. 28
5. E.G. Browne, Article, *Journal of the Royal Asiatic Society*, 1899, p. 933
6. *God Passes By*, p. 55
7. *The Dawn Breakers*, pp. 516-517 (Footnote)
8. A.L.M. Nicolas, *Siyyid 'Alí-Muḥammad dit le Báb*, pp. 2-3-204, 376
9. *The Dawn Breakers*, pp. 516-517 (Footnote)
10. Mírza 'Abu'l-Faḍl, *Fará'id*, pp. 50-51
11. *The Dawn Breakers*, 522
12. Ibid.
13. Ibid.
14. Ibid.
15. *Appreciations*, p. 36

Chapter 24 — AN ISOLATED THUNDERSTORM

1. *God Passes By*, p. 75
2. Lord Curzon, *Persia and the Persian Question*, Vol. I, P. 501

Chapter 25 — THE SACRIFICE

1. *The Dawn Breakers*, p. 70
2. Ibid., pp. 93-94
3. Ibid., p. 45
4. Introduction to *The Dawn Breakers*, by Shoghi Effendi, pp. xxx-xxxl
5. *The Epistle to the Son of the Wolf*, pp. 141, 152
6. *The Dawn Breakers*, p. 50
7. *God Passes By*, p. 25
8. *Epistle to the Son of the Wolf*, p. 154
9. *The Dawn Breakers*, pp. 371-373
10. *Epistle to the Son of the Wolf*, pp. 156-157
11. *The World Order of Bahá'u'lláh*, p. 103
12. Ibid.

Chapter 26 — THE TIDAL WAVE

1. *God Passes By*, p. 194
2. *The Proclamation of Bahá'u'lláh*, p. 28

Chapter 27 — THE TIDAL WAVE CONTINUES

1. *God Passes By*, p. 220
2. Ibid.
3. Ibid.
4. Ibid.

Chapter 28 — THE TEMPEST

1. Cited in *Thief in the Night*, p. 92
2. Ibid.
3. Ibid., p. 107
4. Ibid.
5. Ibid., p. 108
6. Ibid.
7. Ibid., p. 109
8. Ibid.
9. Ibid.
10. Ibid.
11. *The World Order of Bahá'u'lláh*, p. 111
12. Ibid., p. 128

Chapter 30 — THE CLOUDBURST

1. *God Passes By*, pp. 93-103

Chapter 31 — THE BELOVED MASTER

1. *God Passes By*, p. 267
2. Ibid.
3. *The chosen Highway*, Lady Blomfield, p. 184

Chapter 32 — RISING TIDE: AMERICA

1. *God Passes By*, 283
2. Ibid.
3. Ibid.
4. Ibid., p. 284
5. Ibid., pp. 288-289
6. Ibid., p. 289
7. Ibid., p. 287
8. Ibid., p. 281

Chapter 33 — THE KINGDOM OF GOD ON EARTH, A BEGINNING

1. *God Passes By*, p. 351
2. *The Children of the Kingdom*, p. 6, Bol. #2, March 1921
3. *God Passes By*, pp. 339-340
4. Ibid., pp. 93-94
5. *Star of the West* (Magazine), Vol. 8, p. 93

Chapter 34 — RISING TIDE: THE HOLY LAND

1. *God Passes By*, p. 306
2. Ibid., p. 312

Chapter 35 — FLOOD TIDE

1. Translation Committee, World Center of Bahá'í Faith
2. Shoghi Effendi, Letter of Persia, Nov. 27, 1929

Chapter 37 — HIP! HIP! HOORAY!

1. *Appreciations*, pp. 25-26
2. Ibid., p. 59
3. Ibid.
4. Cited, p. 237, in *Release the Sun*

5. *Appreciations*, pp. 44-45
6. Ibid., pp. 32-34
7. *Advent of Divine Justice*, pp. 21-22
8. Ibid., p. 21
9. Ibid.

Chapter 38 — THE FIRST ATTEMPT

1. *Bahá'u'lláh and the New Era*, p. 281
2. *The World Order of Bahá'u'lláh*, p. 107
3. *Gleanings*, pp. 141-142
4. Ibid., p. 142

Chapter 39 — SECOND ATTEMPT

1. *Bahá'í News*, No. 77, p. 19

Chapter 40 — SUMMON THE NATIONS UNTO GOD!

1. *Gleanings*, P. 254
2. *The Bahá'í life*, p. 2, Compilation of the Universal House of Justice
3. *The Proclamation of Bahá'u'lláh*, p. 29
4. Ibid., p. 63
5. Ibid., p. 34
6. Ibid., p. 21

Chapter 41 — "LOOK CHINAWARD"

1. *Star of the West*, Vol 8, # 3, page 37
2. Talk by 'Abdu'l-Bahá, Assembly Hall, Hotel Sacramento (cited in *'Abdu'l-Bahá* by H.M. Balyuzi, p. 312

Chapter 42 — WONDERFUL! COUNSELLOR!

1. *The Proclamation of Bahá'u'lláh*, p. 70
2. *Gleanings*, p. 333-334
3. *The Proclamation of Bahá'u'lláh*, p. 70
4. Ibid., pp. 87, 86
5. Ibid., p. 92
6. Ibid., p. 78
7. *Gleanings*, p. 39
8. Ibid., p. 252
9. Ibid., pp. 39-40
10. *Selections from the Writings of 'Abdu'l-Bahá*, p. 3

11. Ibid.
12. Ibid.
13. *Tablets of Bahá'u'lláh*, p. 86

Chapter 43 — THE PURE MIRRORS

1. *Gleanings*, p. 46
2. Ibid., pp. 46-47
3. Ibid., pp. 49-50

Chapter 44 — THE LIGHTNING FLASH

1. *God Passes By*, p. 94

Chapter 45 — THE SACRED FOLD OF THE FATHER

1. *Epistle to the Son of the Wolf*, p. 143
2. *The Promulgation of Universal Peace*, p. 318

Chapter 46 — REBORN!

1. *The World Order of Bahá'u'lláh*, p. 114
2. Ibid.
3. Ibid., pp. 114-115
4. *Gleanings*, p. 50
5. Ibid.

Chapter 47 — THE THRUST OF THE SPEAR

1. *The Proclamation of Bahá'u'lláh*, p. 93
2. *The Promised Day Is Come*, pp. 30-31
3. *The Proclamation of Bahá'u'lláh*, pp. 83,85
4. *Gleanings*, p. 101
5. Ibid., p. 102

Chapter 48 — THE EVERLASTING FATHER

1. *The Proclamation of Bahá'u'lláh*, p. 93
2. Ibid., pp. 84-85
3. Ibid., p. 27
4. Ibid., p. 84-85
5. Ibid., p. 92
6. Ibid.
7. Ibid.
8. Ibid., p. 94

9. Ibid., p. 91
10. Ibid.
11. Ibid., p. 93

Chapter 49 — THE BAHA'I PEACE PROGRAM

1. *Gleanings*, pp. 79-80
2. Ibid., p. 80
3. *Bahá'í World Faith*, p. 231

Chapter 50 — THE PROMISED DAY IS COME

1. *Gleanings*, p. 249
2. Ibid.
3. Ibid.
4. Ibid., p. 50
5. Ibid., p. 254
6. Ibid.
7. *Appreciations*, p. 16
8. *The World Order of Bahá'u'lláh*, p.p. 36-37
9. *Gleanings*, p. 96
10. Ibid., p. 253
11. *The Promised Day Is Come*, p. 78
12. Ibid.
13. *Gleanings*, pp. 333-334

Chapter 51 — ADMINISTER THE INFALLIBLE REMEDY

1. *The World Order of Bahá'u'lláh*, p. 38
2. Ibid., p. 37
3. *Gleanings*, p. 286
4. Ibid., p. 286-287
5. Ibid., p. 316
6. *The World Order of Bahá'u'lláh*, p. 106
7. *Bahá'í World Faith*, p. 60
8. *Secret of Divine Civilization*, p. 64
9. *Gleanings*, p. 286

Chapter 52 — SING OUT THE SONG OF THE KINGDOM

1. *Selections from the Writings of Bahá'u'lláh*, p. 3
2. Ibid.
3. Ibid.
4. Ibid.

5. Ibid.
6. *Secret of Divine Civilization*, p.p. 64-65
7. *Selections from the Writings of 'Abdu'l-Bahá*, p. 246
8. *The Promised Day Is Come*, p. 34
9. *Bahá'í World Faith*, p. 198
10. *Advent of Divine Justice*, p. 63

EPILOGUE

Chapter 1 — TWO GARDENS

1. *The Promised Day Is Come*, p. 106
2. *Prayers and Meditations*, pp. 192-193
3. *God Passes By*, p. 153
4. Ibid.
5. Ibid.
6. Ibid., p. 154

Chapter 2 — "O LITTLE TOWN OF BETHLEHEM"

1. *God Passes By*, p. 154
2. *The Promised Day Is Come*, p. 106

Chapter 3 — THE PRINCE OF PEACE

1. *The World Order of Bahá'u'lláh*, p. 104
2. Ibid.

BIBLIOGRAPHY

ADVENT OF DIVINE JUSTICE, Shoghi Effendi, Wilmette Illinois, Bahá'í Publishing Trust, 1939, 1971

APPRECIATIONS OF THE BAHÁ'Í FAITH, Reprint from *The Bahá'í World*, Vol. VIII and IX, Wilmette, Illinois, Bahá'í Publishing Trust, 1947

BAHÁ'Í NEWS, Monthly Publication by the National Spiritual Assembly of the United States, Periodicals Office, Bahá'í National Centre, Wilmette, Illinois, 60091

BAHÁ'Í WORLD FAITH, Selected Writings of Bahá'u'lláh and 'Abdu'l-Bahá, Wilmette, Illinois, 1953

CHRIST AND BAHÁ'U'LLÁH, George Townshend,

THE DAWN-BREAKERS, Nabíl's Narrative of the Early Days of the Bahá'í Revelation, Translated and Edited by Shoghi Effendi, Wilmette, Illinois, Bahá'í Publishing Trust, 1970

EPISTLE TO THE SON OF THE WOLF, Bahá'u'lláh. Translated by Shoghi Effendi, Wilmette, Illinois, Bahá'í Publishing Trust, 1939, 1976

GLEANINGS FROM THE WRITINGS OF BAHÁ'U'LLÁH, Translated by Shoghi Effendi, Wilmette, Illinois, Bahá'í Publishing Trust, 1939, 1976

THE HIDDEN WORDS, Arabic, Bahá'u'lláh. Translated by Shoghi Effendi, Wilmette, Illinois: Bahá'í Publishing Trust.

GOD PASSES BY, Shoghi Effendi. Wilmette, Illinois: Bahá'í Publishing Trust, 1957

MESSAGES TO THE BAHÁ'Í WORLD 1950-1957, Shoghi Effendi, Wilmette, Illinois: Bahá'í Publishing Trust

PROCLAMATION OF BAHÁ'U'LLÁH, Bahá'í World Centre, Haifa 1967

THE PROMISED DAY IS COME, Shoghi Effendi, Wilmette, Illinois, Bahá'í Publishing Trust, rev. Edn. 1961

THE SECRET OF DIVINE CIVILIZATION, 'Abdu'l-Bahá, translated by Marzieh Gail, Wilmette, Illinois: Bahá'í Publishing Trust, 1970

SELECTIONS FROM THE WRITINGS OF 'ABDU'L-BAHÁ, Bahá'í World Centre, Haifa, Israel

STAR OF THE WEST. The Bahá'í News Service, Chicago, 1910-1933. Vols. I — XIV reprinted in *Star of the West*, Oxford: George Ronald, 1978

TABLETS OF BAHÁ'U'LLÁH REVEALED AFTER THE KITÁB-I-AQDAS. The Universal House of Justice, Haifa: Bahá'í World Centre, 1973

WORLD ORDER OF BAHÁ'U'LLÁH, Shoghi Effendi, Wilmette, Illinois: Bahá'í Publishing Trust, 1938, 1980